CALIFORNIA STUDIES IN FOOD AND CULTURE
DARRA GOLDSTEIN, EDITOR

MEDIEVAL CUISINE OF THE ISLAMIC WORLD

MEDIEVAL CUISINE
OF THE ISLAMIC WORLD

A CONCISE HISTORY WITH 174 RECIPES

LILIA ZAOUALI

TRANSLATED BY M.B. DeBEVOISE
FOREWORD BY CHARLES PERRY

UNIVERSITY OF CALIFORNIA PRESS
BERKELEY LOS ANGELES LONDON

The publisher gratefully acknowledges the generous contribution to this book provided by the General Endowment Fund of the University of California Press Foundation.

University of California Press, one of the most distinguished university presses in the United States, enriches lives around the world by advancing scholarship in the humanities, social sciences, and natural sciences. Its activities are supported by the UC Press Foundation and by philanthropic contributions from individuals and institutions. For more information, visit www.ucpress.edu.

University of California Press
Berkeley and Los Angeles, California

University of California Press, Ltd.
London, England

Library of Congress Cataloging-in-Publication Data
Zaouali, Lilia.
   [Islam a tavola. English]
   Medieval cuisine of the Islamic world : a concise history with 174 recipes / Lilia Zaouali ; translated by M. B. DeBevoise ; foreword by Charles Perry.
      p.   cm.
   "Translated from both the original French version and the published Italian edition of the book"—Pref. to the American edition.
   Includes bibliographical references and index.
   ISBN 978-0-520-24783-3 (cloth : alk. paper)
   1. Cookery—Arab.   2. Arabs—Food—History.   3. Cookery, Medieval.   4. Cookery, Islamic.   I. Title.
TX725.A65Z3613   2007
641.5939'49—dc22   2006100930

Manufactured in the United States of America

16   15   14   13   12   11   10   09   08   07
10   9   8   7   6   5   4   3   2   1
This book is printed on New Leaf EcoBook 50, a 100% recycled fiber of which 50% is de-inked post-consumer waste, processed chlorine-free. EcoBook 50 is acid-free and meets the minimum requirements of ANSI/ASTM D5634–01 (*Permanence of Paper*). ∞

CONTENTS

FOREWORD
CHARLES PERRY

Islam has the richest medieval food literature in the world—there are more cookbooks in Arabic from before 1400 than in the rest of the world's languages put together, making possible the wide scope of this volume. In most cultures throughout history, cooking has been taught by apprenticeship, either at one's mother's knee, in the case of home cooks, or in a professional kitchen, for chefs. The medieval Arabs were peculiar in writing recipes down, compiling them into cookbooks, and cooking from them.

This practice seems to have been a legacy of ancient Persia. When the Arabian armies conquered Iran in the seventh century, they found the Sasanian court full of connoisseurs. Someone there had actually written a tale (*Khusrau i Kavātān u Rētak Ē*) that was in effect a handy list of sophisticated gourmet opinions so the reader wouldn't make a fool of himself when mingling with the upper crust.

The tale was translated into Arabic, of course. The caliphs of Baghdad followed Persian court practice in many things, and above all where food was concerned. The Persian kings had organized cooking contests among their boon companions? So would the caliphs. They fattened chickens on hempseed before slaughtering them? Likewise in Baghdad.

The Persian aristocrats had saved their favorite recipes in personal cookbooks (not that they necessarily did any cooking themselves), and Baghdad followed this custom as well. The oldest surviving Arabic cookbook, *Kitāb al-tabīkh*, was compiled in the tenth century by a scribe named Ibn Sayyār al-Warrāq from the recipe collections of eighth- and ninth-century caliphs and members of their courts.

Ibn Sayyār's patron, as he mentions in his dedication, had assigned him to collect the dishes of kings and caliphs and other important figures. The unnamed patron was probably the Hamdanid prince Saif al-Daula, who was eager to add a cultural sheen to his upstart provincial court in Aleppo. One sign of this connection is that Ibn Sayyār includes ten poems by Kushājim, a member of Saif al-Daula's circle, and refers to learning several of them from the poet himself—which suggests that Ibn Sayyār had left Baghdad, already beginning its slow decline, and relocated to up-and-coming Aleppo.

Scribes plundered his book many times—Ibn Sayyār's recipes show up in a number of later cookbooks. Very likely it was this glamorous association of written recipes with the caliphs of Baghdad's golden age, together with the fact that their private physicians had testified to the healthful quality of many of these dishes, that accustomed the Arab world to the idea of writing cookbooks.

Ibn Sayyār's book includes a number of aristocratic stews with Persian names, and even a couple of recipes that claim to have been translated from Persian (they are certainly written in rather clumsy Arabic). The Arabs had also brought a few dishes from their peninsula's rather humble cuisine, such as porridge sweetened with dates (ʿasīda)—but not the humblest ones, such as dates kneaded with locusts (ghathīma). In Baghdad, there was a growing category of new dishes that had been invented by professional chefs. This sort of dish, typically given a name ending in the Arabic suffix -iyya, would predominate in later books.

The Arabs had also learned a great deal from the Nabataeans, as they called the Aramaic-speaking Christians of Iraq and Syria. The Arabic words for cheese, wine, and oil, like the names of many fruits and vegetables, come from Aramaic. They'd learned to appreciate some of the Nabataeans' hearty dishes, and Ibn Sayyār devotes a chapter to stews called nabātiyyāt. A couple of Nabataean dishes are still made, such as harīsa: whole grain stewed with meat until done, and then beaten to a smooth, savory paste.

The caliphs employed Christian physicians who were learned in the Greek school of medicine, and they introduced the idea of serving vegetarian dishes to invalids. In Islam, there is no religious requirement to abstain from meat on any occasion, and this surely explains why meatless dishes were called *muzawwaj* ("counterfeit"). The concept that "genuine" dishes contain meat is still alive—the Turkish word for vegetables stuffed with rice instead of meat is *yalanci*, which also means "counterfeit."

Several condiments may have originated in the Nabataean area—or at least, to judge by their names, somewhere exposed to both Persian and Greek influence. The basis of most of them was *bunn* (Persian *bun*, "foundation"), which was made by wrapping lumps of raw barley dough with fresh fig leaves and storing them in a loosely lidded container, typically for forty days. Mold spores on the leaves would infect the barley, mottling it black, white, charcoal, and several shades of green and giving it the aroma of rotting leaves.

When the barley was thoroughly rotted and had dried out, it would be ground up and one part salt added for three parts grain, along with enough water to give it a porridge-like consistency. After another forty days or so of aging, with more water added as needed, a salty liquid called *murrī* (from Greek *halmuris*, "salty thing," or Latin *muria*, "brine," probably by way of Aramaic *muryā*) would be squeezed out. It tastes like soy sauce.

If, on the other hand, milk was added instead of water, molds of the genus *Penicillium* would rush to the front of the line. The resulting condiment, which has a Persian name, *kāmakh ahmar*, smells like blue cheese; in effect, it's a salty blue cheese spread, reddish-brown in color, with a grainy texture. Nothing could be done about its proverbially loathsome appearance, which rather suggests horse droppings, but flavorings such as herbs, spices, or rose petals were often added to it.

Another condiment, *kāmakh rījāl*, was made without any rotted barley, simply by keeping strongly salted yogurt in an open vessel for several weeks and topping it up with fresh milk as needed. It develops the aroma of ordinary cheese, which is produced by slow-growing bacteria naturally found in milk; in effect, *kāmakh rījāl* is a sharp, salty, semiliquid cheese with a hint of rancidity (since butterfat oxidizes more rapidly in the presence of salt). The rancidity might have been something appreciated by connoisseurs, as it is in the modern Moroccan aged butter called *sman.* To keep other microbes from consuming the milk before the cheese bacteria can do their job, cheese-makers curdle milk and press out most of the moisture. *Kāmakh rījāl* protected the cheese bacteria by a different technique, relying on the acidity of yogurt and a high level of salt.

The caliphs of Baghdad belonged to the ʿAbbasid dynasty, which had come to power in 747 by overthrowing the Umayyads of Damascus. One Umayyad prince escaped to Spain, where his part-Berber ancestry helped him cement a power base of his own. As a result, the Arab world split in half. For the next eight centuries, the eastern and western Arabs would be ruled by rival empires separated by the no-man's-land of Libya. Inevitably, easterners and westerners began to cook differently. The two cookbooks from Moorish Spain and Morocco show influence from the local cuisines, Berber and Spanish (an example of the latter is *fulyātil,* a primitive sort of puff pastry; the name literally means "leafy" in medieval Spanish).

As in Baghdad, novel dishes developed in the courts and large cities of Spain and North Africa. Tunisia and the Mediterranean coast of Spain are far richer in fish than anywhere in the eastern Arab countries, and they developed a wide repertoire of dishes based on fresh seafood (in the east, fish was often salted and dried).

Easterners and westerners were aware of each other's food, to a degree. In the early ninth century, a Persian connoisseur named Ziryāb left the ʿAbbasid court and brought the latest Baghdad dishes to Córdoba, and a number of eastern dishes show up in the thirteenth-century cookbooks of North Africa and Moorish Spain. The easterners were not quite so interested in Maghrebi cuisine, but thirteenth-century eastern cookbooks often gave the North African recipe for *murrī.* All *murrī* was spiced. The Baghdadis flavored their soy sauce mildly, often with nothing but fennel and nigella, but the North Africans were famous for "infused" soy sauce (*murrī naqīʿ*), which contained many more spices and other flavorings such as carob, citron leaves, orange wood, and pine cones.

The eastern books also gave recipes for North African couscous. Before the twelfth century, the Arabs had cooked grain in two basic ways (not counting sweets and baked goods): as porridges and as pasta. There were two main kinds of pasta—*itriya*, of Greek origin, was a dry pasta always measured by the handful, and it may have been a short orzo-shaped pasta like the modern Egyptian *treyya;* and the Persian *rishtā* ("thread"), which was fresh pasta cut into strips.

Another word for fresh pasta, *lākhshā* ("slippery thing"), was also Persian. In Ibn Sayyār's book (the only one that mentions it), the recipe comes with a charmingly unlikely anecdote about how the Persian king Khosrau I offhandedly invented it on a hunting expedition. The name disappeared in the Middle East, but it gave the word for "noodle" in eastern Europe: Hungarian *laska,* Russian *lapsha,* Ukrainian *lokshina* (whence Yiddish *lokshn*), Lithuanian *lakštiniai.* In the thirteenth century and after, when the nomadic Turks began to influence the cuisine of the settled people of the Middle East, we find mentions of their traditional pastas, such as *tutmāj,* which may have been rolled thicker than *rishtā,* because *tutmāj* dough was used for making stuffed pastas, which need to be sturdy; and *salmā,* a coin-shaped pasta made by "stamping" lumps of dough with the finger.

But in the twelfth century, ways of cooking grain were developed simultaneously in North Africa and Iran that produced a nonmushy result. The Iranian invention was pilaf: rice scrupulously washed of all surface starch before boiling and given a final step of steaming so all the grains would cook up plump and separate. In North Africa, cooks devised the couscous technique of stirring a bowl of flour sprinkled with water to create dainty granules that could be steamed to make something supernaturally light and delicate. The eastern Arabs still make couscous—though nowhere as elegantly as the North Africans—and they call it *moghrabiyyeh,* "the North African dish."

With its sophisticated cooking techniques and wide repertoire of dishes, medieval Arab cuisine was far more developed than European cuisine of the time. The Arabs were open to interesting dishes from Europe, notably *sals:*

the concept of spicy prepared sauces for fish (the one area where Europeans may have been ahead was fish cookery, because of the Christian obligation of abstaining from meat on certain days). But to a far greater extent, where Muslims and Christians were in contact, such as in Moorish Spain or Sicily and the Crusader kingdoms of the Holy Land, it was the Europeans who borrowed dishes. For instance, one of the dishes the Arabs most esteemed was *sikbāj*, which consisted of meat stewed with a lot of vinegar and served cold. In the Arabic dialect of Spain, the name was pronounced *skibāj*, and it became the Spanish *escabèche*, a cold dish (usually of fish or vegetables) doused in vinegar.

But folk transmission wasn't the only way Arab dishes influenced Europe. In the twelfth century, Europeans began learning Arabic so they could study books not available in Latin, above all works of philosophy and medicine. As it happened, Arab medical writers often discussed recipes in their books. A famous Baghdad physician named Ibn Jazla compiled an encyclopedia of substances that were considered to have medicinal value, and he included several dozen recipes. They were popular in the Arab world because they were carefully written (being, in effect, prescriptions) and included reassuring medical information. Scribes soon excerpted these recipes from Ibn Jazla's *Minhāj al-bayān* to make a recipe collection, and other scribes shamelessly included many of his recipes in their own cookbooks. In the fourteenth century, his recipes were translated into Latin and later even into German.

His was only one of a number of Arabic medical texts that came with recipes. The Italian scholar Anna Martellotti suggests that the dish *sikbāj* entered European cuisine twice, once on the folk level in Spain and again through one of these Latin translations. The name of the dish was usually written *al-sikbāj*, and translators struggling to render the Arabic words into Latin came up with spellings such as *assicpicium*. Martellotti thinks *assicpicium* gave us our word *aspic*. It's certainly possible—if you make a medieval lamb *sikbāj* and let it cool, the meat juices do turn into a tart jelly just like aspic. (And it suggests why *escabèche* and all its descendants, from Italian *scapece* to Jamaican *scoveitch,* are cold dishes.) A number of other Arabic recipes have been traced in medieval European cookbooks, though, unlike aspic, none is still made.

The cuisine depicted in the medieval books was a rich one: a wide range of breads, preserves, and condiments; a repertoire of sweets that were almost identical throughout the Arab world; and above all, complex stews, fragrant with herbs, spices, nuts, fruits, and other flavorings such as rose water. We naturally wonder what the cuisines of the modern Arab world may have inherited from it.

But we have to be cautious. There's an inevitable similarity between the medieval and modern cuisines just because so many ancient staple crops are still the foundation of the Arab diet. The question is, what degree of culinary continuity does a given similarity show? Newly created dishes would naturally tend to include familiar ingredients. In some cases we can see a continuity of technique, such as the practice of scrupulously removing the scum when boiling meat. Regrettably, this is far from proving the survival of particular dishes.

The real problem is in the nature of these cookbooks. Since they owe their ultimate inspiration to the recipe collections of the Persian court, they concentrate on refined, luxurious, special-occasion dishes (as nearly all cookbooks in the world did until rather recently). In other words, they mostly record fashionable dishes. By nature, fashionable dishes are highly susceptible to becoming unfashionable and forgotten.

In fact, it's a good question how often most people ate these specific recipes. The closest thing we have to a book of everyday dishes is *Kitāb al-tibākha* ("The Book of Cookery"; or possibly *Kitāb al-tabbākha*, "The Book of the Female Cook"), written by a fifteenth-century Damascus legal scholar named Ibn Mibrad.

Its forty-four dishes are written in a rather abrupt manner. A typical recipe reads, "*Tuffāhiyya.* Put meat into the pot. Peel apples, cut them up and put them in it. Then sweeten it." This concise, aide-mémoire style (most of the recipes don't bother to say "and cook," much less "add water") probably accounts for the fact that only six of the recipes mention spices. They couldn't have been omitted because the cook was saving money—a humble sausage recipe incorporates the expensive spice saffron. The writer must have presumed that the cook would add his or her usual spice mixture. At any rate, these very simple interpretations of classic dishes suggest how most people really cooked during the Middle Ages.

Some recipes in the tenth- and thirteenth-century books were really specialist dishes, particularly the candies and sweetmeats that were based on boiling sugar to high concentrations of syrup, such as the soft-ball or hard-crack stage. Such recipes were repeated word for word in cookbook after cookbook, strongly suggesting that they had once been jealously guarded professional secrets of Middle Eastern confectioners, who are even today proverbial for their reluctance to reveal their recipes. It is certainly suspicious that when *Kitāb al-tibākha* gives recipes for the sweetmeats called *halwā*, they don't call for concentrated sugar syrup—date molasses (*dibs*), honey sugar, or boiled-down fruit juice (*rubb*) are all as acceptable as sugar syrup, indicating a rather homey and unambitious product. The book's favorite sweetening, in fact, is inexpensive date molasses.

In the modern world, not even the names of most medieval dishes have survived. The few that have are the sort that could serve as basic, everyday foods: *aruzz mufalfal* (pilaf), *kuskusū* (couscous), *rishtā* (noodles), *hasu* (grain soup), *mujaddara* (a porridge of lentils and rice), *harīsa* (meat porridge), *kammūniyya* (fish cooked with cumin), and *marwaziyya* (lamb stewed with prunes, native to the Persian city of Merv but now best known as the *murūziyya* of modern Morocco), along with a handful of sweets: *qatāʾif* (crepes), *maʾmūniyya* (a rice pudding), *asābiʿ Zainab* (a sweet like cannoli, but filled with nuts).

Where the name survives, the recipe may have changed considerably. The medieval recipes for *shorbā* are a lot thicker and starchier than the soups called *shorbā* today. The modern *muhallabiyya* is a kind of elegant pudding; in the Middle Ages, it included meat. *Fākhitiyya*, a stew of lamb flavored with yogurt, sumac berries, and ground walnuts, took its name from the color that results, because it resembles the purplish throat patch of the wood dove (*fākhita*). In present-day Syria, *fākhitiyya* is an alternate name for *arnabiyya*, a stew flavored with sesame paste and pomegranate juice, though the color match is no longer so exact.

How recipes fare in food history tends to be more complicated—and really more interesting—than simple survival or disappearance. Take the case of *buraniyya*, a dish named for the Lady Būrān, whose marriage to the ninth-century caliph al-Ma'mūn was the most lavish wedding party of the Middle Ages (it went on for the better part of a month). Before her time, the Arabs had reviled eggplant for its bitterness: "Its color is like the scorpion's belly," went a saying, "and its taste is like the scorpion's sting." (Doctors went further and claimed it caused freckles, sore throat, and cancer.) But Ibn Sayyār gives two recipes for "Buran's eggplant" (*bādhinjān būrān*), which contain the innovation that solved the problem of bitterness—the eggplant slices are salted before frying, drawing out the bitter juice. Now the Arabs could learn to appreciate its flavor, though doctors continued to disapprove: "The doctor makes ignorant fun of me for loving eggplant," wrote the poet Kushājim, in probably the only racy poem ever written about eggplant, "but I will not give it up. Its flavor is like the saliva generously exchanged by lovers in kissing."

By the thirteenth century, *bādhinjān būrān* had evolved into *būrāniyya*, a dish of stewed meat mixed with fried eggplant. In North Africa, more elaborate *būrāniyyas* were being made that included whole eggplants stuffed with meat and meatballs with chunks of eggplant in the middle. The basic idea of a stew flavored with fried eggplant survives in Morocco.

In the Arab East, however, the elaboration took a different turn. The thirteenth-century Syrian and Iraqi books show not only eggplant *būrāniyya* but a version made with chunks of gourd, seasoned the same way as the current eggplant version, with onions, coriander, and saffron. Since that time, *būrānī* (as the name has come to be pronounced) has ramified into a category of dishes consisting of all sorts of vegetables cooked with meat and seasoned with coriander and garlic.

Meanwhile, all the Arab countries east of Morocco fell under the control of the Ottoman Empire, where a new cuisine evolved—the one that has influenced Greek and other Balkan cuisines as well as the cookery of its Arab subjects. Its new repertoire of dishes gradually abandoned the medieval stews and emphasized roasted meat, stuffed vegetables, and eggplant dishes. As a result, eggplant is now the most popular vegetable in the eastern Arab countries (in Morocco, it's still mostly used in *braniya*); there are stuffed eggplant dishes, eggplant stews, eggplant casseroles such as *musaqqā*, and eggplant pickles (even dishes combining meat with pickled eggplants). Probably because of all this competition, the eggplant version of *būrānī* has died out and *būrānī* is now made with any vegetable *except* eggplant.

So in present-day Syria, the Lady Būrān's name has become a category of dishes in which nothing has survived from the ninth-century recipe of fried eggplant slices dressed with garlic, caraway, and soy sauce. We might think the garlic is a survival if it weren't for the fact that it doesn't appear in the thirteenth- and fifteenth-century recipes. (This is one more case in which food history benefits from the ringside seat provided by the medieval Arab cookery literature.)

Meanwhile, in Iran yogurt substitutes for meat, and in Turkish *boranis* grain tends to replace meat. Altogether, Būrān's dish has ramified into a wide range of dishes. There is a continuity between the modern versions and *bādhinjān būrān*, a linkage you can trace in its family tree, but no inherited similarity between the ninth-century and the modern dishes.

This sort of ceaseless, lurching, unpredictable change is typical of food history. We happen to be able to observe it in the case of *būrāniyya* because the dish was born in the spotlight of celebrity and later versions were recorded in the thirteenth and fifteenth centuries. If a ninth-century recipe can become unrecognizable within a few centuries, we should not be surprised that the cuisine recorded on Babylonian tablets about 1500 B.C.E. looks totally alien to us, even when its recipes use ingredients that are still common.

It's true that recipe features may survive without the name. In medieval Spain and North Africa, stews called tagines were typically finished off with an egg topping called *takhmīr* and sent to the oven; this practice, but not the term, has survived only in Tunisia. On the other hand, the survival of a name need not indicate any continuity at all. *Kāmakh* has been revived in recent centuries as a fancy word for vinegar pickles, with no awareness that it used to be a category of cheese-like condiments.

In fact, one of the main survivals of medieval cookery would not occur to most observers. Many Europeans and Americans are puzzled by the use of tomato juice in Arab stews, giving no more than a thin, tart tomato flavor. But this sort of tomato sauce is not a failed marinara—it's a survival of the medieval practice of adding a sour fruit juice to stews. The thirteenth-century stews flavored with rhubarb juice, sour grape juice, sour apple juice, and so forth are gone, but their spirit lingers on in the form of an ingredient that arrived from the New World only in the sixteenth century.

Food history is fascinating. The world's cuisines are merely the tips of so many icebergs, and for most of them we can only speculate unconvincingly about what lies outside our sight. We can all be glad that the medieval Arabs recorded so much about their cuisine.

TRANSLATOR'S NOTE

M.B. DeBEVOISE

The dual system of transliteration used for Arabic or Arabized terms in the Italian edition of this book, one for the classical and medieval lexicon and the other for the names of contemporary utensils and recipes, has been abandoned in favor of a uniform system that, despite certain simplifications, closely adheres to scholarly principles. Thus, for example, the Arabic consonant *dād*, whose strict transcription is *ḍ*, is represented in all cases here by a simple *d* (rather than *dh* or *z*). With regard to proper names (Qur'an rather than Koran, Qayrawan rather than Kairouan, and so on), I have followed the practice of the late Albert Hourani and other eminent authors. Dates of historical events and figures in the early centuries of Islam are inevitably to some extent conjectural, or at least a matter of disagreement among specialists; for the most part I have preferred the ones given by Hourani in his *History of the Arab Peoples*.

At the suggestion of the American publisher, I have made a great many changes to the organization of the Italian edition while also adding a good deal of material to the text, glossary, and notes. I am especially indebted to Charles Perry for his careful review of the draft translation, and for calling my attention to variants and inconsistencies in the manuscript tradition as well as to scores of other points of technical detail. I owe thanks, too, to the author for her kind and prompt assistance in answering a broad range of queries, and to Sheila Levine and Laura Harger at the University of California Press for their unfailing encouragement and support.

PREFACE TO THE AMERICAN EDITION
LILIA ZAOUALI

It is important to keep in mind, when considering the roots of modern Islamic cooking, that Middle Eastern recipe books composed between the tenth and thirteenth centuries do not concern themselves exclusively with the cooking of Muslims. They contain recipes for dishes that were typical of the cooking of all the subject populations of the ʿAbbasid Empire, which included not only non-Arab Muslims, but also peoples professing a faith other than Islam. Thus Ibn Sayyār, for example, devotes an entire chapter to the "false" or disguised dishes—cereal and vegetable preparations with the appearance of meat—that Christians cooked during Lent and that were called *muzawwarāt* (a term also used to indicate foods suitable for people in ill health, without regard to their religious denomination). Thus, too, Ibn Razīn al-Tujībī gives a recipe for a dish that the Jews of Andalusia prepared to celebrate the Sabbath, which suggests both personal acquaintance with and acknowledgment of the Jewish contribution to the western Islamic world's culinary tradition.

To be sure, there is no mention in these books of pork, which Muslims consider impure. And yet the recipe book that Ibn Sayyār composed for the use of a Muslim prince contains instructions for making wine and beer.

Moreover, although the authors of these recipe books were all Muslim, the same cannot be said of the authors of scientific treatises from this period devoted to questions of diet and hygiene. One thinks, for example, of the tenth-century Jewish physician Abū Yaʿqūb Ishāq ibn Sulaymān al-

Isrā'īlī, who composed his *Book on Dietetics* in the holy city of Qayrawan, in what is now Tunisia.

I am pleased to take this opportunity to acknowledge my indebtedness to Mohamed Benchecroun, Kaj Öhrnberg, Sahban Mroueh, Sulayma Mahjub, Durriyya al-Khatib, David Waines, and Manuela Marín, whose invaluable editions of the Arabic texts of the medieval manuscripts form the basis of the present book.

I owe special thanks to Kaj Öhrnberg for his careful and generous reading of the draft manuscript, and to Malcolm DeBevoise for his patient and meticulous work in translating from both the original French version and the published Italian edition of the book.

PART ONE

CULTURAL BACKGROUND AND CULINARY CONTEXT

CROSSROADS OF THE WORLD'S CUISINES

One day, one of the sultan's cooks called on a group of friends who were playing chess, and they invited him to have a seat. He sat down and took part in the game, and in this way began to spend time with them on his day off. When the game was over, he accompanied them to the house of the one whose turn it was to receive them for dinner, until finally they asked him to cook for them as he did for the sultan. The young man who was their host that evening wished to have a *sikbāj*.[1] The sultan's cook then asked him, "Who usually cooks for you?" "My servant," the host replied, and proceeded to call him. The sultan's cook asked the servant to bring him the pot in which he was accustomed to prepare this dish. When the sultan's cook had seen it, he ordered it to be well cleaned with clay. The young man cleaned the pot again and again. Each time the sultan's cook smelled the pot, then asked that the operation be repeated, until at last he ordered it to be cleaned with celery. Finally, after having smelled the pot once more, he said, "Good, now it is clean," and, still remaining seated to play chess, instructed the young man to cook the dish in his usual way. The host was unable to understand: he expected to see the sultan's cook get up and go into the kitchen, if only to indicate which spices were to be used, but the cook did not leave his seat.

Finally, the table having been set, the *sikbāj* was served. It was excellent. It gave off an aroma that they did not recognize as that of the *sikbāj* to which they were accustomed. Astounded, the guests wished to know the reason for this splendid result.

"But do you suppose that what I cook in the kitchen of the sultan should be different from that with which you are familiar? The ingredients are precisely the same: vinegar, meat, vegetables, eggplant, sugar, saffron, and everything else that is necessary. For the dish to turn out as it should, the ingredients and the cooking pot must be clean."[2]

This scene occurs not in *The Thousand and One Nights* but in a cookbook, the *Kitāb al-tabīkh*—the oldest of all surviving Arab cookbooks, compiled by Ibn Sayyār al-Warrāq in the second half of the tenth century. The events it describes took place more than a thousand years ago in an Arab city—a princely or royal city, possibly Baghdad. Baghdad was a different place from the one we know today, which has been transformed into a battleground and where chess has given way to war. But in fact its decline began well before the wars of the twentieth and twenty-first centuries, for it had already been destroyed twice by the Mongols—by Hulagu Khan in 1258 and by Tamerlane in 1401. And yet despite all that has occurred in the course of its history, despite the persecution of certain peoples who were unwelcome in the eyes of the government (the flight of the Jews, for example, and the persecution of Kurds and Shiites), the continuous presence in Iraq of other peoples who perpetuate ancient religious practices (such as Nestorian and Chaldean rite Christians), and of ancient languages (such as Aramaic) that still today are spoken in certain circles, is evidence—along with the strong sense of identity they imply—of a rich and complex cultural past.

Founded by the Arabs in 762 not far from the ruins of the ancient Sasanian city of Ctesiphon, Baghdad later became the capital of the ʿAbbasid caliphate. The City of Peace (*madīnat al-salām*) was circular, surrounded by three concentric rings of walls and entered by four gates, with the palace of the caliph and the mosque at the center. It knew its greatest prosperity under the reign of Hārūn al-Rashīd (786–809), in the middle of what was later called the golden age of Islam. At this time it attracted all the world's riches, material, spiritual, and intellectual alike; cultures and languages from the world over came together here, coexisting and, of necessity, blending with one another.

The ʿAbbasid caliphate (750–1258) enjoyed its ultimate moments of splendor in the second half of the tenth century, when political power was in the hands of the Persian dynasty of the Buyid emirs. Baghdad undoubtedly preserved its vitality thereafter, but new rivals began to establish themselves as centers of learning and of Islamic culture and art. Already in the

Muslim West there were Córdoba, Fez, and Qayrawan, and to these were soon to be added Cairo, with its mosque-university Al-Azhar, founded by the Shiite Fatimids in the tenth century, as well as Bukhara in eastern Persia (today Uzbekistan), which became the capital of the Samanids. Islam itself was strengthened far from the Arab centers, in the east with the Samanids (819–1005) in Persia and Transoxiana, and with the Ghaznavids (977–1186) in Afghanistan and the Punjab. In Iranian lands, the Persian tongue asserted itself as the language of literature and poetry, but Arabic remained the universal language of science, so much so that Ibn Sīnā (known in the West as Avicenna), a physician and philosopher from Bukhara whose treatises on food were known to every serious cook in the Middle Ages, wrote his works in Arabic. A native Persian speaker and Arabophone, Ibn Sīnā had been able to study all of ancient science thanks to the translation of Greek and Syriac works into Arabic by scribes at the House of Wisdom (*Bayt al-hikma*) in Baghdad.[3]

At its height, Iraq was an intellectual center of the highest importance for the Muslim world, welcoming the greatest masters of the philosophical and Sufi movements, theologians, scholars of every discipline, and poets from mystics to bards of the gentle pleasures of life. It was under the reign of the Buyid emirs, at Basra, that the mystic philosophical-religious sect the Brethren of Purity (*Ikhwān al-safā'*) was born; among its members' many works was a scientific encyclopedia in fifty-two volumes. The tenth century also saw the spread of the philosophical sciences and the composition of great historical works such as the *Meadows of Gold* (*Murūj al-dhahab*) of al-Masʿūdī. Shortly thereafter the Turks made their entrance on the political scene and—what is of greater interest from our point of view—brought with them a distinctive culinary culture. Contacts among the great centers of learning in the Islamic world during this period were so extensive that a scholar rarely died in his native city.

It is in this dynamic cultural context that we must place those men who gathered in Baghdad to play chess. They represented a certain urban social class, cultured and sophisticated, that devoted itself to the arts of conviviality and literary and philosophical conversation; a leisured class that permitted itself the luxury of having every day at table one of the finest and most beloved dishes of the period, *sikbāj*. Culinary culture underwent its own distinctive pattern of development in these urban surroundings, where it aroused the interest of physicians, dietary specialists, writers, and poets.

The codification of cooking recipes in the Muslim world therefore began in Baghdad. The first books of recipes in Arabic were compiled there from the eighth century onward, and the practice spread to the main cities of medieval Islam: Aleppo in Syria, Cairo in Egypt, Murcia in Andalusia, and so on. A comparison of the culinary heritage of the Islamic Middle Ages with today's traditions in the Middle East and North Africa reveals the persistence of certain medieval—indeed, ancient—customs, but also a very pronounced evolution of tastes and a consolidation of regional dietary preferences, giving rise to so-called national cuisines. This tendency was already apparent in the thirteenth century in the work of the Andalusian author Ibn Razīn al-Tujībī, who distinguished "Andalusian cuisine" from "Eastern cuisine."[4]

Baghdad in the tenth century—the point of departure for our gastronomical exploration—was a cosmopolitan city, then, a meeting place for all manner of cultural expression, not least the culinary arts. Although it stood at the crossroads of Arab, Persian, Greek, Indian, Turkish, and even Chinese and African cultures, the predominant culinary reference points in the second half of the tenth century, as attested by the *Kitāb al-tabīkh* of Ibn Sayyār al-Warrāq, were Arab and Persian. It is true that most of the recipes that have come down to us bear Arab names (*masliyya, tharīd, madīra*) or ones of Persian origin (*sikbāj, zīrbāj*), unless they mention the name of the cook who invented them or of the personage for whom they were made for the first time, or refer simply to the mode of cooking employed or to the most important ingredients called for by the recipe. But these recipes were sometimes Arab or Persian in name only. Thus, for example, one finds new versions of *masliyya* and *tharīd*, two ancient dishes that the Arabs of the Arabian peninsula used to make without sugar or vinegar, prepared in the

Persian style as sweet-and-sour confections. By the same token, new versions of *sikbāj*, a classic Persian dish, were made in the manner of Arab recipes for *tharīd* by the addition of crumbled bread to the sauce.

These novel culinary interpretations from the ninth century onward reflect a long history of cultural borrowing and exchange. The coexistence of Arab and Persian tastes in medieval Mesopotamia—a region historically under the influence of Sasanian culture that long before the coming of Islam had been continually traversed by nomadic Arab tribes from the south—is hardly surprising. The tribe of the Banū Lakhm (the Lakhmids) had founded a kingdom in the late third century around the city of Hira to the south of the Euphrates and were allies of the Persians, whereas the tribe of the Banū Ghassān (the Ghassanids) in the sixth century roamed the region to the west of the Euphrates and were allies of the Byzantines, whose frontiers they protected. In the culinary field, the process of borrowing and mixture among Arabs, Persians, and Byzantines therefore probably began prior to the advent of Islam in the region.

What was new, in the tenth century, was the contribution of peoples who had come from north of China: nomads of the steppes bringing alimentary customs whose mingling with those of Arab nomads was favored by the importance both attached to milk and its derivatives, on the one hand, and to simplicity in cooking on the other. Iraq was the site par excellence of the interaction of nomadic cultures, and the place where the city encountered the desert and the steppe, where gentleness met with harshness, and the sophisticated with the barbarous. This phenomenon was witnessed in all the great cities of Arab Islam, from the Fertile Crescent westward through the Nile delta and as far as Andalusia. At the end of the tenth century, the Berber tribe from what is now Kabylia, in Algeria, accompanied the Fatimid dynasty to settle the new city of Cairo. In the twelfth century, Berbers from southern Morocco crossed the Strait of Gibraltar (*Jabal Tāriq* in Arabic, named after the Moorish general Tāriq ibn Ziyād, who had crossed it in 711 with Arab-Berber troops), seized power in Andalusia, and took up residence in its royal cities. The dynasty of the Almohads reigned from its seat in Seville.

Amid this clash of disparate cultures, the evolution of cooking, above all urban cooking, produced astonishing results. The culinary arts in every region of Islam displayed a variety of tendencies and styles, as did other fields of cultural expression such as architecture, the decorative arts, ceramics, and calligraphy. Every sovereign felt obliged to leave his mark on history, beginning with the introduction, in the feasts prepared in his palace, of his preferences and tastes, which were those his mother had transmitted to him or else those of his tribe or of his native region.

To seek to identify a symbolic dish that epitomizes Arab cuisine, or medieval Islamic cuisine, therefore makes little sense. Although *sikbāj* was the preferred dish of the ʿAbbasid caliphs and, through imitation, of the upper classes of society, there is no need to conclude that the Yemeni or the Berber peoples of the Atlas Mountains in Morocco cultivated the same passion for this dish. Its name no longer figures today in Arabic culinary nomenclature, despite paradoxically having survived in the form *escabèche* or *scapece* in southern Europe. As for the favorite dish of the prophet Muhammad, *tharīd*—which Islamic tradition has sought to impose as the quintessential Arab dish—it seems to have had greater success in Andalusia and the Maghreb, to judge from the many recipes that Andalusian authors of the thirteenth century have left to us, and its comparatively rare mention, by contrast, in eastern books that go back to the same period.

SOURCES OF ISLAMIC CULINARY HISTORY

Medieval collections of recipes are invaluable sources not only for culinary history but also for the social and economic history of the Muslim world. The oldest book of Islamic cuisine dates from the tenth century, as we have noted, but classical Arab literature, both before and after this book, is rich in tales and anecdotes relating to gastronomy—descriptions of lavish banquets and marvelous dishes (and of meager meals as well); rules of good table manners; accounts of the prices of foodstuffs, their quality and place of origin; and so on. The topic of food evidently interested agronomists and physicians, who continued the Greek tradition of Hippocrates (ca. 460–377

B.C.E.), Galen of Pergamum (131–201 C.E.), and Rufus of Ephesus (first century), the last of whom is known exclusively in Arabic translation. Galen's *On the Properties of Foods*, translated into Arabic with the title *Kitāb al-aghdhiya* ("Book on Foods"), was cited in all the works of the physicians of the period—Muslim, Hebrew, and Christian—who were practicing under the reign of the Muslim caliphs. Abū Bakr al Rāzī (865–925), author of *Manāfiʿ al-aghdhiya wa madārrihā* ("Book of the Benefits of Food, and Remedies against Its Harmful Effects"), was Muslim; Abū Yaʿqūb Ishāq ibn Sulaymān al-Isrāʾīlī, author of a *Book on Foods*, was Jewish. Both wrote their works in Arabic.

These literary and scientific sources help us to better understand the books of recipes, which were not always written in the best style, and above all enable us to form some idea of what the people of the medieval period were like and what their food preferences were. The literature of classical Islam—including texts on the life of the Prophet, *The Thousand and One Nights,* and popular writings—is full of information about the mode of nourishment current among Muslims during this time.[5]

As for the specifically culinary literature, it seems appropriate that it should have developed at Baghdad toward the beginning of the ninth century and that a great many collections of recipes should have appeared during the course of that century and the next. Unfortunately, only one collection has come down to us in its entirety: the work by Abū Muhammad al-Muzaffar ibn Sayyār al-Warrāq, known by the abbreviated title *Kitāb al-tabīkh* ("The Book of Dishes"), from which the episode that introduces this chapter is taken.[6]

Texts composed prior to the tenth century have not been preserved, but their existence is nonetheless attested in annals, chronicles, and encyclopedias. In his *Fihrist* ("Index"), finished about 990, Ibn al-Nadīm (d. 995) gives us an exhaustive list of the authors of cooking manuals in Arabic, which for the most part have the same title, *Kitāb al-tabīkh*. Of these the first is the work by Abū Ishāq Ibrāhīm ibn al-Mahdī (779–839), half-brother of Caliph Hārūn al-Rashīd and himself caliph for two years. According to Ibn al-Nadīm, many ʿAbbasid caliphs, among them al-Maʾmūn (d. 833), al-Wāthiq (d. 847), and al-Muʿtamid (d. 892), were keenly interested in cooking and intervened directly in the confection of certain dishes—a surprising hereditary passion, crowned by the work of Ibrāhīm ibn al-Mahdī, that was nonetheless characteristic of a madly passionate age. Indeed, one is tempted to suppose that the caliphs passed all their time in the kitchen or at the table, delegating affairs of state to their vizier. Among the missing books we may also cite, by way of example, the *Kitāb al-tabīkh al-latīf* ("Book of Delicious Cooking") and the *Kitāb fadāʾil al-sikbāj* ("Book of the Merits of *Sikbāj*") by Ahmad al-Barmakī (d. 938).

The medieval recipes contained in the present volume are selected principally from collections that have been published in their original version, that is to say, in Arabic. The first is that of Ibn Sayyār al-Warrāq, which may have been composed at Baghdad in the second half of the tenth century.[7] This book, the *Kitāb al-tabīkh,* will be cited in the recipes as S (for the abbreviated name of the author, Ibn Sayyār) in order to avoid confusion with other books of the same title. The other three go back to the thirteenth century. Two were probably compiled in Syria and Egypt, respectively: *Kitāb al-Wusla ilā l-habīb fī wasf al-tayyibāt wa-l-tīb* ("Book of the Relation with the Beloved in the Description of the Best Dishes and Spices"), henceforth *Wusla* (W), and *Kanz al-Fawāʾid fī tanwīʿ al-mawāʾid* ("The Treasure of Useful Advice for the Composition of a Varied Table"), henceforth *Kanz* (K). The third, almost certainly compiled at Murcia, in Andalusia, is titled *Kitāb Fadālat al-khiwān fī tayyibāt al-taʿām wa-l-alwān* ("Book of the Excellent Table Composed of the Best Foods and the Best Dishes"), which will be indicated by the abbreviated name of its author, Ibn Razīn (R).

There exist many other cookbooks whose recipes will occasionally be mentioned, for example the *Kitāb al-tabīkh* of Muhammad ibn al-Karīm al-Kātib al-Baghdādī, composed at Baghdad in the first half of the thirteenth century. This book is well known among researchers because it was the first to be published in its original version, by the Iraqi scholar Daud Chelebi in 1934 at Mosul (this edition is now regrettably out of print), and immediately afterward translated into English by A. J. Arberry in 1939, a version (recently reissued with commentary by Charles Perry in an edited volume published in 2001) that is widely consulted today.[8] *Manuscrito anónimo*, another book that also goes back to the thirteenth century, was written in Andalusia and translated in its entirety into Spanish and partially into English and French.[9]

These cookbooks reflect the salient aspects of the societies of their time, inasmuch as they respect the conventions of their predecessors and perpetuate the models of the ʿAbbasid tradition that their authors knew from their own reading. There was no break with the old traditions, then, but rather an accumulation of knowledge and an enrichment of the culinary art that went hand in hand with the broader aim of cultural enrichment under Muslim rule. But each author introduced features that were typical of his age and of his region; and each one offered a selection of recipes that must either have satisfied those who had tasted them, as for example in the case of Ibn Sayyār, or have responded to personal culinary preferences, as with the author of the *Wusla*. The Andalusian Ibn Razīn, on the other hand, had a much different objective, which was to save from oblivion the culinary heritage of his native region.

Authors and Their Works   Ibn Sayyār al-Warrāq, as his name indicates, was a scribe or copyist (*warrāq*), but of a particular kind.[10] A gifted compiler, trained in medical and dietary matters, he was well acquainted with the literature of his age in all fields. Ibn Sayyār makes an inventory of food products, not omitting their dietary properties, and gives all the relevant rules and prescriptions for the proper maintenance of kitchen equipment and cooking utensils, as well as rules of hygiene relating to the handling of foods, the hands of the cook, table manners, and so on. In the introduction to this book he says,

> You ordered me—may God grant you long life—to write a book in which I was to put together dishes cooked for kings, for caliphs, for lords, and for chiefs. Thus I wrote for you—may God grant you long life—an

honest, complete, and elegant book that treats of the benefits of food for the body and the harm [it may possibly cause]; treats of all roasted meats and dishes cooked with meat, . . . all the cold appetizers of feathered game and freshwater fish, after having consulted—may God sustain you—books of ancient philosophy, and texts of wise men.[11]

Keenly interested in matters of health, though not himself a cook, Ibn Sayyār did his best to describe complicated cooking procedures, illustrating the recipes with poetry and tales that might give a more precise idea of the appearance, odor, and flavor of a dish. To be sure, the details are sometimes insufficient, particularly with regard to proportions and cooking times—as, for example, when he says to take "enough" flour or "sugar, as much as one likes," or when he recommends cooking for "one hour" (whose duration is not necessarily sixty minutes)—but on the whole his work is praiseworthy and remains the fundamental source for the culinary history of the ninth and tenth centuries. Moreover, it is thanks to Ibn Sayyār's text that we are acquainted with the recipes created by the most famous of all Arab cooks, Abū Ishāq Ibrāhīm ibn al-Mahdī, author of the first Arab cookbook, now, alas, lost to us.

Ibrāhīm ibn al-Mahdī was an ʿAbbasid prince, born in 779 in the palace at Rusāfa, the beautiful eastern quarter of Baghdad on the left bank of the Tigris, who became caliph without wishing to be one. He was an eccentric character of many talents, a cook, poet, and musician—the sort of figure who is apt to strike us today as rather improbable, but who was most likely not considered very unusual by his contemporaries. It was an age, after all, that knew a great many men who were no less curious and innovative. Ibn al-Mahdī appears to have passed the better part of his time in the palace kitchens in the company of his companion Bidʿa, a specialist in *sikbāj* and cold appetizers (*bawārid*). All Arab cookbooks of the medieval period have perpetuated Ibn al-Mahdī's memory, and his recipes—such as the one bearing his name, *ibrāhīmiyya*—were reproduced, transformed, and reworked. He may well have been the first to attempt to codify the cooking of his age, including dishes that he and Bidʿa each created.

The work of Ibn Sayyār al-Warrāq evokes what later came to be called the ʿAbbasid golden age, famous for the sumptuous cuisine of its caliphs and the extravagance of their recipes. But it was written as non-Arab rulers were beginning to exert their authority over Iraq, with the advent first of the Shiite dynasties of the Buyid sultans, and then another non-Arab but nonetheless Sunni dynasty, that of the Seljuk Turks.[12] As a consequence, the culinary culture of Baghdad came to be ever more exposed to oriental influences. By contrast, no recipe from Umayyad Andalusia or the Maghreb is recorded by Ibn Sayyār. Iraq was resolutely turned toward the east.

The succeeding cookbooks are all from the thirteenth century and are characterized by the first evidences of Turkish influence in the east and in Egypt, and of Berber elements in Andalusia. The culinary art of the thirteenth century reflects the diversity of the Muslim peoples. The Crusades in Syria and Palestine, the invasion of the Maghreb by the Arab tribe of Banū Hilāl, and the Mongol invasion of Iraq brought new waves of immigration and, with them, new eating habits.

Our three thirteenth-century authors may be said to have followed in the tradition of Ibn Sayyār in the sense that they brought cooking into closer relation with dietetics and medicine. All of them had a certain training in matters of science and the safe handling of food, and they knew the rules for a healthy diet and the hygienic measures recommended by physicians, whose books circulated among the great centers of the Muslim world. Such medical prescriptions constituted a common fund of knowledge no less than Islamic dietary proscriptions did, but by this time a number of distinct cuisines had managed to establish themselves. Even if one finds recipes in each of the three cookbooks attributed to the culinary traditions of Baghdad, and to famous gourmets such as Ibrāhīm ibn al-Mahdī, this does not mean that they occupied a preponderant place in the popular cuisine of the thirteenth century in Cairo, Tunis, Fez, or Seville.

The new cooking had acquired an identity that was not explicit in the collections of the tenth century: the names of its dishes evoked particular cities, regions, ethnic groups, and sometimes referred to religious affiliation.

Thus in the *Kanz*, which was compiled in Egypt under the reign of the Mamluks toward the middle of the thirteenth century, we encounter a succession not only of Egyptian and regional recipes but also of foreign dishes: a *Kishk* from Khorasan, recipes for a condensed yogurt product (*qanbarīs*) from Mosul, Baghdad, and Damascus; a cheese of the Turkoman type; turnips in the Greek style; Frankish condiments (*salsa*) served with fish; and so on.[13]

Authorship of *Wusla* is customarily ascribed to Ibn al-ʿAdīm of Aleppo (1192–1262), who is said to have immigrated to Gaza and then to Egypt after the Tatar occupation of Aleppo.[14] If this attribution is accurate, the work would have been compiled sometime between the end of the Ayyubids' reign and the beginning of that of the Mamluks. The Crusades are recalled by one recipe, *shiwā ifranjī*, a meat dish in the Frankish manner; but the great novelty was the introduction of North African dishes, such as couscous, of which the *Wusla* furnishes three versions. Recipes identified with particular regions, such as "cooked vinegar of Abyssinia," "Indian wine," the "Turkoman recipe," "recipe of Basra," or "recipe of Asyut," confirm the integration of diverse and increasingly deeply rooted cultures within Islamic society. Even though Muslims constituted the majority of Islamic society, Christians and Hebrews formed quite substantial minorities that respected different alimentary norms, though surely they followed the gastronomical fashions of the age as well.

In Baghdad, by contrast, the Iranian fashion persisted along with an Iranized Arab heritage, as the book of Muhammad al-Baghdādī (d. 1239) testifies. I will mention some of his recipes in what follows, though without going into great detail. Al-Baghdādī's book opens with a *sikbāj*, followed by an *ibrāhīmiyya*. Then come a *jurjāniyya* (from the city of Jurjan, in Persia), a *zīrbāj*, a *sughdiyya* (from the name of a part of Persia located between Bukhara and Samarkand in what is now Uzbekistan), a *rishtā* (which means "thread" in Persian and is made with a vermicelli-like pasta), and a few Arab recipes such as *madīra*, *masliyya*, *hays*, and *khabīs* (although *tharīd* is strangely absent).

Finally, we possess two texts from Andalusian authors that go back to the thirteenth century. The first is anonymous,[15] whereas the second is by an author from Murcia. The recipes from southern Spain that appear in the present volume are taken from the latter book. It needs to be noted, first, that Andalusian cuisine at this time was less open to Turkish influence than that of Baghdad and, by contrast, more open to Berber and sub-Saharan African influences, above all after the Almoravid conquest. Obviously the Roman and Visigothic traditions must be taken into consideration as well.

Kitāb Fadālat al-khiwān fī tayyibāt al-ta'ām wa-l-alwān was compiled by Ibn Razīn al-Tujībī in Murcia during the first half of the thirteenth century. For Ibn Razīn, "the passion for cooking . . . is a sign of generosity and holds at bay the spirit of avarice." God, he says, is to be praised for "having given to man the faculty of inventing and excelling in the culinary art." In the introduction to his collection of recipes he states that he wishes to devote himself mainly to Andalusian specialties, including only a limited number of eastern dishes. Oriental peoples he considers to be lacking in good taste ("They eat revolting things"). But Ibn Razīn does finally concede that tastes differ. The cuisines of the Muslim East and West are clearly distinguished in his work, oriental recipes being qualified by the term *mashriqī* ("eastern").

But where did the East end, or where did it begin, in the Andalusian mind? Was Egypt considered part of the *Mashriq*? And why were certain eastern recipes treated as native to Andalusia, whereas others remained foreign? At the time the book was compiled, Murcia was a Castilian protectorate (1243–1266), a circumstance that may be deduced from this remark of Ibn Razīn: "The Andalusians were once in the vanguard, but no longer; by now they have fallen behind in the field of culinary creation, ever since their lands and their homes were occupied by the enemy of Islam." The people of Murcia had a glorious past; under the reign of Ibn Mardanīsh (1147–1172), whom the Christians called *rey lobo* (the "wolf king"), it was the Murcians who directed the resistance to the invasion of the Almohad Berbers. But even under Berber domination the city continued to maintain relations with the republics of Genoa and Pisa. It negotiated alliances with Christian kings and recognized the caliphate of Baghdad. The book of Ibn Razīn, along with the *Manuscrito anónimo,* illustrates the vitality of its culinary arts, which developed with the mixing of cultures.

Whereas only one cookbook from the tenth century has been preserved, and none has come down to us from the eleventh or twelfth centuries, the thirteenth offers five books.[16] Among the manuscripts of this period that are conserved in Arab and European libraries are a certain number of anonymous texts (causing one to wonder whether they may have been written by women). With regard to those authors or copyists whose books are signed with their own names, however, our sources furnish no information, so they are as unknown as the authors of the anonymous texts. All these books were composed in Arabic, no cookbook having been written in Persian, Greek, or Latin between the tenth century and the beginning of the thirteenth.

With rare exceptions, as we shall see in a moment, the authors are male: by and large it was men who cooked, men who commented, men who wrote. The stories they tell us relate exclusively to encounters between men, as consumers and as cooks.

GASTRONOMY AND THE SEARCH FOR THE EXOTIC

The cult of cuisine and gastronomy coincided with the cultivation of new agricultural products, such as rice and sugarcane. The cultivation of cotton and silk dates from this period as well. Nonetheless, many food products continued to be imported, such as Afghan sugar; coconuts; spices from China, India, and Africa; and so on. Four centuries before Marco Polo, Arab travelers and merchants regularly visited China, following the rhythms of the monsoon season, usually aboard Chinese junks. Here is what a foreign traveler of the ninth century has to say about the alimentary habits of the Chinese:

> It is rice that constitutes their food. Sometimes, to accompany it, they cook a sauce (*kushān*), which they pour over the rice; and then they eat

it. As for the princes, they eat wheat bread and the meat of all animals, even of swines and others still. For fruits they have apple, peach, citron, pomegranate, quince, pear, banana, sugarcane, melon, fig, grapes, ribbed cucumber, smooth cucumber, persimmon, walnut, almond, hazelnut, pistachio, plum, apricot, sorb apple, and coconut. In the country they do not have many date palms, except for a few (here and there) in private homes. They drink a fermented beverage made with rice, because in their country there is no grape wine: we do not furnish them with any, and indeed they do not know it and do not drink it. And with rice are made vinegar, wine, sweets, and other such things.

These descriptions occur in an Arab manuscript titled *Akhbār as-Sīn wa-l-Hind* ("Notes on China and India") from 851.[17] The author remains anonymous, despite exhaustive researches by historians, who nonetheless suspect that he may have been of Iraqi origin because he pauses to report on the situation of Iraqi merchants at Canton. Other such works dating from the same period were very fashionable in Iraq, such as *The Marvels of India* and *The Marvels of the Sea,* a genre of literature meant to satisfy the curiosity of a cultured urban elite eager for novelty and exoticism.

The same author recounts that, having departed from Muscat and then called at Kulam Mali in India, his boat dropped anchor in front of an island called Langabalus, where the naked and beardless inhabitants ("who understood neither the language of the Arabs, nor [any of] the languages known by merchants") came to offer, without getting out of their pirogues, "coconuts, sugarcane, bananas, and palm wine: [this] is a white beverage that is sweet like honey when one drinks it the moment it is tapped from the coconut palm, but if it is left to sit for a little while it is transformed into wine and, after a few days, into vinegar." Palm wine was drawn in the same way from date palms as from coconut palms; naturally fermented without any treatment, it could always be found near oases—in southern Tunisia, for example, where it was called *lagmi.*

The problems that arose with China after a massacre of the Arab merchants at Canton between 875 and 878 did not lead to a total rupture of commercial relations. Instead there was a change in routes and ports of call, with the result that trading was now carried on at Kalah, on the Malaccan peninsula. Five hundred years later, and despite the Mongol invasion, commercial relations between the Islamic world and the Far East remained strong, according to the Moroccan traveler Ibn Battūta (1304–ca. 1377), who left a description of the Muslim quarter of Canton, then extensively developed with a mosque, an inn, and a bazaar, and subject to the authority of a *shaykh al-islām* (who supervised worship) and a *qādi* (a magistrate or judge).

The importation of foodstuffs, porcelain, and various technologies, carried on for centuries by Arab ships that departed from the ports of the Persian Gulf, the Red Sea, and the Indian Ocean for India and the Far East, on the one hand, and for Africa, on the other, was undoubtedly accompanied by a wide circulation of ideas and tastes. One has only to consider the vogue for china tableware, for example, still today no less lively in the kingdom of Morocco than in earlier times.

CULINARY TRADITIONS AND CONFLICTS OF IDENTITY

It is said that the ancient Arabs valued visual delights and the art of conversation more highly than a good meal. Eloquence was characteristic of the Bedouins of Arabia, by contrast with their disregard for urban fashions of conviviality. This indifference bewildered their fellow Arabs living in the large cities of Syria, but the "authentic" Arabs, still attached to the customs of nomadic culture, did not hesitate to express their disdain for the sophisticated dishes that adorned the princely banquets of Damascus.

Such disputes had long divided not only Bedouins and city dwellers, but also Arabs and Persians. Then as now, eating habits were an index of the cohesion of a particular ethnic, religious, or social group. In the first century of the Islamic era, for example, Maysūn bint Bahdal—a Christian poet, daughter of the chief of the Kalb tribe, wife of the Umayyad caliph Muʿāwiya, and mother of Caliph Yazīd I—never fully accepted the conventions of city life. Although she adapted herself to them, she continued to prefer the rustic bread of the nomads to the refined bread of the city:

A tent buffeted by the winds
is dearer to me than a magnificent palace:
it pleases me to put on a cloak of coarse wool,
if the eye be watchful, and I no longer find pleasure
in wearing fine transparent fabrics;
the restless howl of the winds
is dearer to me than the beating of drums;
a dog that snarls at distant passersby
is dearer to me than a cat that creeps along the walls.
[. . .]
In the tent, I prefer to have under my teeth
coarse bread rather than white bread.
I want only my land,
which alone in my eyes is noble.[18]

In the poetry and satirical literature of the Shuʿūbiyya movement (an anti-Arab campaign appealing mainly to Islamized Persians), uncivilized dietary habits—such as eating lizards, scorpions and other insects, the flesh of dogs and donkeys, and so on—are attributed to the Bedouins, since even Arab city dwellers were considered to be descended from these uncouth denizens of the desert. Denigrating the culture of the Arabs was a reaction against their preeminence in the political sphere. Bashshār ibn Burd (724–ca. 785), one of the greatest poets of his time—born at Basra of Persian parents, blind from birth and repulsive to look at (he worked in a butcher's shop and took no notice whatever of his appearance)—was one of the most outspoken exponents of the anti-Arab and anti-Bedouin movement, well known for his sharp tongue: "We, in our times of glory, ate white bread and drank out of goblets of silver and gold. . . . You, by night, go out to hunt porcupines and rats."[19] Bashshār was put to death, not for his harsh words but because he was accused of Zoroastrianism. His remains were thrown into the Tigris.

Proud of their distinctive heritage, the Arabs did not take the least offense and responded to these slanders by recounting tales that were still more implausible, such as the one of the Bedouin who relished a sandwich made of a fatty piece of wild donkey inserted between two large dates "like the hoof of a small camel born in the spring." The poet Abū al-Hindī expressed the view (both culinary and nationalist) that "nothing is better than an old lizard," claiming that the eggs of this small creature were the food of real Arabs, whereas the rice and fish that the Persians ate made him vomit, and so on. But the bards of the desert were renowned for saying they did things that they did not. Exaggeration and excess compensated for the hardships and plainness of ordinary existence, the unhappiness of everyday life. Surely we are not to believe al-Thaʿālibi when he describes the gluttony of the Umayyad caliph Muʿāwiya thus: "One day he ate thirty chickens and a hundred hard-cooked eggs, drank many glasses of date wine, then took his pleasure with two virgins"? Paradise on earth! The grandiloquence and lyricism permitted by the Arabic language helped transform food into something extraordinary, something marvelous and fantastic. Rubies and stars, diamonds, gold, and silver were evoked to describe dates, sugars, pastries, eggs, and so on; it was feasting with the eyes and savoring with words. Another author, named Ibn Sīrīn, who wrote prose works, used the language of dreams to interpret food.

DIETARY OBSESSIONS AND PHOBIAS

The Muʿtazilite writer al-Jāhiz (d. ca. 868) is an inexhaustible source of information on the dining habits of men and their relationship with food. Eating is an obsessively present theme in all of his works, especially *Kitāb al-Bukhalā* ("The Book of Misers"), which tells fabulous stories about misers and their cunning in finding ways to eat without spending money.[20] Among the Arabs, generosity was measured primarily by the quality and abundance of the meal offered to guests; by the gifts of food made to strangers, travelers, and the needy; and, as in the Christian tradition, by the sharing of bread. Al-Jāhiz's miser is a man who, despite his ample means, deprives not only himself of good food but also his own family, and offers none to anyone else. His behavior calls to mind that of a certain Abū Yaʿqūb al-Dhaqnān, who claimed that he had never gone without meat since becoming rich. But we see in what manner:

Every Friday, he purchased beef for a *dirham*, onions for the value of a *dāniq*, eggplant for a *dāniq*, and zucchini for a *dāniq*, and, when carrots were in season, he also bought carrots for a *dāniq*. He cooked them all together, making of them a *sikbāj*. On this day, with his family, he ate with bread that which floated on the surface [of the dish], thus leaving at the bottom all the onions, eggplant, carrots, zucchini, fat, and meat. On Saturday they ate bread soaked with broth. Sunday they ate the onions, Monday the carrots, Tuesday the zucchini, Wednesday the eggplant, and Thursday the meat. This is why he said that he had not deprived himself of meat since the day he had become rich.[21]

Worse still than the miser is the freeloader (*mutataffil*) who takes advantage of the generosity of others. Al-Jāhiz tells of one such man who loudly and shamelessly proclaims his success in this regard:

Every day I wander through the square of the quarter, attracted, like the flies, by the aroma of roasted meat. If I see the signs of a wedding, or of a circumcision, or of a party among friends, I do not hesitate to [find a way to] get in, paying no mind to the insults or the blows of the doorkeeper, brushing aside the hosts of the house, feeling no fear whatever. Then you see me circle like an eagle in the sky, before attacking the foods that are laid out [there]. It is more profitable than spending [money], running up debts, and suffering the arrogance of the baker and the butcher.[22]

Islam does not issue injunctions against enjoying the pleasures of food, but satirical moralizers and ascetics have always censured epicurean delights. The Syrian author Abū'l-ʿAlāʾ al-Maʿarrī (973–1057)—blind from the age of four, poet and philosopher, moralist, ascetic, and pessimist—was more than a vegetarian, for he not only ate neither meat nor fish, but abstained from milk, eggs, and honey as well. His vegetarianism brought upon him the charge of heresy from a certain Abū Nasr ibn Abī ʿImrān, a Shiite, for whom the refusal to eat lawful foods, which God had created for man, was blasphemous.[23]

Others, by contrast, excessively cultivated the arts of the table. One such man was Thawb ibn Shahma al-ʿAnbarī, a curiously protective lover of birds who prohibited hunting on his vast estate while declaring himself ready to die of hunger rather than be forced to eat mediocre food.[24] This cannot fail to call to mind the conception of earthly life held by the Roman epicure Marcus Gavius Apicius, who chose death on discovering how little was left to him after spending a few million sesterces on food.

THE ANCIENT CULINARY HERITAGE

Remove the entrails from a chicken, boil it, take it out [of the water], sprinkle it with asafetida and pepper, and roast it. Grind up in a mortar pepper, cumin, coriander seed, asafetida root, rue, crushed dates, pine nuts; moisten with vinegar, honey, *garum* [fish sauce], and oil. Mix together. Bring to a boil, then thicken the sauce with starch, pour it over the chicken, sprinkle with pepper, and serve.[25]

This ancient Roman-Berber recipe is attributed to Apicius, whose life straddled the first century B.C.E. and the first century C.E. "Chicken in the Numidian fashion"—boiled, roasted, and then napped with a spicy sweet-and-sour sauce thickened with a pesto of fresh herbs, pine nuts, and mashed dates—is not so very different from the *bārida* of chicken created by Iraqi gastronomes in the early ninth century, many recipes for which are associated with the ʿAbbasid caliphs.[26] The ingredients are practically the same: vinegar, oil, aromatic herbs, honey (sometimes substituted for by sugar), nuts, and spices such as pepper, cumin, and coriander (also, depending on the recipe, cinnamon, ginger, spikenard, and so on). The difference is that the Islamic dish has *murrī*, another salty fermented condiment, in place of *garum*.

The various sauces for fish, which the cooks of Baghdad called *sibāgh*, certainly had an ancient basis as well. They were flavored with vinegar, spices, and sweetened ingredients, which recall the Alexandrine sauces ascribed to Apicius. Unlike these earlier sauces, however, they incorporated other spices and ingredients—pomegranate seeds, for example—that contributed new flavors and a variety of colors.

Zīrbāj and the *sikbāj* were also prepared with vinegar, a sweetener of some kind (honey, sugar, or fruit juices), and both nuts and desiccated fruits, but the cooking procedure differed: the meat was cooked in its broth, with all the ingredients being added one after the other. The fact remains that the dominant flavor of all these dishes continued to be sweet-and-sour, similar to that of Apicius's chicken and, more generally, to that of the cuisine of the Berbers from the northeastern Maghreb (Latinized Berbers and Berberized Latins) at the beginning of the Christian era. Whom, therefore, are we to credit with devising such sweet-and-sour dishes? The Greeks? The Romans? The Iranians? Wine vinegar, which forms the basis of this flavor, derives from wine, and wine comes from the grape. Where, and when, were grapes first cultivated?

Already by the end of the fourth millennium B.C.E., the presence of both wine and vinegar is attested in Egypt. From there they spread to two areas of northern Mesopotamia, Iraqi Kurdistan and Syria—two regions, then, that were practically adjacent to each other, where commercial exchange was intensively developed. Inevitably, the tumult of military conquest and the complexity of mercantile networks blur our picture of culinary diffusion in the ancient Near East. But it is clear that the Phoenicians were the first to control the Mediterranean and that the establishment of trading centers along its shores and on its islands had the effect of reducing the distance between cultures and encouraging the circulation of culinary traditions, fashions, and technologies. The first mention of the use of vinegar in the cooking of foods goes back to the Old Babylonian period, about 1700–1600 B.C.E. One recipe found on a cuneiform tablet from this period calls for a kind of vinegar called *tabatu*.[27] Three such culinary texts are known, indicating the ingredients to be used, the type of fire required, the process of preparation, and the cooking of dishes intended as sacred offerings. A number of dishes provide evidence of the advances made in devising techniques of cooking and creating particular flavors in ancient Mesopotamia—for example, *mersu*, a kind of cake filled with dried fruit and seasoned with fragrant herbs. The soups made from dry legumes and cereals seem to have differed little, if at all, from the ones that the Arabs made in the medieval period. *Shiqqu,* a condiment made from pickled fish and shellfish, may have been the ancestor of the

Roman *garum* and of the Iraqi fish *sahnā*. And *samnu* calls to mind the Arab *samn*, a clarified salted butter that is still abundantly used today in both the Middle East and North Africa. The blood of sacrificed animals was found in a number of sauces of the ancient Near East.

More than two thousand years later, the extensive use of spices and of contrasting seasonings such as vinegar and honey, so characteristic of Roman cooking, was to become the distinctive trait of the cuisine of medieval Islam as well. More particularly, the combination of pepper, cumin, and coriander, almost invariably found in the seasoning of the dishes of Apicius and of the medieval Islamic period, is a constant feature of present-day cuisine in the Maghreb. This combination seems quite foreign, however, to the taste of the Romans' descendants in modern Italy. Tastes and flavors that go back to antiquity, that were long common to all the peoples of the Mediterranean, are now associated in the Western mind with a completely alien and different world. Dishes cooked with saffron or with turmeric, with cardamom or with ginger, and so on, evoke the East in the broad sense— the Orient of China, India, Iran, Morocco, the Arabs, and Islam—and need today to be discovered in "ethnic" restaurants. And yet I have found the sweet-sour and sweet-salt flavors of the Maghreb in several regional Italian cuisines: *l'agnello alle prugne* (lamb with plum sauce) in an old trattoria in Venice; *le zucchine alla napoletana* (zucchini with vinegar, currants, and onions) in Naples; a pie made with olives, onions, and raisins in Andria, in Puglia—these among many other examples, all of which unfailingly remind me of the flavors of certain Tunisian dishes, such as *mdarbil, sharmūla, murūziyya,* and so on.

Between the time of Apicius and that of Ibrāhīm ibn al-Mahdī, centuries passed without any cookbook being written, during which cooking made its way in silence. Culinary styles spread in the wake of conquests and the seasonal displacement of populations: with the Romans, who dominated the entire coastal periphery of the Mediterranean, and the Persians, whose power expanded as far as Egypt (albeit for a very short time); and with the migrations of nomads in search of new pasturage or driven out of their own lands by rival tribes. Only the original territory of Islam, the Arabian peninsula, escaped foreign domination. The Romans had arrived at its borders with the annexation, at the beginning of the second century C.E., of the kingdom of the Nabataean Arabs, whose capital, Petra (today in Jordan), lies between the rocky gorges of northern Hijaz. It was from the kingdom of Hijaz, known to the Romans as Provincia Arabia and to the Arabs as "the Barrier," that Islam set off to conquer the world at the beginning of the seventh century. From the second century B.C.E. the Roman presence in North Africa had been well established, particularly in the region that extended from Carthage to Algeria, which they called Numidia—whence the name Apicius gave to his chicken dish. Here the Berbers had at first adopted the Punic language, and then, with the coming of the Romans, Latin. During the time of King Masinissa (d. 148 B.C.E.), Berber was declared an official language along with Latin and Punic. Known afterward as Africa Nova, the province rapidly became Christianized in the second century. In the Near East, Mesopotamia had been a Roman province since the end of the second century, and still today is home to very ancient Christian rites. The Egypt of the pharaohs, for its part, succumbed to the supremacy of the Romans for a long period before finally passing under Byzantine domination. Today the country's population includes some ten million Coptic Christians.

The regions conquered by Islam—Berber, Coptic, Arab, and so on—were therefore profoundly influenced by Greco-Roman culture in the west, and by both Persian and Greco-Roman culture in the east. It was in this ancient, rich, and sophisticated cultural context that Islamic culinary culture first flowered.

ARAB CUISINE:

THE TRADITION OF THE PROPHET

But what did the Arabs of the seventh century eat, in the early days of Islam? There were many tribes of Arabs, nomads and city dwellers alike, Arabs of the north and of the south, Arabs of the Gulf and of the Red Sea, dispersed across the vast spaces of the Arabian peninsula. Their alimentary habits are known to us through accounts of the life of the prophet Muhammad, born at Mecca in Hijaz, a region that extends for hundreds of miles along the coast of the Red Sea, from the port of Aqaba in the north to the port of Al-Līth in the south. Hijaz consists of high desert plateaus where rainfall is rare and unpredictable, but it is not totally barren for all that; it is dotted with oases, as for example at Medina, where a settled population cultivates the date palm and, to a lesser extent, vineyards. Wheat was grown a bit farther south, in Asir, the best-irrigated region. Owing to the climate, caravan trade and stock breeding based on the dromedary and the goat were more important activities than agriculture. Relations among the nomadic masters of the desert trade routes and the settled peoples, who controlled the centers of commerce, were rarely peaceful, however, though some degree of harmony was necessary to assure mutual survival in a hostile environment. But even if their roles were complementary from the economic point of view, the Bedouin way of life, simple and plain, was predominant across the great expanses of the Arabian peninsula.

The Arabs remained faithful to this ancestral way of life from both principle and necessity, but perhaps out of a love of independence as well. Nonetheless, they were not indifferent to the influences of neighboring cultures; they knew the civilizations that had grown up around them: Iraq and Sasanid Iran, Byzantine Syria with its Greco-Roman heritage, Christian Abyssinia. The great poets of Arabia, who traveled the length and breadth of the peninsula, disseminated information in much the same way that the press does today; that is, they not only acted as spokesmen of their tribe, but served a function that was in some sense comparable to that of merchants. A sixth-century poet, al-Nābigha al-Dhubyānī, of the Murra tribe, for example, had contacts with the Ghassanid and Lakhmid monarchs, whose peoples had emigrated northward from Arabia a few centuries before the advent of Islam. He lived in Hira in Iraq, at the court of the king Nu'mān III ibn Abī Qābūs (581–602). Al-Nābigha al-Dhubyānī's poems recount tales of Bedouin life, but also of the cultural life he discovered in the Persian court of the Lakhmid kings. At Mecca, despite their xenophobia, the Arabs of the

Quraysh tribe (the tribe of Muhammad) allowed themselves to be tempted by Sasanid pastries, above all by *falūdhaj*, which was, in its simplest version, a cake prepared with starch and honey. We know that this cake was offered to guests by ʿAbd Allāh ibn Jadʿān, who prepared it according to a recipe that he had acquired during his visit to the court of Khosrau II, and was served in ebony bowls.[28]

Yemen, or Arabia Felix as the Romans called it, controlled the sea lanes to and from the Far East. Incense and fragrances came into ports in southern Arabia and Ethiopia. Mecca—which from time immemorial had been the spiritual center of the pre-Islamic Arabs, who made pilgrimages to worship at the temple of Kaʿba—was a center of the caravan trade for merchants coming from the coast of Yemen and bound for Syria and Egypt. Is it imaginable that their cargoes of incense and spices could have passed one another without the inhabitants of Mecca acquiring some of these things? Could Arab women have remained indifferent to such exotic merchandise? Surely not! While the pre-Islamic period is called *jāhiliyya,* the "age of ignorance," this term refers to the Arabs' ignorance of true religion, Islam, not to ignorance in general, and still less to ignorance of the pleasures of life.

With Islam the idea of tradition as a fixed standard of behavior became radicalized, in accordance with the norms derived from Qurʾanic prescriptions and *sunna*. The term *sunna* designates the tradition of Muhammad and his way of life, which were adopted by his companions and the first caliphs as the ideal model to be followed and universally accepted by the Muslim community. To eat as the Prophet ate—in the Arab style, seated on the ground, with the right hand—and to eat what the Prophet ate became an act of faith. The tradition of the Prophet, so far from being the invention of Islam, was a product of the Arab practices of his time and place, practices inherited from the age of *jāhiliyya,* to which some modifications suggested by the Revelation were made. Following the example of the Prophet meant, apart from a few exceptions (pork, blood, and wine), having to reproduce the ancient manners and customs of the Arabs.

Muhammad took it upon himself to respond to questions asked by new converts to the faith when the answer was not found in the Qur'an. The early Muslim community joined together at Medina was made up of individuals from every part of the Arabian peninsula. The Prophet established alliances, ratified by marriage, with distant Islamized tribes. In his role as unifier of the Arabs, and despite efforts to adapt to foreign habits, he did not always succeed in concealing his distaste for a particular dish. One that the Prophet found unappetizing, locusts, was unknown to his tribe, but the religion did not forbid it. He therefore declared it lawful.[29] All the Prophet's arguments concerning dietary matters were gathered by al-Bukhārī (d. 870) in the chapter "al-Ghidā" of his collection of the *hadīth* (the sayings of the Prophet).[30] There exist six official collections of the *hadīth*, compiled by different authors during the ninth century after long and meticulous labors of authentication. Nonetheless, it is by no means impossible that practices from neighboring Islamized provinces may have found their way into this corpus of Arab-Muslim traditions, which was constituted well after the death of the Prophet on the basis of oral transmission.

However this may be, respect for culinary traditions associated with the Arab tradition of Medina contributed to the diffusion in the Muslim world of certain Arab dishes, in particular *tharīd*, the Prophet's favorite meal. A few dishes from this period are known: *masliyya*, mutton and kid cooked in whey (*masl*) and sometimes sprinkled with dry cheese; *madīra*, in which meat was cooked in curdled milk; and *tharīd* itself, meat cooked in a broth with crumbled flat bread added to it just before serving. The Arabs cooked with both fat from the tail of the sheep and clarified butter (*samn*), whereas in other Islamic regions of the Mediterranean these two types of fat were supplemented by vegetable oils, especially olive and sesame oils. Bread was cooked either beneath coals or on red-hot stones, ideally ones that had first been used to roast meat or to melt a piece of sheep tail fat, so that the bread became saturated with the fat that remained stuck to the stone. A dish called *hays*, made with dates and milk, was an Arab specialty that Abū Hind, the

Prophet's barber, had made for him and his companions to celebrate victory after a battle.

MUSLIM CUISINE:

THE QUR'ANIC PROSCRIPTIONS

All foods are permitted, except for the blood and flesh of the pig. Each year Muslims must fast from sunrise to sunset for the entire duration of the lunar month of Ramadan. Ramadan is not a penance but a purification. During the rest of the year Muslims are free to eat as they please, to consume anything they desire, within the limits of the law, at any time of day. There are no meatless Fridays, nor any Sabbath meal, nor any other special regime. Compared to the dietary rules obeyed by Christians and Jews during the time of the Prophet, the Muslim prescriptions must have seemed a gift from heaven. To be sure, pork was strictly prohibited; but is it likely that pigs were ever raised by the Hijaz Arabs? In the sweltering climate of the Arabian peninsula swine have a hard time surviving, for the lack of water causes their skin to dehydrate rapidly, all the more since they are rather sedentary animals. In this part of the world, animals can be raised at all only by transhumance (the seasonal migration of animals and their herders between lowlands and adjacent mountains).

The few Islamic proscriptions there are regarding food were revealed to the Prophet at Medina, after his departure from Mecca, in 622. They are summarized in the following verse from the Qur'an: "[Prophet], say, 'In all that has been revealed to me, I find nothing forbidden for people to eat, except for carrion, flowing blood, pig's meat—it is loathsome—or a sinful offering over which any name other than God's has been invoked.'"[31]

As in the Hebrew religion, swine was considered impure; nor was it lawful to consume the blood shed in killing animals, which in any case had to be ritually slaughtered. Accordingly, an animal was prohibited that had been "strangled, victim of a violent blow or a fall, gored or savaged by a beast of prey, unless you still slaughter it [in the correct manner]."[32] An exception was made in the case of quarry: "They ask you, Prophet, what is lawful for them. Say, 'All good things are lawful for you.' [This includes] what you have taught your birds and beasts of prey to catch, teaching them as God has taught you, so eat what they catch for you, but first pronounce God's name over it."[33]

The new alimentary norms laid down by Islam appeared to the Jews and Christians of the seventh century to liberate its adherents by relaxing and simplifying traditional obligations. The number of dietary restrictions was reduced to two, as against the dozens insisted on by Jewish law, and the period of fasting was set at thirty days rather than the forty days of Lent, in addition to the elimination of meatless Fridays and the changing of the day of worship from the Jewish Saturday to the Muslim Friday. The Qur'an explains why God imposed so many prohibitions on the Jews: "We forbade for the Jews every animal with claws, and the fat of cattle and sheep, except what is on their backs and in their intestines, or that which sticks to their bones. This is how We penalized them for their disobedience: We are true to Our word."[34]

In a certain sense, the Muslim stands nearer to the Jew in rejecting pork and spilled blood, and further from the Christian, who, in addition to consuming the meat of impure animals[35] and enjoying blood sausage, kills oxen by clubbing them on the head and wrings the necks of chickens. On the other hand, both Christians and Muslims indiscriminately consume horse meat, snails, locusts, rabbits, and every type of fish (exception being made for the Iranians, who, having their own opinion on this subject, had to devise a *fatwa* making it lawful to eat sturgeon, which caused offense for its lack of scales). So adamant is the insistence on the obligation to eat everything that God has made lawful—that is, all animals except the pig—that one may wonder whether a vegetarian could be admitted to the community of believers. The problem had already been posed in the eleventh century in connection with the poet and philosopher Abu al-Alaʿ al-Maʾarri, whose avoidance of meat caused him to be accused of heresy. His behavior contradicted the Qurʾanic injunction "You who believe, do not forbid the good things God has made lawful to you—do not exceed the limits: God does not love those who exceed the limits—but eat the lawful and good things that God provides for you. Be mindful of God, in whom you believe."[36] By luck, reason prevailed over fanaticism and Abu al-Ala° al-Ma°arri was permitted to continue to observe an ascetic regime and to devote himself to the composition of his philosophical works.

On earth, food is a gift from God to human beings; in the hereafter it is the occasion of divine reward. Heavenly foods are sweet, refreshing, and intoxicating. Fruits in paradise are "plucked directly from the tree," as the Qur°an says, and the "trees" are palms, pomegranates, and grapevines, always laden with marvelous fruits having no need for human attention: "Here is a picture of the Garden promised to the pious: rivers of water forever pure, rivers of milk forever fresh, rivers of wine, a delight for those who drink, rivers of honey clarified and pure, [all] flow in it; there they will find fruit of every kind; and they will find forgiveness from their Lord."[37]

In saying little about food, and nothing at all about cooking, the Qur°an leaves us free to indulge our appetite, or rather to exercise unlimited creativity in this domain—so long as no lard is used!

"They Ask You about Intoxicants . . ."   With regard to intoxicating beverages, the Qur°an lays down a few proscriptions associated with the revelations of the Medina period, but they do not seem to constitute a prohibition as categorical as the ones that apply to pork and spilled blood: "They ask you[, Prophet,] about intoxicants and gambling: say, 'There is great sin in both, and some benefit for people: the sin is greater than the benefit.'"[38]

Wine is more or less forbidden depending on one's denominational allegiance within Sunni Islam, which counts four rites (or juridical schools) recognized by the highest religious authorities. For instance, the Hanafi rite, followed by the majority of Turks, does not prohibit it altogether. Interpretations vary, but a lay reading seems to suggest that it is above all the abuse of alcoholic beverages that the Qur°an condemns and not moderate consumption. Moreover, wine is not considered "impure" in the way that pork is—otherwise why should it be included among the pleasures that are promised to pious Muslims on entering Paradise? "The truly good will live in bliss, seated on couches, gazing around. You will recognize on their faces the radiance of bliss. They will be served a sealed nectar, its seal [perfumed with] a fragrant herb—let those who strive, strive for this—mixed with the water of Tasnim, a spring from which those brought near will drink."[39]

Muslim laws restricted the consumption of alcohol but rarely its production, which was supervised for the most part by Christians and Jews. The municipal inspector of customs (*muhtasib*) was charged with intervening in the event of public displays of drunkenness, and particularly against persons who came inebriated to the mosque. In practice, for the whole of the medieval period, from Iraq to Andalusia, the consumption of alcohol of any kind— whether wine from the grape, palm wine, date wine, honey wine, or any other kind—though it was never officially authorized, was more or less tolerated depending on the attitude of the government at any particular time.[40] There were always those in favor and those against, as numerous medieval writings on the subject attest; nevertheless, support for the anti-alcohol position grew in the aftermath of the Crusades in the Middle East and the Almohad conquest in the Maghreb and Andalusia. A pair of Andalusian authors, writing two centuries apart, expressed passionate views about wine: Abū Maslama, in the eleventh century, exalted it in his *Garden of Joys in the Description of the Reality of Wine,* and Ibn Zarqūn, in the thirteenth, condemned it in his *Burning of the Embers for Prohibiting Wine.*[41]

Ibn Sayyār, the author of our earliest culinary record, dedicated the final pages of his book to the art of *munādama,* a term that indicates conviviality or the tasting of wine by a group of educated men capable of holding interesting conversations, especially in the presence of the king. This is evidence that a tradition of sociable behavior was openly perpetuated in the tenth and eleventh centuries. It is clear that the state of drunkenness was considered shameful. For this reason Ibn Sayyār insisted on respect for certain rules of decency, in order to avoid objectionable conduct:

The *nadīm* [boon companion] who drinks with the king must occupy the place that has been assigned to him, without seeking to put himself in a higher or lower position; he must not lie down, but rather hold himself in an upright position. . . . He must not yawn, . . . nor persist in argument under the effect of drink, because whoever behaves in this way is boorish. . . . He must drink by taking small sips, inhaling the fragrance [of the wine]. He is not to drink more than he is capable of supporting, [stopping] before he loses his judgment and encounters difficulties in controlling his actions. He is not to hoist his glass before the king, nor to fill it before that of the king, [taking care to] drink only after the king or at the same time. May he not begin to speak, nor to sing or to play a musical instrument, nor jest while the servant hands him his drink: he is to take it without asking for it to be filled more or less, without discussion or argument. Should he feel himself overcome by inebriation, let him get up and leave while he is still in control of himself. Let him not touch the hand of the wine server when he offers the glass, nor look at him excessively while [the server] is occupied with the wine, nor gesture to him, neither winking at him nor speaking in his ear.[42]

A century earlier, learned men had been divided over the effects of wine. Al-Rāzī, a Muslim physician of Persian birth and director of the great hospital at Baghdad, took issue with Arab physicians of the period who condemned not only its consumption but also its medicinal use: "The usefulness of wine, for the protection of health and the improvement of digestion, is assured if one grants it its due place, and if its quantity and its quality, as well as the moment when it is consumed, are in keeping with the rules of art. It renders the body fertile, expels all excesses, causing them to leave the body, and increases the innate heat [of the body]."[43]

It seems plain that the taboo against wine fell less heavily upon non-Arab than Arab Muslims. For the Turks of the Seljuk tribe, assembled in Iraq after their migration from central Asia toward the middle of the eleventh century, the consumption of wine was permitted, as it had been under the reign of the Buyids. Of this there can be no doubt, for it is the Seljuk sultan's own vizier who furnishes us with proof. Nizām al-Mulk, born into a Persian family and murdered by a member of the sect of the Hashishiyyīn (the Assassins), protector of al-Ghazālī (one of the most celebrated theologians of Islam), and founder of the institution of the madrasa (school of higher education in the religious and secular sciences), was the author of *The Book of Government*, addressed to the Sunni Turkish sovereigns who reigned over all the Islamic East, Arabia included. He dedicated one chapter to the "Organization of Gatherings Devoted to the Pleasures of Wine: Rules to Be Obeyed":

> It is customary for each person to attend the gathering dedicated to the pleasures of wine, accompanied by a single slave. He is forbidden to bring with him a cupbearer and cruets of wine . . . since, [the sultan] being the supreme father of the universal family and [the guests] being the human members of his family and his servants, whoever receives sustenance from [the sultan] must not bring from his own house either his food or his wine. If [nonetheless] he brings some, because the cellarmaster of the palace does not provide any [of good quality], then one must harshly reprimand him.[44]

Ramadan: A Spiritual and Gastronomic Event With the appearance of the new moon marking the start of the month of Ramadan, Muslims enter into a holy period of obligatory fasting (*sawm*) that constitutes one of the five pillars of Islam. It involves total abstinence from all food and drink, from sunrise to sunset, for the entire month. It also excludes the taking of medicines, as well as the use of tobacco and all sexual relations.

Ramadan is the ninth month of the Muslim lunar calendar, one of three holy months of the year—the holiest of the three, in fact, since it is to the night between the twenty-sixth and twenty-seventh days of this month that tradition assigns the first revelation of the Qurʾan to Muhammad. The Qurʾan calls it the Night of Glory: "The Night of Glory is better than a thousand months; on that night the angels and the Spirit descend again with their Lord's permission on every task."[45] This month, whose name means "incandescent" or "reduced to ashes" because it coincided with the hottest month of the year before the modification of the lunar-solar calendar (converted to a lunar calendar by the command of the Prophet shortly before his death), had been sacred for the ancient Arabs from the earliest times, no doubt because it represented the hardest and most dangerous period of the year for survival in the desert regions, where thirst is apt to be fatal. With the new system of computation inaugurated by the Prophet, the month dedicated to fasting began to fall ever earlier, by eleven days per year (the lunar year being shorter than the solar year). Hence the chance that the month would coincide with August—that is to say, with the hottest month and the longest days—was reduced to three times every thirty-three years. The wisdom and humanity of this decision were worthy of a prophet who cared for the health and safety of his people.

Before the institution of the month of Ramadan, Muhammad had obliged Muslims to fast on the day of the Hebrew festival of Kippur ("atonement"), but this tradition was abandoned after the break with the Jews of Medina.

The rhythm of Ramadan alternates between abstinence and unrestrained consumption; between hunger and satiety, retreat and sociability, prayers and festivities. Anyone in a Muslim city during this time, Muslim or not, observant or not, is unavoidably aware of the exceptional contrasts of its days and nights, and invited to share the lavish evening meal that marks the breaking of the fast, the desserts and refreshing beverages that are served throughout the evening, and, last but not least, the final meal, *sahūr*, which must be eaten just before the rising of the sun. This meal is very important, for it provides an ample supply of energy for the day of fasting ahead: "Eat and drink until the white thread of dawn becomes distinct from the black. Then fast until nightfall."[46]

The evening meal of Ramadan is prepared in silence in the last minutes before the firing of the cannon that immediately follows the muezzin's cry announcing the end of the fast. The table is decorated with the most refined and varied dishes, beginning with specialties that Muslim women learn to prepare with passion and care, and serve on the most beautiful china plates. The fast itself must be seen not as a penance but as evidence of obedience to God and of gratitude to Him. Nor must it be supposed that the spiritual observance of Ramadan is somehow incompatible with good cheer and the pleasures of the table. It is, of course, a month of piety and of solidarity; but it is also a gastronomic event unique in the world, lasting twenty-nine or thirty days in a row. Food markets are abundantly stocked with the best local and exotic products during this period, spice merchants and nut vendors exhaust their supplies before the end of the month, and pastry shops make a fortune. In the evenings the mosques and mausoleums are never empty of the faithful, who come to hear Qur'anic chants and Sufi songs, and to participate in group prayers. The cafés and nightclubs are filled as well, with men who smoke the hookah while listening to the music of Umm Kulthum, the legendary Egyptian singer who passed away in 1975.

What still remains today of the ancient culinary tradition? At least a number of simple gestures that recall those of the Prophet: breaking the fast with water and dates and drinking curdled milk with the meal. The dishes typical of Ramadan differ from country to country, apart from *zulābiyya,* a honey fritter that has been found on tables every year in almost all the Muslim countries of the Mediterranean since medieval times.

The month concludes with the festival of *ʿid al-fitr* (called Seker Bayram by the Turks), an occasion for offerings and the exchange of cakes that little by little gives way to the resumption of the normal rhythms of daily life.

THE EXTRAVAGANCE OF DAMASCUS

Traveling from Medina to Damascus, the Arabs passed from one oasis to another—and what oases! Irrigated by the Barada River and lying near the coast of the Mediterranean, to the west of the Ghuta oasis, Damascus, gateway of the Fertile Crescent, turns its back on the desert. Overlooking the waters that nourish cultivated lands and periodically upset the life of its inhabitants, Damascus—with its fields of grain, vineyards, orchards of apple, plum, and apricot, pines, and rose gardens—promises a happy end for journeys from less hospitable regions.

The Muslim caliphate, once transferred to Damascus, broke with tradition in introducing the dynastic principle. The new rulers of the Umayyad dynasty (661–750)—who, like their predecessors, belonged to the Quraysh tribe, the tribe of Muhammad—also broke with the austere Arab alimentary traditions of Islam's early days. The image of the Umayyad dynasties preserved by ʿAbbasid historiography, of a gluttonous, bulimic, and dissolute people, is altogether plausible.

Muʿāwiya ibn Abī Sufyān, the first Umayyad caliph at Damascus, was little inclined to deny himself the pleasures of food. Having discovered the refinement of Syrian cooking, he was able, thanks to the wealth of his office, to give free rein to every wish. The staff of the various administrative departments of state were native Syrians, as were the cooks of the caliph's kitchens, to which the heritage of the Byzantines had been bequeathed. Banquets were organized and menus drawn up in accordance with the fashions of the Byzantine and Sasanid courts (the Sasanids had occupied Syria from 612 to 627, shortly before the arrival of the Arabs) without, however, completely renouncing certain Arab culinary traditions. These were maintained, in more or less modified form, throughout the medieval period and beyond. The Arabs' predilection for Persian cuisine, evident since the pre-Islamic period, increased still more owing to their fondness for sweet desserts such as *falūdhaj*, a pudding made from sugar, starch, and nuts and flavored with musk and rose water, long a favorite of the leisured classes of Damascus.

The Umayyads, wishing to make a show of their generosity to the conquered population, continued the Byzantine practice of public food distribution. Tables for the people were laid every day, and in some cities twice a day.

As in all great empires, the affluence and abundance enjoyed by the upper classes of the Muslim world stood in contrast both to the precarious circumstances of the greater part of the urban population and to the extreme simplicity of life in the countryside. The economy of the state rested in large measure on the exploitation of slaves and on the collection of taxes, which grew ever more burdensome. All the subjects of the Muslim world paid a sort of tithe, known as *kharāj*; farmers paid it in kind. The *dhimmī*, or infidel subjects—Christians, Jews, and Zoroastrians—were obliged to render to the state a supplementary tax, the *jizya*, which was dedicated to protection of non-Muslims. Believers, for their part, paid the *zakāt*, an obligatory donation meant to assist members of the Muslim community that was presented directly to its beneficiaries near the end of the month of Ramadan.

Peasant revolts are recorded in the late seventh century, first in Egypt, where Coptic farmers rose up three times within twenty-five years in protest against difficult economic conditions. Later, in 841, under the reign of the ʿAbbasids in Syria and Palestine, a great revolt led by Abū Harb ("father of war") broke out. But a larger and more significant revolt was launched in 869 by the Zanj, the black slaves who worked Iraqi agricultural estates. Angered by their treatment during the ʿAbbasid campaign to reclaim marshlands in the south of Iraq, undertaken in order to introduce new crops such as sugarcane, they were not suppressed until 883.

THE GASTRONOME PRINCE AND HIS MUSE

At the beginning of the ninth century, in the royal palace at Rusāfa near Baghdad, a prince and his concubine, united by a grand passion for the culinary arts, passed most of their time before the stoves. A sensuous cuisine such as that of Ibrāhīm ibn al-Mahdī is inconceivable without romantic inspiration. The muse in this case, a woman named Bidʿa, was particularly valuable, for she was a great cook. Theirs seems to have been an extraordinary partnership, which assumed tangible form in the creation of a genuine laboratory of flavor. The historian David Waines is not wrong to call this cooking the "new wave" of its time.

Here is what Yūsuf ibn Ibrāhīm, a slave freed by Ibrāhīm ibn al-Mahdī, tells us about Bidʿa:

> Ibrāhīm al-Mahdī had a blonde concubine born of a non-Muslim mother. She had been offered to him by al-Rashīd on his return from Damascus. This concubine was the best cook among the women of her time, had the greatest experience in the preparation of cold appetizers

and desserts, and was infinitely skillful. Her fame reached as far as Caliph al-Amīn, who had heard so much about her that he told Abū Isḥāq [Ibrāhīm al-Mahdī] of his desire once again to sample a *sikbāj* made with her own hands. [It had to be] a dish prepared with the best veal, mutton, kid, and poultry, and on this occasion there were to be no dishes other than this one; if he were to be served something beforehand or afterward, he would not taste it. His desire was to eat the *sikbāj* and drink at table until he was drunk, and only afterward would he wash his hands.

Ibrāhīm took his leave of al-Amīn and summoned the concubine. The woman appeared; she was called Bidʿa. He said to her, "Bidʿa, your lord, the emir of the believers, wishes to eat a *sikbāj* and calls on me to satisfy his desire. He says that one day al-Rashīd made him taste a *sikbāj* that you had cooked. He esteemed it very highly. It was made with all the meats." She replied, "I hear and obey the emir of the believers." Therefore Ibrāhīm ordered the manager of the kitchen to procure [for Bidʿa] all that was necessary, without omitting anything. This supervisor did not delay in bringing everything that she had ordered, and in the morning Bidʿa set to work. She asked for a *mithqāl* of amber and of Indian aloe wood in order to smoke the meats together with the other ingredients, after they had been washed. . . . The cooking pot was blackened with smoke after having been well washed, . . . as well as the *tayfūra*, in which a little musk was placed before filling it [with the food] to [be] serve[d].[47]

It was essential that the olfactory and visual sensations of the dish be registered before the actual tasting. The odor, color, and appearance of the dish provoked astonishment and wonder. The ingredients having been cleaned and scented with amber, aloe wood, and musk, to say nothing of the profusion of spices added during and at the end of the cooking, in accordance with the rules of art, the result was dazzling. Al-Amīn was amazed by the aesthetic perfection of the dish, whose harmoniously arranged garnishes combined to create a spectacle "like a flowering garden, a bride on her wedding night, or a decorated sword." The variety of garnishes made them the equivalent of thirty main courses—better even than the feast that she had made for Hārūn al-Rashīd. It will be recalled that, according to Ibn Sayyār, *sikbāj* had been the favorite dish of the Sasanid king Khosrau I

Anūshīrvan ever since his cook had created it to combat his lack of appetite. For this feast Bidʿa was rewarded with a necklace valued at ten thousand *dirham* and a poem composed by the caliph paying tribute to her cooking.

Why so much fuss about a dish of meat in a vinegar sauce? It needs to be kept in mind that this is only one example among hundreds reported by Iraqi authors of the ninth and tenth centuries, such as al-Jāhiz, who was born a few years before Ibrāhīm al-Mahdī and who died twenty-eight years after him. His many works have left us a portrait of a social elite in Baghdad that nourished an immense interest in the pleasures of the table. This is not really so very different from what we read today in newspapers, magazines, and culinary novels, to say nothing of television shows and films, that recount the lives of the great cooks and pastry chefs. The world has not changed. Cooking continues to cause rivers of ink to flow.

This recipe, Bidʿa's *sikbāj* for al-Amīn, is reproduced by Ibn Sayyār in complete detail. It calls for an incredible quantity of giblets, a sheep cut up into large pieces, a whole lamb, three hens, five chickens, five chicks, thrushes, eggplants, carrots, onions, a great deal of vinegar and saffron, various spices, cheese, herbs, and wheat-flour cakes for the *tharīd*. The extravagance, ostentation, luxury, and lavishness are typical of the banquets of medieval princes. (One might note in passing that the official luncheons and dinners sponsored by European governments today, with caviar, foie gras, champagne, and so on, are no less sumptuous than the banquets of the ʿAbbasids.)

But the recipe for *sikbāj* that enchanted Caliph al-Amīn was not merely the product of a cook's fancy or of a king's whim. Instead it represented the marriage of two culinary traditions, Arab and Persian, the classic preparation of meats and vegetables in vinegar that constitutes the *sikbāj* proper being accompanied by *tharīd,* bread cakes that have been crumbled and soaked in a broth—in this case, the broth of the *sikbāj.*

Many original recipes are attributed to Bidʿa and Ibrāhīm al-Mahdī, some with poetic names such as *ʿāshiqa* (the beloved), *narjisiyya* (narcissus), and *bustāniyya* (orchard). The *aruzziyya* of Ibrāhīm al-Mahdī is a dish of rice cooked in milk flavored with cinnamon and galangal, and then combined

FIGURE 1. Medieval Arab cookbooks reflected the culinary habits of courts and elites, lovers of good meals and of eating in company. It was at one of the convivial meals that followed a friendly game of chess that Ibn Sayyār reports the sultan's cook revealing the rule of good cooking to his companions: "The secret of success is a well-washed casserole." Detail of the ceiling of the central nave of the Cappella Palatina del Palazzo dei Normanni, Palermo, ca. 1143.

FIGURE 2. The exceedingly refined craftsmanship and precious materials used in making tableware and cookware were (and still are today) evidence of the elevated social position of the host who offered a meal to his guests.

a. Incised brass bowl with black bitumen inlay (height 21 centimeters). From Egypt or Syria, 1467–95. Regione Siciliana, Assesorato Beni Culturali Ambientali e P.I., Dipartimento BB.CC ed E.P., Galleria Regionale della Sicilia di Palazzo Abatellis. Palermo, inv. no. 7280.

b. Wrought brass pot (height 9 centimeters). From Egypt or Syria, late thirteenth century or first half of the fourteenth. Regione Siciliana, Assesorato Beni Culturali Ambientali e P.I., Dipartimento BB.CC ed E.P., Galleria Regionale della Sicilia di Palazzo Abatellis. Palermo, inv. no. 7332.

c. Domestic jar with base. From Murcia (Andalusia), twelfth or thirteenth century. Historical Museum of the City of Murcia (Andalusia). Photograph by Philippe Maillard.

FIGURE 3. Peacock-shaped vessel in embossed bronze containing water for washing one's hands before and after meals. Córdoba [?], late tenth or early eleventh century. Photo Institut du Monde Arabe, Paris. Collection Davos, Fondation Furusiyya.

FIGURE 4. (*left, top*) The physician Ibn Butlān (d. 1063) is shown waking up to discover that his hosts (also doctors) are dining without him. Food was evidently a central concern of physicians in the medieval Arab world, as it had been in the Greek world of Hippocrates and Galen. Probably of Syrian origin, 1273. Rights reserved by the Biblioteca Ambrosiana. Reproduction prohibited. Authorization no. F159/04. A. 125 Inf., fol. 35*v*.

FIGURE 5. (*left, bottom*) In this scene from the tale of Bayād and Riyād, the courtier Bayād entertains Riyād and her handmaidens, who listen to his song while refreshing themselves with a cool beverage. From Spain or Morocco, thirteenth century. © Biblioteca Apostolica Vaticano, Vatican City, MS Ar. 368, fol. 10*r*.

FIGURE 6. (*above*) Banquet scene. Seated on the ground around a sumptuously laid table, the guests (all of them male) eat with their hands. From the *Maqāmāt* of al-Harīrī, eleventh century. Oriental Institute of the Academy of Sciences, Saint Petersburg, Russia, MS S.23, p. 205.

a.

b.

c.

d.

e.

f.

FIGURE 7. (*left*) Examples of elegant and costly tableware.

a. Bowl from Raqqada (near Qayrawan), ninth or early tenth century. The little bird, drawn with a certain naturalistic flourish, occurs rather frequently as a decorative motif. Dépos de Raqqada, photo C.R.A.H.

b. Ceramic cup from Egypt, eleventh century. Museum of Islamic Art, Cairo. © IMA 1998. Photograph by Philippe Maillard.

c–d. Ceramic dish from Andalusia, tenth century; inside of the dish (*left*) and bottom outside (*right*). Davids Samling, Copenhagen. Photographs by Ole Woldbye.

e. Glazed ceramic bowl with monochrome decoration (height 10 centimeters). From Tunisia, twelfth or thirteenth century. Museo Nazionale di San Matteo, Pisa, inv. no. 292.

f. Ceramic dish with vegetal decoration, first half of twelfth century. Historical Museum of the City of Murcia (Andalusia). Photograph by Philippe Maillard.

FIGURE 8. (*above*) Decorated ceramic cup from Basra, Iraq, ninth century. Tareq Rajab Museum, Kuwait City.

FIGURE 9. Examples of kitchenware for daily use. Except for *d* and *e*, all the pieces shown are part of a lucky find in a well in the San Nicolas quarter of Murcia, in Andalusia, and date from the second half of the twelfth century to the first half of the thirteenth.

a–b. Bowls with convex covers. Historical Museum of the City of Murcia (Andalusia). Photographs by Philippe Maillard.

c. Apparatus for cooking couscous, consisting of two superimposed pots: the lower one is a normal casserole, the upper one (having a diameter at its base smaller than that of the opening of the pot below) has a perforated bottom. Strictly speaking, the couscous steamer (*kiskas*) is the upper part. The date for this piece coincides with the composition in the mid-thirteenth century of Ibn Razīn's *Fadālat al-khiwān,* which gives a recipe for couscous. Historical Museum of the City of Murcia (Andalusia). Photograph by Philippe Maillard.

d. Bowl with steeply sloping sides in glazed terra-cotta. Iraq, tenth century. Private collection, Treviso.

e. Glazed terra-cotta bowl. Iraq, ninth century. Courtesy of the Ministero per i Bene e le Attività Culturali, Rome. From the Museo Nazionale d'Arte Orientale, Rome, inv. no. 2643.

f. Small terra-cotta stove with saucepan on top, from Murcia. Historical Museum of the City of Murcia (Andalusia). Photograph by Philippe Maillard.

a.   b.

FIGURE 10. (*above*) Two more pieces of expensive tableware.

a. Highly refined glass with base. Syria, first third of the ninth century. Museum of Damascus, Syria.

b. Small ewer of cut rock crystal. Egypt, early eleventh century. Courtesy of the Ministero per i Bene e le Attività Culturali, Rome. Special permission of the Polo Museale, Florence. Further reproduction by whatever means prohibited. All rights reserved. Palazzo Pitti, Museo degli Argenti, Florence, inv. no. 1917.

FIGURE 11. (*right*) A curious mechanical wine dispenser, mentioned in the *Kitāb fī maʿrifat al-hiyal al-handisiyya* of al-Jazarī, Iraq, 1206. This device is evidence of the taste for mechanical inventions that was so widespread during the period, and suggests that the convivial consumption of wine was not as rare as is usually supposed. Topkapi Sarayi, Istanbul, MS A. 3472, fol. 88*v*.

a.

b.

FIGURE 12. (*above*) Ceramic table- and kitchenware. Historical Museum of the City of Murcia (Andalusia). Photographs by Philippe Maillard.
a. Open and covered bowls of various sizes.
b. Small jars and containers from Murcia (Andalusia), twelfth or thirteenth century.

FIGURE 13. (*right*) Scene of a woman making pasta while other women next to her tend the fire. Persia, sixteenth century. Detail of a picture attributed to Mir Sayyid ʿAlī, *Laylī and Manjūn Chained,* illustrating the love story by the Persian poet Ilyas b. Yūsuf Nizāmī (ca. 1140–ca. 1209). © The British Museum, London, Or. 2265, fol. 157ν.

a.

b.

c.

FIGURE 14. The recipes transmitted by medieval cookbooks provide evidence of the extraordinary variety of fruits and spices used to lend highly prized scents and colors to various dishes. These illustrations reflect the great interest shown by the Islamic world in botanical study and the use of natural products, particularly in the culinary arts and medicine, but also in other fields.
a. Quince tree in a thirteenth-century drawing by Ibn al-Baytār. Quince was widely used in cooking. Al-ʿUmarī, *Masālik al-absār fī mamālik al-amsār* (20 volumes), copy from the fourteenth century. Cliché Bibliothèque Nationale de France, Paris.
b. Lentil plant, from a fourteenth-century Iraqi copy of Dioscorides' *De materia medica.* Mosul 1228, MS A. III 2127, fol. 80*r.* Topkapi Sarayi, Istanbul.
c. Harvesting essential oils, from a fifteenth-century Persian copy of Dioscorides' *De materia medica.* Topkapi Sarayi, Istanbul.

FIGURE 15. Representation of various types of plants in a book of natural history from Iraq, 1199. Depicted in the upper panel (*from left*) are Chinese cinnamon, the plant from which galbanum (a resin having medicinal applications and used for incense) is extracted, and cardamom; in the lower panel (*from left*), licorice, valerian (identification of this plant is uncertain), and wild carrot. From the *Kitāb al-Tiryāq* or *Diryāq*, attributed to pseudo-Galen. Cliché Bibliothèque Nationale de France, Paris, MS ar. 2964, fol. 54ν.

FIGURE 16. Spice merchant in a present-day market in Cairo. Photograph by Rolando Schinasi.

with smoked beef that has been cooked in sheep tail fat. These two cooks are also responsible for several recipes for eggplant in sauce—stuffed, grilled, fried—as well as new versions of Iranian dishes: a *zīrbāj* with quinces; various kinds of *sikbāj*; a *sibāgh* with fish that, apart from a few details, recalls the sauces of Apicius; and originally simple Arab dishes, now transformed into sophisticated examples of culinary art.

The taste of the ninth century in Baghdad ran toward vinegar and white sugar, nuts, rose water, spices from India and China, and sweet wine made from raisins and dates. It was an age of abundance and ostentation, but also one marked by a quest for new and surprising flavors, and an interest in codifying proper manners at table and rules of dietary hygiene. Caliphs of the ʿAbbasid dynasty contributed as much to this enterprise as members of their courts—one thinks of al-Wāthiq, al-Maʾmūn, Ibn Māsawayh, Ibn Dahqāna, Umm al-Fadl (a woman!), and Abū Jaʿfar al-Barmakī among others, not to mention Ibrāhīm and Bidʿa themselves—whose many recipes were recorded by Ibn Sayyār al-Warrāq.

FROM BAGHDAD TO CÓRDOBA, FROM TUNIS TO PALERMO

Ziryāb is the name of a black-feathered bird. It also means "gold, any yellow thing."[48] And, last but not least, it is the name of a Kurdish musician who brought ʿAbbasid culinary traditions to Andalusia in the ninth century. Ziryāb fled Baghdad in the time of Hārūn al-Rashīd, finally taking refuge in Córdoba after stopping at Tunis. About 820 he was received at the court of ʿAbd al-Rahmān II, descendant of the last surviving member of the Umayyad dynasty in Damascus, and conquered the court with his elegance, good manners, and penchant for sophisticated cuisine. Ziryāb is credited with the renewal of the culinary arts in Andalusia; with its preference for small, low tables, tablecloths of fine leather, and cups made from glass; with introducing the succession of courses in a definite order (by contrast with the habit of serving everything all at once); and so many other novel refinements, as the historian Lucie Bolens has shown in her study of Andalusian cuisine.[49]

It was a curious route—from Baghdad to Córdoba, via the Mediterranean and North Africa—for ʿAbbasid gastronomic fashion to have taken. It is entirely possible that, together with his precious lute, Ziryāb brought with him books of recipes and linen pouches filled with cinnamon (*Cinnamomum chinense*, known to the Arabs as *dārsīnī*) and other spices. Otherwise, without either notebooks or texts of recipes, this solitary fugitive would have had to rely solely on his visual, gustatory, and olfactory memories. One may well imagine him attempting to re-create the flavors he had tasted at a banquet held by Hārūn al-Rashīd in addition to playing the melodies he had heard there. The thirteenth-century *Manuscrito anónimo* remembered Ziryāb with a recipe that bore his name, *baqliyya li-Ziryāb*, a stew of lamb and cabbage and other flavorings, covered with a topping of meat, bread crumbs, almonds, and eggs. In Tunisia this dish is now called *marqit ʿasāfir*, or "bird stew," in which small clumps of cauliflower are soaked in egg batter, dredged in flour, and fried.

The circulation of cookbooks played an undeniable role in preserving and diffusing the Arab culinary heritage. Recipes traveled with the men who carried these books. Although the Muslim West (North Africa, Andalusia, Sicily) did not possess a culinary literature prior to the thirteenth century, it did produce numerous legal and scientific treatises relating to food, not only books on dietetics and agriculture but also ones containing commercial codes (*hisba*), which set prices and standards of quality for the foodstuffs that were sold in urban markets to innkeepers and private hosts. It is interesting to note that in the medieval Muslim world there were no religious or ethnic barriers in the field of scholarship, so a Jew could readily study and teach in the holy city of Qayrawan, writing a treatise on food undisturbed. It was in this city that Ishāq ibn Sulaymān al-Isrāʾīlī (Isaac Israeli), who died at the age of a hundred (or more) about 935, finished out his very long life.[50] He seems already to have been quite advanced in age when he came to Qayrawan from Cairo to study with the master Ishāq ibn ʿImrān, and lived under the reign of both the Sunni Aghlabite dynasty and the first Shiite Fatimid caliph, ʿUbayd Allāh ibn al-Mahdī. A physician and logician, Ishāq ibn Sulaymān was the author of the monumental *Kitāb al-aghdhiya wa-l-adwiya* ("The Book of Foods and Cures"), known in the West by the title *Book on Dietetics*. Translated into Latin during the eleventh century by Constantine the African and later extensively reprinted, it was for centuries a fundamental reference work for Western scientists. In addition to treating of foods and their manner of preparation (how to cook bread and pasta, for example), it gives guidance regarding healthful nourishment and recommends diets and cures for indigestion and other health problems. Ishāq ibn Sulaymān cites a great many sources, among them Galen, Dioscorides, Hippocrates, Rufus, Yaʿqūb ibn Ishāq al-Kindī, Yahyā ibn Māsawayh, and so on. There was no break either with the past or with the culinary traditions of the Mediterranean.

To the contrary, insofar as strictly culinary documentation is concerned, one passes directly from the ninth and tenth centuries in Iraq to the thirteenth century of the Mamluks and the Andalusians. Sugar and vinegar are found in many of the recipes for sour dishes.[51] By this time rice, eggplant, and spinach were cultivated in both North Africa and Spain. If the Andalusian and Maghrebi books of the period are to be believed, the most sophisticated condiments, vinegars, syrups, and aromatic essences (as well as fruit preserves that were more varied than those of Baghdad) were well rooted in the alimentary habits of Muslim society in the Mediterranean area: meat sauces with cherries, apricots, and quinces; seasoned sauces for fish garnished with pomegranate seeds; banana cakes; balls of minced meat mixed with rice and chickpeas; fish in raisin and vinegar sauce; as well as recipes enriched with sugar, honey, and verjuice, and spices and seasonings that were within the means of most families. The same dishes made without meat—and so described as "false" or "counterfeit" (*muzawwar*)—were prescribed for the sick, but they could also be adapted to suit the needs of poorer families.

ʿAbbasid cuisine still occupied a noteworthy place and the old Persian and Arab culinary terminology survived, but a new vocabulary was now added to it, composed of terms from Spanish, Berber, Turkish, and other languages. The obsession with *sikbāj* that one meets with in certain authors was an eastern phenomenon, whereas the passion for *tharīd* was rooted in Andalusia and the Maghreb. Local traditions came to be consolidated, and new specialties made their appearance in Syria, Egypt, Andalusia, and North Africa. Egypt and Syria had many preparations in common, among them a dish made with leaves of the jute plant (*mulūkhiyya*, also known as Jew's mallow [*Corchorus olitorius*]) that went back to ancient Egypt, a puree of chickpeas (hummus, known today as a Lebanese specialty), sesame paste (*tahīna*, comparable to the tahini found in Lebanese restaurants), little balls of rice and meat, fermented cereal preserves (*kishk*), and yogurt (*yāghūrt*), for example, to say nothing of the specialties of the Christian East, Coptic, Greek, and Byzantine. The Muslim West was noted for its small cheese dumplings (*mujabbanāt*), steamed couscous (*kuskusū*), various types of pasta (*itriya, fidāwish,* and so on) cooked in broth, semolina cakes filled with date paste (*maqrūd*), and mutton sausages (*mirqās*, better known today as *merguez*), as well as for its love of snails and crayfish and the like. Over time, as ethnic identities became more precisely defined, culinary traditions came to be differentiated and diversified: in the East, recipes were now styled Kurdish, Turkish, Indian, Ethiopian, Moroccan, Maghrebi, and so on; in the West they bore the names of Berber tribes—Kutāma, Lamtūna, Sanhāja— or else were associated with Slavic mercenaries (*saqāliba*), Jewish rituals, or cities in Spain and North Africa such as Toledo, Ceuta, Bougie (now Bejaia in Algeria), and Tunis.

In Europe, the names of certain medieval dishes betray their Arab origin: *festiggia* (from the Arabic *fastuqiyya*, a dish made with pistachios); *fidei* and *fidellini* (from *fidāwish*, a type of pasta)—whence the Italian word *fidelari*, referring to a class of artisans in Genoa who specialized in the manufacture of pasta; *romania* (from *rummāniyya*, a dish made with pomegranates); *limonia* (from *līmūniyya*, denoting various lemon dishes); *somacchia* (from *summāqiyya*, meaning "sumac"). The Arabic word *sikbāj*, which, as we have seen, designates a vinegar-based dish, spread across the Mediterranean in various forms and survives today in several regional Spanish dialects (*escabèche* in Castilian, for example, and *escabeig* in Catalan) and in all the Italian dialects of the Tyrrhenian coast: *scabeccio* in Genoese, *scapece* in Neapolitan, *schibbeci* and *scabbici* in Sicilian, and so on.[52] Slightly sour flavors became popular throughout Europe, as cookbooks from the fourteenth and fifteenth centuries testify. In France, a taste for acidity was satisfied by vinegar, verjuice, and ginger, whereas in Italy preferences inclined toward sweet-and-sour, the result of combining sugar, honey, or raisins with vinegar.

Zibibbo (from *zabīb*, "raisin"), a white grape variety also known as Muscat of Alexandria, gave its name to a strong sweet wine made from raisins that is associated especially with the island of Pantelleria and with Sicily (where it is called *vino passito*), though it is also produced elsewhere. Arab domination brought to Sicily the cultures of the Middle East as well as those of the Berber and Arab worlds: the sweets, almond pastries, syrups, and sherbets found there today undoubtedly go back to the Muslim period. Books of Arab scientific knowledge entered Europe through Spain, Sicily, and the medical school at Salerno, notable among them the *Kitāb al-aghdhiya wa-l-adwiya* by Ishāq ibn Sulaymān and the *Taqwīm al-sihha* by a Christian physician in Baghdad named Ibn Butlān (d. 1066). These served as models for the first European cookbooks, which appeared under the generic title *Tacuinum sanitatis*, taken directly from the Arab title of Ibn Butlān's treatise.

While the first written recipes for couscous go back to the middle of the thirteenth century and are furnished by Andalusian authors, it was via Sicily rather than Spain that couscous came to be definitively incorporated into the alimentary heritage of Europe. In the area of Trapani, in particular, it continues today to be prepared and steamed in exactly the same manner as that of the medieval Andalusians (following the recipe given by Ibn Razīn). The Cuscus Fest of San Vito is the best evidence of the permanence of this tradition and of the Sicilians' attachment to it.[53]

Italy is acquainted with other kinds of couscous, also the couscous of diaspora. In Tuscany, *cuscussù* was introduced by Jews from Spain and Portugal who came to settle in Livorno at the end of the sixteenth century; and in Sardinia, more precisely at Carloforte, a version was introduced during the eighteenth century by families from Liguria who had lived on the small island of Tabarka, off the coast of Tunisia.

FROM THE MEDIEVAL PERIOD TO THE PRESENT DAY

What has become of the thousands of medieval recipes that have come down to us in written form? Have they also survived in the collective memory of generations of cooks, passed along by the skillful labors of women who, until not so long ago, passed half their lives in the kitchen? Eating habits have undergone great changes with the adoption of agricultural products from the Americas, above all the tomato, chile, and potato, now essential ingredients in Mediterranean cuisine. Nonetheless, a great many things still recall the Islamic Middle Ages. First of all, spicy flavors continue to be universally appreciated. In Morocco, in the United Arab Emirates, in Yemen, and in the markets of Arab cities everywhere, the shops of the ʿattārīn are overflowing with spices from around the world: black pepper, cubeb (an Indonesian pepper variety), coriander, caraway, cumin, anise, dill, fennel, cardamom, ginger, cinnamon bark, rosebuds, cloves, saffron, turmeric powder, nutmeg, gum arabic, and so on. Clarified and salted butter (*sman* in dialect, Arabic *samn*), sheep tail fat, and dried meat cooked and reserved in its own fat are used less in daily cooking than in the past, but they are essential ingredients of holiday meals. Medieval aromas remain an indispensable part of Arab cooking, especially in the Maghreb, where annual stocks of aromatic essential oils continue to be made in artisanal fashion, and rose water, orange-blossom water, wild mint, wild rose, and the like are frequently distilled in the home.

By contrast, *murrī* and *kāmakh*—condiments made from fermented grains, or sometimes marinated fish, the manufacture of which required months of preparation—have completely disappeared. The lack of these condiments makes it difficult (though by no means impossible) to re-create authentic medieval flavors; a great deal of patience is required.[54] Nor is the use of honey in salted dishes common any longer. On the other hand, the cooking of meat and fish with nuts and dried fruits has remained a lively tradition in North Africa, and Moroccan mutton tagines with plums or apricots and almonds are famous around the world. Many dishes in the same style are less familiar because they are prepared only on special occasions and only at home, never in restaurants—for example, salted fish in a sweet-and-sour sauce with raisins that has been seasoned with cinnamon, cloves, cubeb, saffron, and rosebuds, which the inhabitants of Sfax, in Tunisia, prepare for the end of Ramadan, ʿid al-fitr.

As elsewhere in the Islamic world, vinegar is frequently used in the Maghreb, in *mdarbil* (veal and eggplant) and *sharmūla* (made with fried zucchini), for example, and in certain boiled dishes made with meal as well as *kabkābu* (fish and pickled vegetables), to say nothing of salads. Lemon, either freshly squeezed or candied, is much more commonly used in vegetable or meat stews and in soups.

Nowadays one no longer speaks of Arab cuisine or Islamic cuisine, but rather of national cuisines: Egyptian, Lebanese, Palestinian, Algerian, Yemeni, and so on. The tradition of writing cookbooks was revived only toward the end of the nineteenth century with the development of printing, belatedly introduced to the Muslim world. At first they bore the classical title of *kitāb al-tabīkh* ("cookbook"), to which was then added—after the fall of the Ottoman Empire—the term *sharqi* ("eastern"), and finally—in the second half of the twentieth century—the name of the country whose cooking it described. Probably Tunisia was the first country to produce a book of national cuisine, in 1922, *La véritable cuisine tunisienne* by Jacques-Victor Lévy, who wrote under the name Jacques Véhel.[55]

Those dishes of the medieval Islamic kitchen that have survived down the ages are now less fatty and less highly seasoned than their original versions, and are apt to be accompanied by tomato sauces rather than the vanished *murrī* and *kāmakh*. They include couscous and various kinds of handmade pasta (in the Maghreb), vegetables pickled in brine (found everywhere), meat and sausages (Tunisia), fish that has been coated with salt and dried flat breads made from milled wheat with the addition of minced meat (Iraq, Arabia), *mulūkhiyya* with jute leaves (Egypt), salty-sweet pies and cakes (Morocco), and meatballs and stuffed vegetables (Maghreb, Lebanon, Syria, and so on). I have gathered thirty-one contemporary recipes that recall the flavors of the Middle Ages in a separate section at the end of the book, following the selection of original recipes drawn from our four sources for that period.

MATERIALS, TECHNIQUES, AND TERMINOLOGY

COOKWARE AND HYGIENE

The success of a dish, as the sultan's cook emphasized at the outset of our story, depends first of all on the proper cleaning of the cooking utensils and of the food. Ibn Sayyār and other authors insist particularly on the importance of the quality of the water used to wash the ingredients and on the method followed in this regard; only secondarily do they mention the quality of the oil and spices, the type of wood used for the stove, proper cooking techniques, and so on. Hygiene was a foremost concern of all our authors from the medieval period. The average air temperature, in Baghdad or Cairo, did not allow fresh foods to be preserved, especially meat and fish; indeed, the prescriptions for the handling of these items are continually repeated, along with advice for eliminating "foul odors." Ibn Sayyār recommends rinsing meat with clean, cold water, and never immersing it directly in boiling water, since this "keeps the blood from escaping and retains the filth, . . . and so the meat becomes evil-smelling."[1] Meat must be carefully washed in case the butcher's hands are unclean or he has rinsed them with dirty water. Nor should it be cut up with the same knife used to cut up the onions, leeks, eggplants, or any other vegetables. In the event that these expedients prove to be insufficient to eliminate whatever disagreeable and bothersome odors may persist, it is necessary then to blanch the meat in boiling water, skimming the foam from the liquid, before proceeding with the recipe.

Bad odors were often caused by the pots in which the food was cooked. The authors of these books refer to various utensils and products to be used for cleaning them, keeping in mind the number of times that a particular pot has been used for cooking. The use of chipped, split, cracked, or broken casseroles, along with ones that had been repaired, was strictly forbidden, because food residues become progressively encrusted and rot, so that their odor permeates the material from which the pot is made, diffusing through successive rounds of cooking and altering the flavor of the dish. According to the Jewish physician Ibn Zuhr (d. 1162), who practiced in Andalusia, these unwholesome residues were liable to cause fevers.[2]

With regard to materials, gold and silver remained an unobtainable ideal in the fabrication of cookware: because they were considered unlawful under Islamic proscriptions, cooks had to content themselves with more common materials (carved soapstone in the East, pottery in the West). Clay pots were to be used just once, glazed pots not more than five times.[3] Iron pots were acceptable as long as they were carefully cleaned and dried after every washing to prevent the formation of rust; generally, however, they were used only for frying food, not boiling, so the problem did not arise. (According to Ibn Zuhr, food cooked in iron "strengthens the limbs, improves the tone of the erection, and stimulates sexual desire.") Copper, by contrast, was absolutely advised against, unless it was tin-plated, and the same went for lead.

Although the terminology relating to kitchen utensils and tableware is rich, the description of individual items is regrettably vague. Certain adjectives recur: small, medium, or large; high or low; round; thick or thin. In the absence of more detailed information, it is difficult to imagine the precise dimension and form of the various pots and casserole and serving dishes— *qidr, tājīn, tājin, miqlā, tābiq, qidr al-kuskusī, dast, maʿjana, mājūr, ghadhāra, mithrad, jām, tayfūra, askarja,* and so on—without visiting museum collections of Islamic art and artifacts. An exhibit of Islamic art in Italian museums, mounted at the Palazzo Ducale in Venice in 1993, brought together a wide range of very beautiful pieces associated with the arts of the table dating for the most part to the period that concerns us here, namely, between the tenth century and the thirteenth. Many were originally from Andalusia,

Arab Sicily, and Tunisia, with others coming from the Middle East and Persia. Of particular interest are the examples of what Ibn Razīn called *mithrad*, a type of pottery used to serve *tharīd*, monochrome or polychrome as the case may be and bearing naturalistic, calligraphic, or abstract decorations, with curved walls sloping downward toward an annular base.

All the serving dishes at this exhibition, large and small, including soup bowls and cups, were of this form. The term *mithrad*, like the objects it refers to, is still in use in Tunisia: yellow and green ware in the southern part of the country, blue and white with floral designs in the area of Nabeul. The same exhibition featured a series of precious carafes of rock crystal, finely chiseled and set with stones, dating to the early eleventh century under the Fatimids. These pieces are dispersed among museums around the world and are almost never presented as items used in the kitchen or at table, being classified instead according to the nature of the material from which they are made: glass, copper, bronze, and so on. In Spain, however, the Ibn Arabi Center for Arab Archaeological Studies in Murcia possesses a set of kitchen utensils from a single dwelling, including pots, jars, table settings, and portable ovens. This excavated material dates from the second quarter of the thirteenth century, that is, from the era of Ibn Razīn. The highlight of this collection is a perfectly reconstituted apparatus for making couscous, composed of two superimposed pots and a lid. The upper pot, made of unglazed heat-resistant porcelain with a bottom perforated with holes, has a diameter slightly smaller than the opening of the lower pot, into which it must be fitted for steam cooking. The base of the lower pot is made of heat-resistant porcelain with a glazed lining. Both pots are rounded and have two handles each. The other examples of pots with curved sides are probably related to the *qidr*, similar in form to a jar. A pot with straight sides is called *tājīn*.

UTENSILS AND STOVES

Medieval recipes mention a variety of cooking utensils: metal spits, skewers made of willow wood or wicker, copper bowls for washing with hot water, copper funnels for filling sausages (in gut casings), a large knife for carving, an ax for breaking bones, a knife for cutting onions and vegetables, a knife sharpener, colanders, sieves of various materials and gauges, wood and metal skimmers, a wicker colander for straining water and salt, a long wooden meat mallet, dishcloths for drying washed plates, casserole lids, a mortar for spices, a stone mortar for pounding meat, a wooden chopping board for cutting meat, a table for rolling out pasta, small and large rolling pins for making pastry (the best ones, according to Ibn Sayyār, are made from wood of the jujube tree), goose feathers for brushing dough with milk or egg, a walnut bowl for kneading dough, a wooden vessel for yeast, carving forks and ladles, trays, cylindrical and other molds decorated with designs for making pastry, a grater, scissors, a still, glass jars and leather pouches for keeping spices, and so on.

The fireplaces for cooking described by Ibn Sayyār are of three types. The basic oven (whether fixed in place or portable is not specified) is "of rectangular shape, inclined and half as high as a man, with openings to disperse the smoke and to allow air to enter."[4] For the cooking of sweets, syrups, and caramels, he recommends a round stove. A third type of oven, called *tannūr*, should be deep, of medium height, with a west-facing opening through which the prevailing wind can pass, fanning the coals.

ODORS, COLORS, AND FLAVORS

Michel de Montaigne, describing the meal prepared by the cooks of the Hafsid sultan of Tunis on his arrival in Naples, relies solely on olfactory recollection: "They stuffed his foods with aromatic substances, so sumptuously that one peacock and two pheasants came to a hundred ducats to dress them in that manner; and when they were carved, they filled not only the dining hall but all the rooms in his palace, and even the neighboring houses, with sweet fumes which did not vanish for some time."[5]

"Aromatic substances" were the essence of the medieval Islamic kitchen: the fragrance of a dish announced its flavor and color. Some forty natural flavorings obtained from local and exotic spices, herbs, leaves of trees, seeds, berries, roots, resins, bark, and rosebuds were absolutely necessary in medieval cooking. Most of these ingredients are still used today, not only in the regions where this cuisine originated but also in Europe, where immigration and an interest in ethnic cuisines have expanded the commercial availability of foreign products. The use of spices is more widespread than it was in the Middle Ages, in part because they are now less costly. Nonetheless, their appeal to the lower and middle classes has been limited by local tastes, which cause supply to vary from one region to another. Cardamom and ginger, for example, are used mainly in the Middle East, but scarcely at all in the Maghreb. Sumac is an eastern preference. In place of saffron, still the most expensive of all spices and rare in most modern Arab cuisines, safflower (or bastard saffron) is frequently used as a coloring. Nutmeg, mace, resin, and gum arabic are seldom used. Black (or round) pepper has replaced the other types of pepper used in the Middle Ages, among them long pepper and very probably Szechuan pepper. Coriander, caraway, cumin, turmeric, and cinnamon, on the other hand, are still found in most parts of the Arab world, as are cloves.

The appearance of food in the presentation of dishes was important, and enticing colors were desired. Before the importation of artificial coloring agents, "coriander [cilantro] water" was used for green coloring and, in Tunisia until not very long ago, "spinach water." Saffron and turmeric were used to impart a yellow color. Raw pomegranate seeds, which resemble precious stones, were used for the color red. Fennel-flower or nigella (*Nigella sativa*, also sometimes called black cumin) seeds, sprinkled on fresh cheese, created the impression of black dots on a white background. Egg—yolk and albumen—reproduced the colors of the poet's narcissus (*Narcissus poeticus*) with its white petals and yellow center.

SPICE MIXTURES AND FERMENTED CONDIMENTS

Because compound seasonings and fermented condiments made from curdled milk and vinegar cannot be found in markets, it is necessary to make them in batches from time to time. But since proportions are not indicated in medieval cookbooks, it is difficult, for example, to re-create an authentic *atrāf ṭīb*. According to *Wusla*, this condiment contains a dozen ingredients, among them spikenard, betel, bay leaf, nutmeg, mace, cloves, rosebuds, pepper, ginger, and cardamom; other recipes (there were many) call for "familiar" or "common" spices to be used.

In addition to numerous varieties of seasonings, sweeteners, and flavored liquids—scented salts, vinegars and oils for dressing salads, exotic spices, white and unrefined sugars, honey, aromatic herbs, rosebuds, musk, rose essences, mint and coriander (cilantro) waters, citrus juices, verjuice, rose syrup, almond milk, and grape, date, and pomegranate jams—the medieval kitchen used condiments whose flavor is yet distantly imaginable to us, such as *murrī* (similar to soy sauce), *kāmakh* (a sort of cheese spread), and *bunn* (analogous to the thick paste from which soy sauce is pressed). These condiments were essential in cooking, above all in Baghdad during the tenth century, but also in Andalusia and Egypt, where we know of their use only from the thirteenth century. Re-creating them today would discourage all but the most intrepid cooks; indeed, it would be easier to concoct a magic potion than the simplest *murrī* or *kāmakh*, which are based on the long and involved fermentation of cereals or salted fish.

These condiments seem to have been comparable to East Asian sauces such as Chinese soy sauce and Vietnamese *nuoc mam*, themselves re-creations, using modern food technologies, of ancient artisanal products. Preservation by salting or brining was widespread throughout the medieval world. The sauces mentioned by Apicius, *garum* and *liquamen*, were for centuries considered indispensable in Greco-Roman cooking. *Garum* was obtained by marinating fish intestines; *murrī* (in one of its several versions) by marinating small dried fish (*sīr*) in salt, aromatic herbs, must, and wine; and modern *nuoc mam* by marinating salted fresh anchovies.

The Andalusian author Ibn Khalsūn, writing in the late thirteenth century, tells us, "*Murrī* is [served] cold, [having been] dried for a suitable time. It assists the passage of undigested foods and arrests secretions of the phlegmatic humor. It whets the appetite and warms the blood, but weakens sight and favors scabies. The best [kind of *murrī*] is *naqīʿ* [i.e., the product of prolonged infusion with spices]. It is eaten together with fat and oil."[6]

Understandably, perhaps, no contemporary expert on medieval Islamic cuisine (apart from Charles Perry) seems to have tried to make this condiment. Not only would it be necessary to have a great deal of time at one's disposal—from three to six months for a special *murrī*, carefully supervising the entire process—one would also have to begin preparing it at the right time of year and under the proper conditions. To precisely duplicate the conditions under which Ibn Razīn executed his recipe, one would have to go to Murcia, in Spain, and pass three months there, from the spring equinox until the summer solstice. "One must begin making the infused *murrī*," he says, "toward the end of the month of March of the solar calendar"[7]—the necessary condition of success in the fermentation of this precious condiment, which was meant to be preserved for a long time.

The recipes for *murrī* in our three thirteenth-century sources are virtually identical. Another version is given by the Iraqi author al-Baghdādī, who indicates that it was used in various preparations of meat, chicken, and fish dishes, even omelets. (He also gives a recipe for *kāmakh* [*rijāl*], in which a hollowed-out bottle gourd is used to age a mixture of yogurt, milk, and salt, according to a procedure that begins in the month of June and ends in October.) The most treasured of all condiments was the *murrī* obtained after an extended period of infusion. One recipe calls for subjecting handfuls of barley to a first fermentation, wrapped up in fig leaves for two periods of twenty days each. It is then cleaned of all traces of mold, split, and ground to flour before the first rotting. The powder thus obtained is mixed with a large quantity of salt and dissolved in very soft water, scented with various aromatic herbs and fennel and coriander seeds, before being left to macerate in oil for twenty days in a jar sealed with animal hide. There follow numerous other operations, at variable intervals of between one and ten days, one of which consists in adding every three days bread that has been barely cooked, dried in the oven, and then grated. The resulting preparation is to be stirred twice a day until the end of the autumn. The first extract, obtained by straining and filtering the mixture, is a concentrate of *murrī* (known as "the mouth" [*fam*]), which surely was considered the best part. It is preserved in a porcelain dish glazed on the inside. The residue is reused to prepare another batch. The author of this recipe insists on the importance of respecting the intervals indicated, and on the state of cleanliness required of the men and women who handle this delicate condiment, which is liable to be ruined by the least negligence.

This procedure recalls the preparation of the Vietnamese *nuoc mam*, where a first concentrate of superior quality, rare and extremely expensive, is obtained after three months of maceration, while the ordinary product intended for commercial distribution is left to macerate for another three months. It also recalls the manufacture of soy sauce, which is the product of the natural fermentation of soybeans, steamed alone or together with roasted, crushed whole wheat. This fermentation yields a first liquid, *koji*, to which salt and water are added; aging in cask for six months produces a second liquid, *moromi*, which is pressed in its turn, yielding soy sauce and, after another filtering, tamari and shoyu. *Murrī* was a liquid of decidedly dark color, if not actually black, bitter-salty in flavor, with notes of herbs and spices depending on the recipe. Unlike *kāmakh* (a condiment for bread particularly favored for picnics), it was used during cooking in small quantities or else as a sauce served with the meal.

THE SEQUENCE OF COURSES

Meals were served on a low wooden table or directly on a tablecloth stretched out on the ground. All the cooked dishes were presented together, hot and cold, main courses, starters, sauces, *murrī* and *kāmakh* with vinegar and flavored salt, all served in small bowls. The ʿAbbasids liked to begin with fruit, dates being particularly preferred. Then they moved on to the cold salted dishes. Hot (or rather, because they were eaten without utensils, warm) dishes—lamb, veal, poultry, fish, and so on—were served together with vegetables preserved in vinegar or brine. Breads of varying thickness, shape, and texture—*ruqāq, raghīf, jardaq, fatīr*, and so on—that could be easily folded by hand, or torn apart, were served to assist diners in picking up last bits of food and cleaning the bottom of the bowl. At the end of the meal, sweets and syrups were offered. The Andalusian author Ibn Razīn advised beginning with the heavy foods, because the bottom of the stomach was thought to digest them more easily than the upper part. Heavy foods included dairy products, tharīd, pasta, fatty meats such as beef and mutton, dried meats, fish, roasted seeds, and the like. One then turned to the vegetables. All very salty foods were "to be put in the center of the stomach," and desserts, mature fruits, and sweet beverages consumed last.

This manner of approaching a meal resembles the practice still followed in Arab countries today, where one readily eats with the hands, preferably the right hand. Some commentators have claimed to find the use of a fork attested by al-Jāhiz, but the violation of table etiquette it would seem to involve (being repeatedly inserted into the diner's mouth and then into food) casts doubt on such an interpretation.[8]

Etiquette during the ʿAbbasid era was very strict with regard to cleanliness of the hands, which were to be carefully washed before and after the meal with special soaps and powders. One was not to suck bones noisily, or to put back on a plate a piece of meat that had already been chewed. It was also necessary to dispose of fruit rinds discreetly, without drawing attention to oneself. Rather than bite into fruits, one was to cut the desired amount with a knife, and to avoid dirtying one's hands with the juice. At the end of the meal, it was customary to clean the teeth with a toothpick, and lozenges made from musk, sandalwood, amber, spikenard, cloves, aloe wood, roses, cinnamon, and the like were sucked in order to guard against bad breath.

A NOTE ON CULINARY TERMINOLOGY

The recipes that make up the second part of the book are taken from four medieval works written in Arabic by authors from different countries. We therefore find ourselves faced with a culinary vocabulary that varies from one work to another. It is not my purpose here to set forth the difficulties of translating from Arabic (more precisely, from four varieties of this language), but merely to explain the inclusion in the text of a nomenclature foreign to English, together with a certain number of Arabic terms that are transcribed rather than translated. These include certain ingredients typical of medieval Islamic cuisine, which are referred to by their original names: salted and clarified butter (*samn*), sesame paste (*tahīna*), spice mixtures (such as *atrāf tīb*), and condiments made from fermented cereals or fermented fish (*murrī*), as well as a few milk derivatives (*shirāz*) and special breads (*fatīr*). The same goes for certain measures of weight such as *ūqiya* and *dirham*, and various utensils and items of tableware such as *mithrad* (already described) or *dast* (whose shape is unknown to us).

The definition of these and other terms is given in the brief glossary at the end of the book. Readers will quickly become comfortable with them, just as they have come to know words such as *couscous* and *tagine* that have entered Western languages, and many others related to Islamic culture in general. To simplify reading, the transliteration of medieval Arabic terms only partly respects the system adopted in scholarly editions.

A few expressions referring to the manner and duration of cooking are found in all four works, and are reproduced here without interpretation: "one boiling," "two boilings," "three boilings," "cook for an hour," "the necessary time," "the necessary amount," and so on.

As far as possible, the style of the translation is faithful to that of the various authors, although minor interpolations in brackets have frequently been necessary to give a logical order to the operations involved in making a dish, or occasionally to fill a gap in the text of the recipe that otherwise would be incomprehensible.

A NOTE ON THE ADAPTATION OF MEDIEVAL DISHES

Many recipes do not require any modification or substitution for ingredients that can no longer be obtained. For these it is enough to follow the instructions and guess at the appropriate proportions. As with cooking times, I leave it to the reader to settle on the right measure, to learn from practice to use the right amount of oil or butter, to use fewer or more spices, to salt and to season with vinegar according to one's own personal taste. "Do as you please!" our medieval cooks often say. In fact, if the quantities of sugar and fats are reduced, while certain disagreeable types of fat are eliminated altogether, practically all the recipes for sweet-and-sour dishes, meats cooked with fruit, sweet chicken pies, cheese pastries, couscous, various types of pasta, fish (without *murrī*), pancakes, and marmalades and mustards are perfectly suited to modern tastes. It must be said that most young people today find the taste and smell of sheep tail fat utterly disgusting, as well as that of *samn,* so it is difficult to recommend these ingredients. I say nothing, then, of *murrī,* though one might consider substituting soy sauce for it. It is more from this—our wariness in the presence of unfamiliar flavors—than from a lack of certain ingredients that the difficulty of recreating some of the characteristic dishes of the medieval period arises. Where it is impossible to reproduce the authentic flavors of a bygone age, however, I look to these recipes for inspiration in order to make something new and pleasing, as the original custodians of this cuisine did.

Experimenting with many of these recipes brings out their direct relation to Arab cooking today. For this reason I have found it more interesting in some cases to present contemporary Arab dishes rather than offer personal interpretations of older recipes. The cuisine of every Arab country today is rich in dishes that may be ascribed without the least hesitation to the heritage of medieval Islam. The modifications that have been made to older recipes are not recent; they have been refined over time not only in response to changing culinary fashions, but also as a consequence of shortages of food supply, the interruption of ancient caravan routes, and the introduction of foods native to the New World such as tomatoes, chiles, and potatoes. In making a selection of contemporary recipes for part three of the book, I have (with only a few exceptions) chosen dishes that do not call for the use of foods that came to Islamic lands following the discovery of the Americas.

With regard to medieval cooking, the challenge was first of all to extract from the thousands of known recipes a small number (fewer than 150) of representative examples. Then there was the additional problem of selecting dishes that were representative of an entire age and, within that age, various historical periods in each of the four regions of the medieval Islamic world represented by our authors, even if the creative cuisine of the ʿAbbasids is assigned a preeminent position. One must choose among a great many characteristic preparations, including pasta and couscous, soups made with grains and vegetables, marmalades and cakes made with honey or sugar, sweet-and-sour sauces, fermented condiments, rice and eggplant dishes, and so on. I have successfully experimented with a number of these recipes myself; others proved to be complete failures, forcing me to exclude them from the present collection. I have not dared to try my hand at condiments made from fermented cereals. Readers will understand why once they have examined the recipes for themselves.

Re-creating these dishes is an adventure for the cook and a risk for those who are bold enough to sample the "novel" tastes and flavors of a culinary heritage that goes back more than a thousand years—an opportunity and a challenge both, not only for recreational cooks but also for the greatest chefs of our time.

PART TWO

—

THE MEDIEVAL TRADITION

NOTE: The recipes that follow are numbered and their origin indicated by a letter in parentheses: [K]=*Kanz;* [R]=Ibn Razīn; [S]=Ibn Sayyār; [W]=*Wusla.* (See "Sources of Islamic Culinary History," in this book's first chapter, for further details on the source texts.)

COLD APPETIZERS

The dishes known by the name of *bārida* were served at the beginning of the meal as cold appetizers. In Baghdad—so authors of the ninth and tenth centuries tell us—first courses typically featured chicken or fish, but numerous recipes based on vegetables, especially eggplant, were also quite popular. The style of *bārida* associated with Baghdad recalls several of Apicius's recipes. The principal ingredient was cooked separately and then sprinkled with a slightly sour sauce, which frequently contained the same herbs and spices used in the Roman versions: asafetida, rue, coriander seeds, caraway, and cumin.

The most original cold starters are the fish recipes suggested by Ibn Sayyār, such as a fish whose flesh is ground up and stuffed back into its skin (later recalled by Ibn Razīn; see recipe 68); a fish that is boiled and its skin peeled off by pressing it between two boards, the flesh then being marinated in wine vinegar; a fish omelet; a fish whose head is roasted, its belly stewed, and its tail fried (without the three parts being separated); a fish tongue marinated in vinegar, cooked, and flavored with cinnamon; and finally, a live fish drowned in grape juice (recipe 4). Ibn Sayyār may have been joking when he said that the eccentric Ibrāhīm ibn al-Mahdī would not eat any part of fish but the tongue; if not, this was surely the ultimate in luxury and snobbery.

1. COLD CHICKEN WITH SPICES AND HERBS [S]

This bārida *recipe originally occurred in the recipe collection of Caliph al-Maʾmūn, now lost, from which Ibn Sayyār reproduced it.*

Take some vinegar and *murrī* and in them macerate coriander [seeds], Chinese cinnamon, pepper, dried and fresh thyme, cumin, caraway, fresh coriander [cilantro], mint, rue, celery, the pulp of a cucumber, and elecampane. Put everything in a grinder, mix, and pour over the grilled chicken.

2. CHICKEN WITH WALNUTS AND POMEGRANATE [S]

This bārida *recipe appeared in the book, now lost, of Caliph al-Wāthiq.*

Take a chicken that has already been cooked on the grill, divide it up into pieces, and arrange the pieces one on top of another in a serving dish [*jam*].

Beat some mustard with a good wine vinegar, a little *murrī*, and sugar. Add to this rather sour-tasting mixture some crushed walnuts and a bit of asafetida. Pour generously over the chicken so that it is well covered, then season with oil, sprinkle with chopped rue, and finally garnish with pomegranate seeds, God willing.

3. BLACK APPETIZER [S]

This dish is called black bārida *for the color of the pulp of a dark raisin variety. It is very similar to the sauce used today to season cold fish in Bizerte and salted fish in Sfax, both cities in Tunisia (see recipes 160 and 161).*

Carefully crush some black raisins, mix with a little vinegar, strain, and add [to the liquid thus obtained] a little cinnamon, just enough galangal, and a little ginger, oil, and chopped rue. Pour [this sauce] over the chicken.

4. FISH DROWNED IN GRAPE JUICE [S]

This bārida *from Ibn al-Mahdī is certainly unusual. It must be said that there is occasionally something cruel and perverse about fine cooking—one has only to think of the suffering of geese from which foie gras is made.*

Take a large live fish. Put it in black grape juice in a vessel deep enough for it to be completely immersed. It will thrash about and swallow the juice until its body is filled with it. When the level of the juice goes down and the belly and gills are saturated with it, remove the fish, clean it, cook it on the grill, and serve. One eats it with *sibāgh*, which is prepared with asafetida, *murrī*, wine vinegar, celery water, mint water, and caraway.

This fish, like all fish, is served with *sibāgh*, because without *sibāgh* no fish can be appreciated.

5. MARINATED OLIVES WITH THYME [S]

This recipe is attributed to Ibrāhīm al-Mahdī. Along with fresh water and bread, olives are served with every meal in much of the Muslim world today, especially in the lands of the Fertile Crescent and North Africa. Most Arab families along the coast of the Mediterranean prepare batches of pickled olives from the beginning of the harvest season.

Take some black olives and some green olives, knowing that the black ones are better; put them in a jar, add salt and thyme, and then cover with oil of good quality [i.e., olive oil]. They are preserved so they can be eaten as the occasion arises.

6. PUREE OF CHICKPEAS WITH CINNAMON AND GINGER [K]

Chickpea puree was flavored with vinegar and pickled lemons during the Middle Ages, just as it is flavored with lemon and sesame paste in today's hummus bi-tahineh. *Making it is no problem at all because all the ingredients are readily available, except for rue. In certain respects it is better and lighter than the modern version, which is made with tahini.*

Cook the chickpeas in water, then mash them in a mortar to make a puree. Push the puree through a sieve for wheat, unless it is already fine enough, in which case this step is not necessary. Mix it then with wine vinegar, the pulp of pickled lemons, and cinnamon, pepper, ginger, parsley of the best quality, mint, and rue that have all been chopped and placed on the surface of the serving dish [*zubdiyya*]. Finally, pour over [this mixture] a generous amount of oil of good quality.

7. FAVA BEANS IN SOUR SAUCE WITH HAZELNUTS [K]

Fava beans (fūl), *which today form the basis of Egyptian diet, were seldom used in the medieval recipes that have come down to us, probably for the simple reason that they belong to popular cooking. Our authors are interested particularly, if not exclusively, in the cuisine of the elite classes of their societies.*

Clean the beans and cook them in water. Let cool and then drain. Mix *tahīna* with oil of good quality, vinegar, *atrāf tīb*, mint, coriander [seed], and some roasted crushed hazelnuts.

Chop parsley, mint, and rue root and mix everything together in vinegar.

Color the beans with a bit of saffron. Let them [soak] in this mixture before serving them in a dish. They have a good flavor as well as a splendid fragrance.

Anyone who likes dried fava beans should first boil them, then shell them and prepare a sauce with vinegar, coriander [seed], scented oil, and a little sumac and thyme. They are then ready to serve.

8. PUREE OF EGGPLANT WITH YOGURT [K]

The best-known eggplant puree in the Arab world is the Syrian-Lebanese baba ghannouj, *which is mixed with tahini, if one likes, and enriched by a few drops of sour pomegranate syrup* (dibs rummān). *The modern Tunisian recipe is closer to the medieval version, owing to the slightly sour taste imparted by the vinegar (recipe 159).*

Cut the eggplant into small pieces; put them in a jar for cooking [*dast*] together with whole cleaned onions. Add some sesame oil and oil of good quality and a little water. Reduce over a slow fire. When the ingredients are cooked, put them through a sieve and combine with a very small clove of garlic, yogurt, and chopped parsley.

9. CARROTS AND LEEKS WITH SESAME PASTE [K]

Tahīniyya, *the original name of this recipe, derives from* tahīna, *the term still used today to refer to sesame paste. Tahini can be found ready-made in the international section of many markets, as well as in shops stocking Arab or Asian products.*

Get some carrots, [the] white [part of some] leeks, sesame butter [*tahīna*], wine vinegar, and *atrāf tīb*. Slice the carrots and boil them. Take the [green] tops of the leeks and boil them separately, then drain them and soften them in sesame oil. Put the *tahīna* in a dish, sprinkle it with boiling water, and mix it by hand so that the sesame oil can express itself; then add a little vinegar, honey, and some *atrāf tīb*. Put the drained carrots and leeks in a serving dish and add the *tahīna*. You must do [this] in such a way that the quantity of carrots and leeks suits that of the condiments.

BREAD AND BROTH

Tharīd (or *tharīda*) was a kind of national dish of the Arabs in the early years of Islam. It symbolized what it meant to be Arab, just as *sikbāj* embodied Persian identity. The prophet Muhammad declared it the best of all dishes, going so far as to compare its excellence to his favorite wife, ʿAʾisha. And yet there is hardly anything special about this dish, which is nothing more than crumbled bread soaked in meat broth. Once the bread crumbs have thoroughly absorbed the broth, they are arranged in a pyramid, pieces of meat are set around it, and the dish is ready to be served. But because it was the preferred dish of the Prophet, it entered into Tradition (*sunna*), which every Muslim had to respect, maintain, and hand down. Remarking on the fondness for this dish of Muhammad's people, the Quraysh tribe, the scribe al-Jāhiz claimed with a deceptive pretense to objectivity that the nickname "Hashim" given to ʿAmr bin ʿAbd Manaf, a very close and important kinsman of the Prophet, came from the term *hashama*, which means "to break" or "to crack," precisely because he was the one who broke the unleavened flat bread used to make *tharīd*.

Notwithstanding all the variations it underwent over the centuries, having crossed so many borders, this dish remained associated with a procedure called *thard*, which consisted of crumbling the bread—by hand, by grating, or by some other method—and then moistening it with broth.[1] The nature and quality of the bread varied, depending on the recipe and the available ingredients, from hard, stale bread to thin flat bread made with white flour. The broth was more or less rich, depending on the proportions of meat, fat, vegetables, and spices; and the amount of bread and more or less meat likewise depended on the generosity of the host. The consistency of the *tharīd* had to be such that it could be taken by hand directly from the platter, without a spoon, which also meant that it could not be too hot. The meat needed to be sufficiently tender from long cooking that it could be pulled from the bone with only one hand, since the Arab way of eating is exactly this—of serving oneself with the right hand alone.

The recipes for *tharīd* that figure in the cookbooks differ from one another; they have in common only the crumbled bread soaked in broth, except in the case of a Tunisian version that consists of a sort of crepe cooked first on a griddle, then cut up and cooked a second time by steaming. As for the rest, a few are spicy, others not at all; some are made with cheese, others with curdled milk, vinegar, or sugar. There is something for every taste.

Ibn Sayyār mentions a dozen versions of *tharīd,* some of which are attributed to cooks at the beginning of the ninth century; among the authors of the thirteenth century, only Ibn Razīn assigns the dish a prominent place, giving some twenty versions. The following brief selection of recipes will give an idea of the great liberties taken by cooks in modifying a dish that represents the most ancient and sacred Arab tradition.

The second *tharīd* described by Ibn Sayyār uses meat and tripe sausages cooked in broth and bread made with dough that has been kneaded the day before. The third uses hot bread just out of the oven. The fourth uses hard bread and broth containing vinegar and yeast. In another version, the broth contains raisins and pomegranate seeds in addition to meat, and the bread crumbs are obtained from a bread made from thin dough. This last *tharīd* was sprinkled with white sugar, which must have given it rather the appearance of a cake. Sugared meat dishes of this sort, formerly much appreciated in the Levant, are no longer found where they seem to have been created, but instead survive in Morocco, Algeria, and Tunisia. There they are called tagine or *marqa hluwwa* (sweet stew), a few recipes for which are given later in the book, in part three, which is devoted to contemporary dishes.

10. SYRIAN *THARĪD* [S]

A cousin of this dish, said to have been made by "certain Christians" in Syria in the tenth century, calls for smoked meats and sliced white bread. From the same period comes a tharīd *with vinegar-flavored meat that united the Arab and Persian styles, in which the sourness of yogurt was softened by the addition of sugar. There was also a white* tharīd *consisting of grilled chicken and hard-cooked eggs covered with crumbled bread and cooked in milk.*

Take some mutton and poultry, such as chickens and capons or the like; you can also use mutton by itself or chicken by itself. Cut [the meats] into medium-size pieces, remove the entrails, discard the heads and necks, rinse, and arrange in a clean pot. Some water will be needed in which to soak some cleaned truffles overnight. Cover the meat with this liquid after having strained it. In the absence of truffles, use honey that has been darkened by boiling and the addition of a little *kāmakh*. Add chickpeas and salt, then increase the fire under the pot. Prepare a fragrant bundle of fresh rue, Greek or Nabataean leeks, and fresh coriander [cilantro], and put it in the pot. Then you must add the crushed spices, coriander [seeds], cumin, caraway, and pepper, and fan the fire beneath the pot in order to cook the meat. Next, crumble the white bread and sprinkle it with enough broth for the bread to be soaked, then take the meat [and arrange it on the soaked bread] and garnish with sausages all around the dish.

11. *THARĪD* WITH TRUFFLES [R]

This recipe is cited by Ibn Razīn under the name of shāshiyyat Ibn al-Rafīʿ *and, in a roughly similar version, by the anonymous Andalusian author under the name of* shāshiyya Ibn al-Wadīʿ *(or else "shāshiyya in the style of Bougie," a city in what is now eastern Algeria). The association with Ibn Wadīʿ appears to derive from the fact that the melted butter, when poured over the* tharīd *and the vegetables, seeps into them and spreads over the edges, forming a white fringe that brought to mind the cap (shāshiyya) that Ibn Wadīʿ customarily wore—presumably a green cap having a conical shape with a white border.[2] In Ibn Razīn's version, the bread crumbs were incorporated directly into the broth even though, according to his own definition of* tharīd, *"it is necessary to crumble the leavened bread as finely* as possible, then moisten it with broth from which the wadk [*the greasy liquid that floats on the surface of the broth*] has been removed and let it rest for a little while."[3]

Choose meat of the best quality from a young fat mutton or spring lamb in sufficient quantity. Cut up and wash. Arrange the meat in a large casserole; add salt, oil, pepper, coriander [seeds], and a little chopped onion, and cover with an ample amount of water. Put on the fire. When the meat is almost cooked, add fennel, shelled fresh fava beans, truffles, and a little fresh coriander [cilantro], having first washed all of these things and cut up the truffles. Cook [them] with the meat.

When all of it is cooked, break up [in the broth, which will have been poured into a *mithrad*] any kind of bread, into the smallest crumbs possible, and remove the casserole from the fire, placing it on a hot plate. Cut fresh cheese into pieces and add it to the broth; [the broth] will be ready when [the cheese] has been well soaked. Boil fresh butter in an earthenware pot and skim. Take the vegetables that are in the casserole and strew them over the *tharīd*, add the meat and the cheese, pour the butter on top, and sprinkle with cinnamon. Enjoy your meal and may good health be yours, God willing.

12. *THARĪD* OF TUNIS [R]

This thirteenth-century recipe from Tunis is one of the most original of the recipes for tharīd *because it introduces two new procedures: the confection of a rough puff paste* (demi-feuilletage, *as we would call it today) and the cooking of this paste in what the author calls "the couscous pot" and what would later be called a couscous steamer. In this version, the semolina dough brushed with butter and* samn *is stretched out with a rolling pin similar to the one used in Tunis today to prepare fresh pasta that is to be cooked by steaming; this pastry, moreover, is cooked twice, first in the skillet and then in the steamer, and then at the end sprinkled with chicken broth and so forth.*

A few centuries later, Tunis boasted of a rather similar specialty, al-fatīr wa mā yatīr, *a dish of pasta and chicken that was prepared on the eve of the Muslim festival of ʿAshūrāʾ. According to the brief description given by Ibn Abī Dinār, a seventeenth-century chronicler of Tunis, it was "chicken accompanied by a prepa-*

ration called dawīda, *which is similar to the* kunāfa *of the Egyptians, except that the Tunis version is thicker"*[4]—*a forerunner of the dish known as* nuwāsir, *which today the people of Tunis prepare on the occasion of* ʿĀshūrāʾ *(see recipe 165). The* fatīr *of the thirteenth century resembles the modern* khobz ftir *made by mixing an unleavened dough with oil, butter, and milk and cooking it in a ceramic pan called a* ghannāy.

The candied lemons and olives that garnish this dish are typical of Tunis as well, and are invariably found on the tables of families from Andalusia in particular. Lemons, olives, turnips, carrots, celery, and capers are all preserved in brine, water, and salt, though rarely in vinegar, as is customary (except in the case of lemons and olives) in the Middle East. It is not by chance that in Tunisia they are said to be umāllah (*"salted"*) *and not* mukhallalāt (*"seasoned with vinegar"*).

Take very fat chickens and capons, slaughter them, blanch them, eviscerate them, and remove the entrails. Cut into little pieces and put them in a large terra-cotta casserole dish that has first of all been well washed. Add to the chicken salt, oil, pepper, coriander [seeds], an onion halved or sliced, and chickpeas that have been soaked. Cook on the fire.

[Preparation of the *fatīr,* or very thin unleavened flat bread:] In the meantime, take the semolina and moisten [it], energetically mixing with a little water and salt. Divide the dough into pieces and knead each piece with clarified butter. Roll it out, first by hand and then with a rolling pin, fold it, add clarified butter, and roll it out again to obtain a very thin layer. [For this purpose] use a *shaubak,* which is a piece of carved wood, thick in the center and thin at the extremities. Small lumps of dough can be rolled out three at a time, placing one on top of the other with clarified butter between each layer.

Heat an iron skillet or one of unglazed clay. Take a piece of the rolled-out dough and heat it until it has become white and lost all its moisture, at which point remove it from the fire and beat it with the hands in order to separate the layers, then break it up into medium-size pieces and put them in a *mithrad.* Take another piece of dough, do the same, and continue in this way until all the dough has been used up.

Finally, take the contents of the *mithrad* and arrange them in a couscous pot; place it on top of the pot in which the chicken is cooking. Stick a piece of dough all around at the point of contact between the two casseroles and cover the couscous pot [on top] with a cloth to keep steam from escaping. Let [the dough] cook with the steam, which rises from the lower pot and passes through the holes of the couscous pot.

When the chicken has been cooked to perfection, check the level of the oil that has formed on the surface of the broth; if it is not abundant, add some good *samn* and fresh butter and bring to a boil, then move the casserole away from the fire and place it over the glowing coals so that the oil collects on the surface. Skim off the greasy liquid and reserve it in a separate dish. Moisten the *fatīr* with a good quantity of broth but not too much, since an excessive amount of broth will dissolve the *fatīr* and ruin it. Remove the pieces of chicken, the chickpeas, and the onion and arrange them over the *fatīr*, setting all of these things in the center of the *mithrad*. Garnish with hard-cooked eggs, good olives, and candied lemons placed all around inside the pot. Afterward, baste with the greasy liquid that has been reserved and sprinkle with cinnamon and ginger.

This dish with *fatīr* is the exclusive specialty of the people of Ifrīqiya [ancient Tunisia] and particularly of the citizens of Tunis, for whom it is a feast dish and a source of great pride.

13. *THARĪD* OF NAWRŪZ [R]

The ingredients are few—chicken, walnuts, cheese, crumbled flat bread—but the preparation is sophisticated. This is a feast-day meal, a special tharīd to celebrate Nawrūz, the Persian New Year's Day, which falls on the first day of spring. That it should have been celebrated in Andalusia is not surprising, nor that Andalusians (Muslims and Jews alike) should have carried the tradition with them to North Africa following their expulsion from Granada in 1492. The seventeenth-century Tunisian author Ibn Abī Dīnār discusses at length the devotion of the inhabitants of Tunis to this festival, and their decision to move its date to the first day of May.[5] This tradition has been lost today; by way of compensation, the Maghrebi continue to commemorate the old new year (the new year of the Julian calendar, called ʿajmi in Tunisia and yannāyir in Algeria and Morocco, which corresponds to 13 January in the Gregorian calendar).

Take some fat chickens, slice them open, and remove their entrails; after having plucked them, and emptied and rinsed them with salted water, clean them inside and out and make them ready with the wings and feet folded back. Put them in a casserole with water and salt and place it on the fire.

First, blanch the walnuts so that they may be peeled more easily. Peel the garlic and boil it to remove the odor. Grate the cheese with an iron grater to reduce it to a powder, putting aside the remainder to be added [later] to the walnuts and garlic; and, finally, crush everything well.

[Preparation of the flat bread (*fatīr*):] Next, make a dough with semolina, water, and salt, but without yeast. Mix well with a little water and form [the dough into] thin cakes, wiping off the water from one side and perforating them with holes. Cook them halfway through in the oven.

When the chickens are almost done, remove them from the pot, brush them with oil, place them in dishes of glazed terra-cotta, and put these in the oven. Check them from time to time to make sure they are roasting [as they should], without burning.

In the meantime, reduce the walnuts, garlic, and the remaining cheese to a puree and dilute this mixture in a bowl containing warm water and much oil.

Cut up the chickens and put the pieces in the bowl with the [walnut and cheese] sauce. Then break the flat bread into medium-size pieces, not too small. Sprinkle the grated cheese on the bottom of the *mithrad,* add the thin crumbled flat bread, sprinkle again with grated cheese, and so on until the *mithrad* is full.

Take the [sauce] mixture—if the quantity is not sufficient, add some grated cheese to thicken it and make it white, thanks to the abundance of cheese—and pour it over the *tharīd.* Then drizzle sweet fragrant olive oil [over it] and moisten it [further], little by little, with the hot chicken broth [from the casserole]. This step is complete when the broth has reached the bottom of the *mithrad;* if there is not enough of it, add boiling water that was prepared beforehand. Mix the *tharīd* [and the other ingredients] during this time, [stirring] from the bottom toward the top, so that everything is perfectly moist. Sprinkle again with grated cheese.

Remove the pieces of chicken from the bowl and arrange them on top in the *mithrad*. Sprinkle with grated cheese and oil. Enjoy your meal and may you be in good health, God willing.

The chickens can be roasted on the spit instead of being cooked in the oven. The same thing may be done with rabbits and quail instead of chicken.

14. SABBATH *THARĪD* [R]

This was a dish for the Sabbath or for a great feast that followed a period of fasting. It still occupies a prominent place in the cuisine of Andalusia, a land of many cultures and religions. Originally bequeathed to the tradition of the prophet Muhammad, and then to both Islamic tradition and Arab identity, tharīd *was also a feast dish of Persians, Jews, and Christians.*

Take fat hens, fattened capons, and whatever may be found in the way of geese, pigeons, partridges, and [other] birds. After they have been slaughtered, cleaned, and eviscerated, arrange them in a pot containing oil, salt, pepper, coriander [seed], and a chopped onion. Place the pot over a low fire. Stir the meat and cover with water. When it is almost cooked, remove it from the pot and run it through with spits.

Prepare a sauce with vinegar, *murrī*, and oil with which to brush the meat, which is next grilled over a medium fire.

In the meantime, take great care in preparing semolina flat bread that is pierced with a sharp iron so that the cooking in [either] the *furn* or the *tannūr* will be a success. After having removed it from the oven, cut into pieces as large as a *dīnār*.

To the broth that is in the pot add cheese that is dry and fragrant, grated with a grater [*iskirfāj*] in sufficient quantity, and add enough crushed garlic that the flavor really comes through. Bring to a boil, then soak the *fatīr* [the pieces of flat bread] with some broth. When they have well absorbed it, lay them over the poultry, which has been cut up into small pieces, and cover with chopped eggs. Sprinkle with peeled almonds, walnuts, fresh olives and [olives] that have been preserved, grated cheese, cinnamon, and spikenard. [The dish] is to be eaten by the will of great and mighty God.

SWEET-AND-SOUR DISHES

Vinegar cooked with sugar or honey yields a syrup that is more or less thick depending on the length of time it is cooked. It caramelizes if you have the patience to heat it long enough and do not mind the suffocating smell of evaporated vinegar. The flavor is pleasing, sweet and slightly acidic. In the recipes for sweet-and-sour dishes, vinegar and sugar are added in the course of cooking when the meat is almost done, with a little starch if a thick or caramelized consistency is desired. The addition of small amounts of vinegar and sugar in stewed meats—beef with carrots, for example—gives good results. Honey may be substituted for sugar, however, or otherwise one can use fruits with high sugar content such as dried figs, raisins, and apricots, all familiar sweetening agents in Arab (and especially Moroccan) cuisine.

Acidity can also be contributed by some fruits, such as pomegranates and sour cherries. The bitter taste of quinces, reminiscent of vinegar, is balanced by the addition of honey and raisins. Almonds, pistachios, and walnuts, well crushed in the mortar, seem to have been used, along with chickpeas, to thicken sweet-and-sour sauces.

By virtue of its sweet-and-sour notes, North African cooking, more than that of the Middle East, has remained faithful to its medieval origins. Indeed, all the modern adaptations of these recipes found in part three belong to the Maghrebi culinary tradition, and above all to the heritage of Andalusia, which spread southward with the hundreds of thousands of Muslims and Jews who were expelled from Spain from the late fifteenth century onward and sought refuge in the cities and countryside of North Africa.

In any case, the recipes for salty-sweet and sweet-and-sour dishes that follow do not insist on the use of particular condiments, with the exception of certain spice mixtures, and so they are easily modified to suit personal tastes. I leave it to readers to decide whether to follow tradition or to create a new version of each dish themselves.

15. *SIKBĀJ* WITH EGGPLANT [K]

Sikbāj (a Persian term denoting a dish made with vinegar) was the most fashionable dish in Baghdad during the ʿAbbasid period, as we have already seen. The recipe presented here, from Kanz, provides evidence of the diffusion of sikbāj and of its continuing popularity during the thirteenth century. Despite its lack of detail, this recipe readily lends itself to experimentation, without the need to make substitutions, since almost all the ingredients are easily obtained. The only difficulty lies in determining the proper quantities of vinegar, sugar, grape juice, and honey, as well as how long they should be cooked with the meat; it must be kept in mind, of course, that the final result depends on the degree of acidity of the vinegar and grape juice, about which the recipe is silent. But one should not be discouraged by these small omissions. Still, it would probably be wise to add olive oil to the list of ingredients, which the author seems to have forgotten to mention.

One may therefore proceed as follows. Brown about a pound of lamb and two chopped onions in four teaspoons of olive oil, then cover with water and cook over low heat. In another pot, cook two or three eggplants (depending on their size) in salted water, having first pricked them with a knife or fork; then strain them and add the puree to the meat when it is almost cooked and the liquid has reduced enough. Crush some coriander seeds and cinnamon in a mortar and add together with salt. A few minutes later, dissolve a teaspoon of sugar in a teaspoon of vinegar and a small cup of grape juice, and to this add a teaspoon of starch. Mix well and stir the solution into the meat and vegetables. Let it cook a few minutes longer; sprinkle with rose water and remove from the heat. Transfer the sikbāj to a serving dish and garnish with peeled and roasted almonds, dried figs, and raisins.

Considering that sikbāj in its original form owed its distinctive character more to the flavor of vinegar than to that of sugar, the nearest present-day version may be mdarbil, another dish of meat and eggplant that belongs to the culinary heritage of Algeria and Tunisia (see recipe 145).

Cut some fatty meat into pieces of medium size, put them in a pot, and cover with water. Add a little salt, ʿud [galangal, or possibly aloe wood], and cinnamon. Bring to a boil, skimming to remove all fetid impurities. Then add coriander seeds.

Take some white onions or leeks or Syrian garlic, carrots, and, if they are in season, eggplant. Peel the vegetables, cut the eggplant into four pieces, and boil in salted water in a separate casserole. Next, drain [the vegetables] and arrange them over the meat with some spices, and adjust the salt. When [the meat] is almost cooked, make a moderately sour-sweet mixture with the right quantities of vinegar, verjuice, and honey, and pour this into the pot. Cook for an hour and thicken with a little starch or rice. Then take some peeled almonds broken in two, some jujubes, dried figs, and raisins; scatter them over [the vegetables] and extinguish the fire. Cover and let rest for an hour. Then wipe the pot dry with a clean towel. Sprinkle [the *sikbāj*] with rose water and, when the temperature has cooled, serve.

16. *RUMMĀNIYYA:* MEATBALLS IN POMEGRANATE JUICE [K]

The name rummāniyya *means "dish with pomegranate." It is found in a* Liber de coquinaria *dating from the late thirteenth or early fourteenth century, as well as in four Italian translations from the fourteenth century, where it appears under the name* romania.

It may be wondered whether the absence of oil from the recipe is a deliberate omission or merely an oversight. Nor is salt mentioned. The difficulty in re-creating this recipe lies in finding a balance between opposed flavors, sour and sweet; and in determining the right proportions of atrāf tīb *(pepper, cloves, ginger, and other spices) and mint leaves, which when dried have a rather intrusive flavor. Anyone who wishes to try reproducing this autumnal dish can find rose water syrup (jul-lāb) at Syrian-Lebanese markets.*

Cut the meat into pieces, put it in a pot, and cover with water. Bring to a boil while removing the fetid scum. Next add small meatballs the size of a hazelnut. The quantity of broth must be reduced so that when the cooking is done only a residue of light and velvety juice remains. In the meantime, take some sour pomegranate juice, sweeten it with rose water syrup, add some mint leaves and pistachios crushed in the mortar to thicken it, color it with a little saffron, and season with all the [ingredients of] *atrāf tīb*. Sprinkle with rose water and [diluted] saffron, and serve.

17. *MARWAZIYYA* WITH CHERRIES [K]

In most medieval recipes, the essential ingredient of this dish was prunes. A modern Tunisian and Moroccan dish having nearly the same name, murūziyya, is likewise made with vinegar and raisins, but calls for dried chestnuts and almonds instead of cherries and jujubes. Cherries were a luxury item, known as "fruit of the king." Substituting chestnuts gives the dish a less sour flavor and a creamier consistency. According to another recipe, the dish is to be prepared with or without meat, but in either case with squash, raisins, chickpeas, and sugar—a very sweet version re-created below as a vegetarian dish (see recipe 162).

A pound and a half of meat, four *ūqiya* of cherries, half a pound of onions [grown in sandy soil] (*basal ramli*), half a *dirham* of saffron, two and a half *ūqiya* of raisins, and, if you like, four *ūqiya* of sweet wine vinegar. Boil the meat without spices. When the meat is cooked, add a pound and a half of water and, when it boils, rinse the onions, cut them, and then rinse them again with water and salt, then with water alone. Add them to the meat and cook. When the onions are half cooked, add the cherries, having first soaked them in water, as well as the raisins and jujubes. Let the cherries and raisins cook. If you like, add three *ūqiya* of sugar at the first boiling, together with some diluted saffron. When everything has been well boiled, throw in mint and *atrāf tīb*, and damp the fire.

18. *TABĀHAJA:* BEEF WITH PISTACHIOS [K]

Certain dishes that originally were made with pistachios (another expensive item that showed honor to guests) are prepared today in Tunisia with peas, for reasons of economy.

You need meat and mint. Blanch the meat, brown it in a little oil, and then pour its broth [i.e., some of the liquid in which it was blanched] over it. Mix honey, pistachios, *atrāf ṭīb*, some starch, saffron, and pepper in a little vinegar. Add this mixture to the meat and cook until it thickens.

19. *ZĪRBĀJ* WITH QUINCE [W]

Quinces are used in either meat or fish dishes, often paired with raisins. The most original modern example of their use is couscous with gilt-head bream and quinces, a classic autumnal dish prepared when the season for catching sea bream coincides with the ripening of the fruit.

Take some cooked meat, add some coarsely crushed chickpeas, and cook [some more]; then add the broth of the meat, vinegar, honey or sugar, some saffron, some quinces [cut] into pieces, and some new apples, also cut into pieces. If you like, [put in] some peeled almonds and some jujubes, or else pistachios and mint. Let thicken over the fire and serve.

Another version: follow the same procedure, with a little starch to thicken [the sauce]; the color remains yellow.

20. *ZĪRBĀJIYYA* WITH ALMONDS [R]

Almonds are sold everywhere. First you should blanch and peel them. Then, depending on the recipe, they are lightly toasted and either cut in half or sliced, or else transformed into almond flour, almond paste, or even almond milk. All these versions are easily prepared at home or can be found in markets, with the exception of almond milk, whose availability is limited in Europe and the United States.

Take a large hen, fat but young. Keep it whole, cutting off the neck and folding back the wings and feet. Put it in a new casserole together with salt, sweet olive oil, pepper, coriander [seeds], and a little cumin along with chopped onion, citron leaves, and fresh water. Place the pot on the fire. When the cooking is almost done, brush the hen with some saffron crushed in the mortar and diluted in water, then pour some good vinegar into the pot, however much you like. Take four *ūqiya* of almonds, peeled and finely crushed in the mortar to the consistency of a paste; take a look at the hen and, if it seems to be cooked, put the crushed almond [paste] in the pot and mix it so that it melts, then leave the pot over a medium fire. After one or two boilings, take some good sugar in a quantity equal to that of the almonds, dissolve it in rose water or fresh water, then strain it and add it to the pot. If you find the flavor too sweet, add some vinegar; if it is not sweet enough, add some sugar [as much as you like]. Let the pot simmer over glowing embers. Then transfer the [zīrbājiyya] to a serving dish and add some chopped eggs.

21. MEAT STEW WITH CARAMELIZED ONIONS [W]

This is the best [kind of] caramel, and more fragrant than many other dishes!

Take dry onions and remove the outer layers; wash them and cook in water until they are soft. Let cool and reserve the cooking liquid. At this point, take the meat and cook it first in water and then in oil. Make simple little [meat] balls in the shape of a taro, then fry them with the meat until everything is well cooked. Take wine vinegar and bee's honey or sugar, and put them on the onions, which must be cooked over a slow fire with saffron and *atrāf tīb*, immersed in sheep tail fat. Thicken over a slow fire until it has achieved a starchy consistency like that of pudding [*khabīs*]. This plate will have a sweet-and-sour flavor that influences the mood of the person who eats it. After that, boil the meat twice so that the flavorings thoroughly permeate it. Put in fresh mint and remove the meat, thicken the onions [until they are] like caramel, and remove from the fire.

22. *JŪDHĀBA* WITH APRICOTS AND CHICKEN [S]

This dish involves spreading a layer of dried or fresh fruit (apricots, bananas, and so on), sweetened with sugar and flavored with spices and rose water, over an already baked flat bread and then covering the mixture with another cooked flat bread. All the medieval collections include recipes that call for a chicken to be hung over the jūdhāba so that it absorbs the fat from the bird, or else incorporated with the filling, as is typically done in Andalusia. The recipe given here is attributed to the ʿAbbasid caliph al-Wāthiq.

Take some sweet and mature apricots; detach [the fruit] from the pit. [Mix it with sugar.] In a clean baking pan . . . spread out [an already baked] flat bread [and place the mixture of apricots and sugar] on top. [Cover this with another cooked flat bread.] If you wish to add a bit of saffron, do so and sprinkle with rose water; then hang an excellent hen over [the dish], may it please God.

23. JŪDHĀBA WITH BANANAS AND CHICKEN [S]

This recipe was created by Ibrāhīm ibn al-Mahdī. An almost identical version from the thirteenth century is found in Wusla, *though there the banana pieces are batter-fried.*

In Tunisia, what goes under the name of banana pie (tājin mūz) is actually a potato pie. Neither sweet nor made with puff pastry, it is thickened with eggs and colored with saffron, and also contains meat and grated cheese.

Peel some bananas and set them aside. Take a baking pan, spread out [an already baked flat bread] in it, and arrange some bananas [over the bread]. Sprinkle with purified sugar, then take another [cooked flat bread] and put it on top. . . . Drown everything in rose water and place an excellent hen on top, may it please God.

24. ANDALUSIAN PIE [R]

The Andalusian recipe for this dish is much more sophisticated than the one from Baghdad—a sort of pie filled with a whole chicken, highly spiced, sweetened, and scented with rose water. It calls to mind not only the Moroccan and Algerian bestilla (see recipe 154), but also the simpler Tunisian tājin malsuqa.

Take a fat young hen. Clean it, cut it along the breast, and put it in a pot. Pour over it some sweet oil; add salt, pepper, cinnamon, spikenard, and cardamom, and put it on the fire. Instead of water, add some good rose water and cook everything without broth.

Take . . . two thin layers of dough, and spread them out in a ceramic pot whose sides and bottom have been smeared with sheep tail fat that has been pushed through a sieve and crushed [so that it resembles] marrow. Make sure the layers [of dough] adhere to the walls of the pot so that they cover them [as well as the bottom]. Dust the [dough] that covers the bottom of the pot with some sugar, peeled almonds, cloves, and a spoonful of spikenard. Sprinkle a good amount of sweet oil [on it], and moisten everything with sweetened rose water in which you will already have diluted a little camphor and musk. Cover with one or two more layers [of dough] and repeat the same operation until half the height of the pot has been reached.

Take the cooked hen, rub it with some saffron diluted in rose water, put it in the pot, and cover it with some layers [of dough]; sprinkle with sugar and almonds as indicated above. Continue in this way, adding [more layers], until the pot is full and the hen is buried within. At the end, sprinkle with much sugar, add some oil and rose water in ample quantities, cover the [contents of the pot] with the edges of the layers [of dough] that hang over the sides, and then close with a lid and seal it with a piece of dough so that no air can escape. Put [the pot] in a medium-hot oven. Leave [it] in the oven long enough to cook a dish of meat, then take [it] out of the oven and remove the [dough] seal: a delicate aroma will come out from it. Remove the layers [of dough] that cover [the contents of the pot], in case the heat has ruined them, as well as the ones that line the sides of the pot, and turn it over [to empty the contents] onto a [serving] dish.

This dish is served as it is; [it is a dish] of absolutely delicious flavor, whose unusual preparation makes it a regal dish, a dish of harmonious and well-structured combinations, an excellent meal.

This *jūdhāba* can be made without chicken or meat, using simply a layer of dough and a layer of almonds, cracked and then crushed in a mortar with sugar and Indian ingredients and saffron, and covered with rose water and sweet oil; after the cooking [is done] it is arranged on a [serving] dish and accompanied with rose syrup and fresh butter. One can also dispense with syrup.

25. MEAT WITH FRIED BANANAS [W]

There is no end to the comparison here between bananas and taro (the edible corm, or root, of the stemless plant Colocasia esculenta). *The author concludes by likening his recipe to a meat dish made with taro known as* sitt al-shanā ͨ (*a puzzling* name, roughly "the lady of loathsomeness"), the recipe for which is found in Kanz (see recipe 40),[1] but no explanation is given of the manner of preparing and frying this tuber, which is typically associated with Egyptian cooking. The name is probably meant to recall the ugliness of the taro, whose skin is wrinkled and hairy.

Peel some green bananas lengthwise and cut them as one does taro. Fry in an abundant quantity of sesame oil to color it well, as one does with taro. Then cut the meat, blanch it in boiling water, and cook it as one does taro, with fresh coriander [cilantro], crushed garlic, and onions. When the meat is well roasted, arrange the fried bananas on top along with a little broth and some hazelnuts that have been peeled, toasted, and very finely crushed in a mortar, in accordance with the description I gave at the beginning of this book, and let the broth reduce. Serve. This dish has the flavor and the appearance of *sitt al-shanā*ᶜ.

26. *RUTĀBIYYA:* MEAT WITH DATES [W]

This dish is within the reach of every cook. It bears comparison with the Moroccan dish of squab with dates, a genuine delicacy that is flavored with cinnamon (see recipe 155).

Cook some red meat cut into small pieces in a pot with some water. When it is cooked, strain it and brown it in fat. Add salt and spices. When the cooking is done, add however many dates you desire, leave [the pot] on the fire for a moment, and then set [it] aside. Remove the pits from the dates and substitute parboiled [and peeled] almonds for them.

You can also prepare this dish by making small meatballs in the shape of the date pit, colored with saffron and fried. In truth one proceeds in this way when dates cannot be had, and you may add beets, vinegar, and saffron [as well].

27. CHICKEN WITH DRIED FRUITS AND ALMOND MILK [K]

This dish has a curious name, sitt al-nawba (*or* sitt al-nūba), *which may mean "the lady of the procession," or "the Nubian lady," or possibly "lady misfortune." The recipe is complicated but nevertheless worth a try, all the more since it has no equivalent in present-day cooking.*[2]

Take some chickens and cook them in water. When the cooking is two-thirds done, strain them and brown them in sesame oil, then set them aside in a container.

Take some [parboiled and] peeled almonds. Toast them, crush them in a mortar, and push them through a sieve in order to obtain the milk of the almond. Put this [in a pan] on the fire with some white sugar. Dilute the saffron and cook it together with the almond milk and the sugar until it thickens. Arrange the chickens [on top of this preparation] and add jujubes and dark raisins that you will already have soaked in rose water with musk, along with parboiled pistachios, peeled and halved.

Pour oil from toasted almonds on top and it is ready.

28. MEAT WITH THE JUICE OF COOKED APRICOTS [K]

A similar version of this dish is made in North Africa today (see recipe 147).

Cut some fatty meat into little pieces and put it in a casserole with very little salt. Cover with water, [heat over the fire], and skim.

Wash onions; cut them and arrange on top of the meat along with the most common spices. Take some fresh apricots, crush them and boil them well, then wash them and crush them by hand, strain them, and add their juice to the meat. Some cooks thicken [the preparation] with water flavored with safflower that has been crushed in the mortar and dissolved. This is a good idea. Leave [the casserole] over the fire until boiling, then wait until the boiling stops and serve.

ROASTS, MEATBALLS, AND SAUSAGES

Meats roasted in an oven (more specifically, a *tannūr*) or cooked in ceramic frying pans were often treated beforehand with vinegar. In a recipe mentioned by Ibn Sayyār, half of a completely eviscerated sheep was marinated for an entire night in vinegar, salt, and spices (crushed coriander seeds, cumin, pepper, and cinnamon). Just before it went into the oven, the meat was sprinkled once more with vinegar. Another recipe calls for cooking it halfway through in very strong vinegar in a frying pan, letting the meat cool, and then draining off the vinegar and adding the spices before putting it in the oven.

But in general the most common procedure was first to heat the mutton in flavored water and skim off the foam of the blood that rises to the surface after boiling, and then to roast it. The water used for this operation was seldom thrown out. Instead, having been cleaned of the "fetid scum," it was saved, and reused as a broth for the cooking of meats in oil and other purposes.

29. POUNDED MEAT [S]

The author calls this recipe a "very original madqūqa." *The Arabic term refers to meat that has been pounded with a wooden utensil or in a mortar until it has acquired the texture of mincemeat. The majority of such recipes in Ibn Sayyār's book call for small meatballs. Their shape could be round (a ball the size of a hazelnut in the case of* banādiq; *see recipe 149), long (like a small sausage), or flat (disk-shaped).*

The meaning of the phrase "white of the onion" is obscure. It may refer to a particular variety of onion cultivated in Iraq in Ibn Sayyār's time, or to the immature bulb of a green onion, or perhaps simply to the heart of an ordinary onion.

Pound the meat on a stone until it has the consistency of marrow. Put a little water in a clean pan, and as soon as it boils, throw in the crushed meat. When the water boils with the meat, remove the scum and add some excellent oil, salt, and the white [part] of a chopped onion, and cook. Mix it and add coriander [seeds] crushed in the mortar, some pepper, soaked chickpeas, and almonds that have been peeled, crushed, and reduced to a paste; sprinkle over it [more of] the white [part] of [a chopped] onion and leave on the fire until it has thickened. Then serve, may it please God.

30. FRIED MEATBALLS [K]

These meatballs can be prepared in the Moroccan manner, holding the meat to-gether with egg, which will give you a kofta (see recipe 150). One may skip the step of parboiling and pass directly to pan-frying.

You need meat, pepper, fresh and dry coriander [cilantro and coriander seeds], a little oil of good quality, and a little onion. Crush the meat in a mortar together with a roasted onion, add flavorings, and make as many servings as you desire. Boil a little water in a frying pan. When it boils, throw in the meatballs, cook them halfway through, and then remove from the fire. Next put a [second] pan on the fire with some sesame oil and fry the boiled meatballs. Crush the dry coriander and sprinkle it on the vessels [in which the meatballs are served].

31. MEATBALLS WITH VINEGAR [K]

Much the same flavor can be appreciated in a Tunisian preparation, no longer very common today, that follows the inverse procedure to the one found in the medieval recipe. These meatballs are prepared with meat that has first been cooked and then cut up and mixed with spices, parsley, and chopped onion. The meatballs are dredged in flour and fried in olive oil. Only afterward are they moistened with a vinegar sauce cooked with sugar and finely chopped onion and garnished with veg-etables preserved in vinegar. In another recipe, sausage-shaped meatballs are cooked in a tomato sauce, and the vegetables that accompany them are pickled in brine (see recipe 151).

Prepare the meatballs in the same way, but cook them until they are half done in very strong vinegar. Let them cool in the pan in which you have cooked them and then drain off the vinegar, season with spices, and finish by cooking in the oven.

32. LIVER SAUSAGES IN THE MANNER OF CALIPH AL-MUʿTAMID [S]

This dish is called ʿuṣbān, which means "packets": the livers are rolled up in caul fat (the word thubūr refers to the lacy abdominal membrane that is often used in Europe for making sausages) and baked. In Tunisia today it is prepared in the same manner, but it contains additional organ meats and is left out in the sun to dry before being conserved. In southeastern Italy, in Lecce (Puglia), where small pieces of liver, heart, and tongue are similarly tied up with gut, these little sausages are known as turcinieddhi.

Take some kid and lamb livers, and boil them in water, thyme, and oil without quite cooking them all the way through.

Cut the [half-boiled livers] like thin belts.

Take the nets [*thubūr*] of the kids and lambs and, after having washed them, put them into boiling water until they are stretched, then fill them with the livers, [which in the meantime have been] cooked with *murrī*, rue, and thyme. Now close [the casings] up, tying them with the intestines, [which have been] turned inside out and washed with salt and celery. Soften with oil and put in the oven.

33. SMOKED SCALLOPS OF MEAT IN THE EGYPTIAN MANNER [W]

Cut the meat into thin scallops and smoke them. Then take the smoked scallops, moisten them with water, and put them in a pot [*dast*] that contains sesame oil. During the cooking, spray [them] from time to time with rose water and sprinkle with salt. When the meat is well cooked and has turned brown, sprinkle with dry coriander [seeds] and eat.

34. ANOTHER RECIPE FOR MEAT IN THE EGYPTIAN MANNER [W]

It is sometimes mistakenly inferred from this recipe that the meat undergoes no cooking. In fact, it was first hung in the top of a tannūr oven and allowed to cook until the juices ran; then it was marinated in vinegar or fruit juice. The recipe that immediately follows in Wusla, *and which is almost identical to this one, refers explicitly to cooking in the oven.*

Large scallops of meat are cut and hung from a hook high in the oven to let the blood and liquids drain out as one does with the smoked scallops. Then put the meat in a [covered] dish. Some [cooks] add juice from apples and quinces to the meat before placing it in the dish; others blend sugar, vinegar, mint, olive oil, a rosebud, mastic, three coriander roots, *atrāf tīb,* and cinnamon. Cover [the dish], without adding water.

35. A FRANKISH RECIPE FOR ROAST LAMB [W]

This dish, shiwā ifranjī, *recalls the Crusades. The Muslims called the Franks* ifranj, *as distinct from* rūm, *their Greek and Byzantine neighbors.*[1]

Take a lamb that has been parboiled, salt it, and brush it with sesame oil and rose water. Run a long spit through it. Put wood charcoal in the braziers for the length of the lamb, to the right and the left so that there is no fire under the animal, and roast the lamb slowly and patiently, so that it will be well cooked and tender. From time to time soften [the skin] with sesame oil, rose water, and salt.

36. ROAST LAMB IN THE ARAB MANNER [W]

Here we have a traditional Bedouin method for roasting a whole lamb, using a more sophisticated version of the familiar earth oven.

Take a parboiled lamb or sheep, carve it lengthwise, cutting some slits [in the meat], and brush [it] with a little olive oil, saffron, and strong spices such as pepper, caraway, dry coriander [seeds], and powdered Chinese cinnamon to dispel the fetid odor. Dig a pit as long and wide as the lamb, but still deeper, and carefully place inside it stones or slabs of marble and light a fire with wood or wood charcoal or some other fuel—in short, with whatever is at hand. Fan the fire well and, when the stones have turned red, put out the fire and remove the cinders, very rapidly so that the stones do not have time to cool. Lay down on the stones a plait of green branches of tamarisk or willow or cane and lay the meat over it, spreading out [the meat] so that it does not fall over to one side. Cover it with a copper pan of [the sort used by] the Arabs or else with a tray, and cover its sides with clay. On top of the pan make a fire [in such a way] that [the heat] is uniformly distributed. Leave alone until [the lamb] is cooked, then sweep away the [remnants of the] fire and remove the lamb [from the pit].

37. ARTIFICIAL MARROW [W]

Copper tubes are fabricated in a shape similar to that of the haunch bone, with one end plugged up. A liver is boiled in water to the point that it is [partly] cooked, and then the fat of a sheep tail, in the same quantity as the liver, is chopped in its entirety. The copper tubes are filled [with the liver and fat] and sealed with a bit of dough. They are then lowered into the boiling water and [their contents] cooked. When the cooking is finished, the tubes are emptied on to a serving dish [*zubdiyya*] and [their contents] will be like marrow in color and flavor.

38. SCENTED STUFFING FOR A ROAST [W]

Take the inner part of some stale bread, grate it, and put it through a sieve. Take parsley, mint, and rue; chop them and mix them with the bread crumbs. Knead the mixture with lemon juice and verjuice. Mix in toasted and crushed pistachios, strong spices, *atrāf tīb*, pepper, and a little olive oil having a neutral taste, not the burned taste of sesame oil. Mix everything together and use it to stuff the belly of a lamb, which is then roasted after having been exposed to the fumes of incense.

39. *LABANIYYA RŪMIYYA:* GREEK (OR BYZANTINE) YOGURT STEW [W]

A pound of meat is parboiled to eliminate the stench, until it is cooked halfway through; then the chopped leaves of chard are added and cooked. When everything is cooked, the meat, broth, and chard are removed from the pot and a pound of yogurt and a half *ūqiya* of rice are poured [into the pot] and mixed together so that the rice is cooked. At this point the meat and chard are added back, together with a small quantity of broth, and cooked with mint leaves. After having transferred [the contents of the pot] to a platter [*zubdiyya*], the [dish] is sprinkled with crushed garlic.

This can be prepared with turnips or spinach in place of the chard.

MEAT, POULTRY, AND VEGETABLE STEWS

The small selection of recipes that follows is hardly representative of the rich variety of meat dishes incorporating vegetables, salad leaves, and tubers that existed in the medieval Muslim world. A comprehensive listing would have to take into consideration various squashes, spinach, beets, asparagus, desert truffles, carrots, turnips, leeks, and so on. The sample given here emphasizes eggplant, a vegetable that only gradually managed to overcome the distaste that many felt for it in the Islamic world.[1] The Italians long refused to eat it for fear of becoming intoxicated (a danger supposed to be reserved for Christians, until Christian Armenians came to Venice and ate it without falling ill); indeed, eggplant was called *malasana*, meaning "unhealthy"— hence the modern Italian word for it, *melanzana*. Thanks to the Armenians of Venice, it came to be cultivated by the peoples of northern Italy, who gave it the name *petonciano*, derived from the Arabic *bādhinjān*. In certain Arab circles, eggplant was regarded as the queen of vegetables. The Andalusian agronomist Ibn al-ʿAwwām distinguished four kinds: that of Egypt, with white fruits and purple flowers, that is, blue-violet; another from Syria having violet-purple [*sic*] fruits with a reddish sheen; our eggplant [from Seville], which is black [very dark red], slender and long, also with purple flowers; and finally the eggplant of Cordova, brown in color and usually with purple flower.[2] All authors insist, however, that the eggplant must be placed in salted water for a certain time to be purged of its bitter liquor.

The other dishes presented in this selection involve the use of taro (members of the *Colocasia* genus, whose Linnaean name derives from the Greek *Kolokasia*, which in turn gave rise to the Arabic *qulqās*) and the leaves of the jute plant (*Corchorus capsularis*), both of which were typical of Egyptian cooking.

40. SITT AL-SHANĀ: MEAT WITH TARO [K]

This recipe calls for the edible corm of the tuber Colocasia esculenta, *about one to two feet long, which requires cooking in order to rid it of irritating calcium oxide crystals.*

You need meat, taro, hazelnuts, *tahīna*, green coriander [cilantro], and pepper. Blanch the meat, then fry it with the coriander and pepper. Toast the hazelnuts, crush them, and mix them with the *tahīna*. When the meat is cooked, add the [previously] fried taro and the *tahīna* mixed with hazelnuts.

41. BEEF WITH ROSEBUDS [K]

Provide yourself with meat, rosebuds, lemons, onions, pepper, mastic, and cinnamon.

Blanch the meat, then fry it with the onions. When it is ready, add crushed pepper, lemon juice, [mastic, cinnamon,] and rosebuds that have been crumbled by hand. Moisten with the necessary quantity of broth.

42. KIBRĪTIYYA: MEATBALLS WITH EGGPLANT [W]

Cut the meat into small pieces and blanch it. Then form it into small balls as [one does] for *būrāniyya* [a dish of eggplant with meatballs] and fry it with crushed garlic, dry coriander [seeds], and sheep tail fat. Next add caraway, pepper, and Chinese cinnamon. When everything is well fried, add the eggplant, which has previously been purged [i.e., soaked in salt water to remove its bitter taste] and cut first in two, and then each piece into quarters. Now add a little beef broth, along with finely chopped green onions, and let [the broth] boil until it has reduced [in quantity] and the eggplant is cooked. Then serve [the dish].

43. CHICKEN WITH SEVILLE ORANGES [W]

Cook the chickens in boiling water after having cut them into pieces, then brown them in sesame oil and chicken fat with chopped onions until the onions are cooked. The [pieces of] chicken must be very well browned. Take some boiled almonds [probably hulled], and crush them until their oil is squeezed out. Push them through a sieve with the broth of the chickens, then pour [the mixture of almond oil and broth] on the chickens. Next, peel some Seville oranges and press them thus, without the peel. Pour [the juice] in the broth while adding some whole almonds to it, a few leaves of mint, cinnamon, and mastic. Boil again long enough to adjust [or to suit] its degree of acidity. Serve.

If you wish to sweeten it, do, but it is better without sugar.

44. STUFFED EGGPLANT [W]

Ibn Razīn, in one of seventeen recipes for stuffed eggplant, calls for extra stuffing to be spread over the eggplant before it is put in the oven.

Take some of our large eggplants. Remove the head [*rās*] of each eggplant and hollow out the inside in order to extract the pulp while taking care not to cut the skin; indeed, [the skin] should be of a good thickness. Then take some meat and pound it in a mortar and boil it. When it is cooked, pound it in the mortar [again] in order to make it still more tender. Put [it] in a pot [*dast*] and add fresh sheep tail fat, dry coriander [seeds], caraway, pepper, Chinese cinnamon, and fresh chopped coriander [cilantro] and parsley in great quantities. Fry all of it until it is roasted. Add salt and stuff the eggplant with this mixture. Close up [the stuffed eggplants] with what was cut off [i.e., the head]. Insert [in each eggplant] three sticks of good-quality wood that has been smoked [in order to reattach the head], then put them in the pot and cook over a lively fire in the sheep tail fat until they are well cooked. Then put them on a serving dish [*zubdiyya*] and sprinkle with dry coriander. At the moment of serving, remove the sticks and throw them away.

45. EGGPLANT IN SWEET-AND-SOUR SAUCE [W]

Compare this with recipe 145.

The meat is blanched and then cooked. The meatballs are prepared in accordance with the usual procedure. The eggplants are fried, then added to the meat. At this point, pour [in] some *tahīna* that has been diluted with lemon juice and vinegar. Prepare [a mixture of] chopped parsley, green coriander [cilantro], strong spices, mint, and a root of rue. Sweeten all of it with a little sugar, not too much. Enliven the flavor with garlic and add the eggplant to the meat with a little broth. Bring it to a boil three times and then remove it from the fire.

46. EGGPLANT FRIED IN THE INDIAN STYLE [W]

. . . Izz al-Dīn al-Wāsitī has seen the Indians cook eggplant in this way; he says that prepared thus it is extremely delicious. It is necessary to cut each eggplant into four pieces and cook them in sesame oil. One needs to put a quarter-*dirham* of [atrāf] *tīb* for every twenty eggplants.[3] This gives them an exquisite flavor. In order to achieve a similar result [to the Indian version], the cooking pot [*dast*] must be covered once the eggplants have been put in it.

47. *MULŪKHIYYA:* MEATBALLS WITH JUTE LEAVES [K]

See also recipe 153.

You need some meat, fat, and jute leaves. If necessary, use chicken or pigeons. You need some garlic, onion, and pepper. Boil the meat and strain it. In a mortar crush garlic, pepper, coriander [seeds], and caraway and add them to the meat along with the onion [which you will already have roasted]; then crush [the spice mixture] again with the meat to make meatballs. The meatballs are then put in a pot with the broth. When the broth . . . reaches a boil, the chopped jute leaves are added, and one cooks [it] until done.

48. VEGETARIAN *MULŪKHIYYA* [K]

You need some mallow [jute leaves], sesame oil, mastic, cinnamon, onion, and dry coriander [seeds]. Fry the onion in the sesame oil and then cook [it] with all the other ingredients.

FISH

Whether from the sea or fresh water; whether fresh, salted, dried, roasted, boiled, or fried; whether whole, shaped into balls, or skewered and flavored with various sauces; whether served as an appetizer or as a main course, fish occupied a place of honor in medieval Islamic cuisine.[1] There was a kind of imagination brought to the preparation of certain dishes that we no longer find today, to say nothing of the many recipes for condiments incorporating salted fish and the many sauces and marinades, more or less spicy, more or less sour, that accompanied each dish.

The small selection of recipes here is taken mainly from the cookbooks of the thirteenth century. Andalusia stands out for Ibn Razīn's shrimp dish (recipe 70), which occurs between recipes for locusts and snails, practically on the margin of the page. There are no recipes for octopus (large or small), cuttlefish, or squid; no mention of seafood, crabs, or sea urchins. And there are no fish soups.

49. ZABĪBIYYA: FISH WITH RAISINS [K]

Compare to recipe 160.

Get some fresh fish, raisins, wine vinegar, *atrāf ṭīb*, saffron, pepper, almonds, and sesame oil. Wash the fish, dredge it in flour, fry it, and let it cool down.

Boil the vinegar with the raisins along with pepper crushed in a mortar and the *atrāf ṭīb* [and then pour all of it over the fish]. Cook the almonds in boiling water and then sprinkle them with the saffron and scatter them over the fish.

50. *LĪMŪNIYYA:* FISH WITH LEMON [K]

One needs some fresh fish, safflower, lemon, mastic, cinnamon, and a sprig of mint. Crush the safflower in the mortar, strain it, and place it over the fire. Squeeze the lemons, strain the [juice], add the juice to the safflower, and boil [the mixture]. Wash the fresh fish, cut it into pieces, and put [them] with the ingredients that are already [cooking] on the fire. It is necessary to stoke the fire until the fish is perfectly cooked; then strew it with the mastic, cinnamon, and mint.

51. *SĪR:* SALTED AND SEASONED FISH [K]

Take small salted fish and season them with a little of their marinade [*yasīr min marqatihī*], lime juice, good oil, thyme, and lime peel.[2]

52. ANOTHER RECIPE FOR SEASONING *SĪR* [K]

Where the climate permits, the best way to preserve fish is by drying, especially for purposes of export. This practice is still current in small Tunisian ports, despite the advent of refrigeration. The south of Tunisia used to supply the Saharan region as far away as Libya, but today the taking of small fish is tightly controlled and production is limited to supplying the local market. Alevin (a very small fish, called wuzaff *in Tunisia) is dried and then mashed in a mortar with spices for use as a condiment. Sardines and other small fish known as* shāwri *(a specialty exclusive to the northeast of Tunisia) are used as an accompaniment for certain dishes in the absence of fresh fish.*

Remove the skin from some fish, cut them into pieces, and season them with oil; lime juice; dried thyme; chopped parsley, mint, and rue; and a little crushed garlic. Mix everything together and partake of it.

53. FISH *ZĪRBĀJ* [K]

You need fresh fish, vinegar, honey, saffron, *atrāf tīb*, *tahīna*, pepper, raisins, almonds, sesame oil, and flour.

Wash the fish, cut it into pieces, and dredge it in the flour. Put a skillet on the fire, pour into it the sesame oil, [fry the fish,] and let it cool. Mix the vinegar with the saffron, *atrāf tīb*, pepper, and *tahīna*. [Then] fry some onion with a little sesame oil. Crush the other ingredients for the sauce in a mortar and add them [to the onion]. Mix it, and when it begins to boil, pour the sauce over the fish. Blanch the onions and color them with a little saffron, then put them together with a bit of oil on top of the preparation, and serve.

54. FISH *SIKBĀJ* [K]

Provide yourself with some fresh fish, vinegar, honey, *atrāf tīb*, pepper, onion, saffron, sesame oil, and flour. Wash the fish and cut it into pieces, then fry [the pieces] in the sesame oil after having dredged [them] in the flour. When [they] are ready, take them out [of the pan]. Slice the onion and brown it in the sesame oil. In the mortar, crush the pepper and *atrāf tīb*. Dissolve the saffron in vinegar and honey and add it [to the pan]. When [the sauce] is ready, pour it over the fish.

55. LARGE ROASTED FISH [R]

Choose some large fish, such as shad or grouper. Scale them, open their bellies, clean them, and rinse them, then blanch them. Cut them into slices of medium thickness.

In a glazed earthenware skillet, put a good amount of oil, vinegar, *murrī*, and cloves of garlic. In a bowl, put pepper, dry coriander [seeds], cumin, a little powdered saffron, and a little mastic. Mix all this in a little water and pour the mixture into the pan. Immerse the pieces of fish one after another in this marinade, taking care to see that they are thoroughly permeated with spices and the rest.

Once this step is complete, neatly arrange the slices in the pan, add a little water, and put [it] in the oven. The fish is cooked when it is golden brown.

If one wishes to make this dish at home, the pan containing the fish must be covered with an unglazed ceramic plate and placed over a rather strong fire so that the heat reaches the fish. Reduce its juices and let it brown. When it is cooked, take it off the fire, wait for it to cool, and eat with God's blessing.

One may substitute juice made from coriander leaves [cilantro] for the vinegar and *murrī*. With sea bream, add walnuts crushed in a mortar.

56. GILT-HEAD BREAM WITH GRAPE JUICE REDUCTION [R]

Scale the fish [gilt-head bream or striped mullet, depending on availability], clean it outside and inside, immerse it in boiling water, and wash it with care. Cut it into pieces of medium size, put the pieces into a glazed frying pan, sprinkle with salt, pour into it a good amount of oil, and add pepper, dry coriander [seeds], a little cumin, a pinch of mace, a little infused *murrī*, and a little water and citron leaves. Sprinkle the pieces of fish well with these flavorings and with powdered saffron until they take on color.

Take an onion, clean it, cut it into slices of medium thickness, put them in a pot with a little water, and put [the pot] over the fire. When the onion is cooked, remove it from the heat and add it to the pan after having colored it with the saffron. If the sauce is too concentrated, whereas the fish is not yet cooked, add [some of the] onion cooking water. When the fish is cooked, coat it with honey and boiled-down grape juice and put it in the oven so that it takes on color.

Another way: one can also cook it at home. In this case, proceed as described earlier in the book. Let cool and then eat with God's blessing.

57. *MURŪJ*: A RECIPE FOR EVERY TYPE OF FISH [R]

Take some fish, big or small, with scales or without; blanch them, scale them [if necessary], empty them [of their viscera], rinse them, and cut them into small pieces. Salt them and set them aside.

In a frying pan put vinegar, *murrī*, some excellent olive oil, pepper, coriander seeds, a little cumin, a clove of garlic, and a little thyme, and bring the mixture to a boil. Immerse the fish [pieces] in this aromatic broth and cook [them in a] covered [pan] for a very short time.

Another way: with sardines and eels, do the same thing but with a sauce of coriander [seeds], crushed garlic, and a little vinegar.[3]

58. FISH BALLS WITH GINGER AND CHEESE [R]

Take any kind of fish as long as its flesh is firm. Scale it, blanch it, then remove the skin, bones, and viscera.

Grind up the fish in a mortar; put it in a dish and add salt, pepper, cinnamon, ginger, powdered mastic, a little cumin, saffron, dry coriander [seeds], a little onion, garlic, mint water, infused *murrī*, and oil. Mix well.

Take a clean skillet and pour some oil into it.

From the mixture [of fish and seasonings] make little balls, flattening some of them [*quruswa banadiq*], and fry them in the hot oil, carefully turning them so that they are golden brown on all sides, then remove them from the heat. If you like you can also add some cheese.

In a serving dish put some lemon juice or some infused *murrī* with a sauce made from vinegar, oil, and a large amount of crushed garlic. All of it must be boiled in a glazed clay skillet. Do as you please, and eat.

59. SKEWERS OF FISH WITH CINNAMON AND GINGER [R]

Remove the skin from the fish, clean the inside of it, and then blanch it. Then cut it into pieces of medium thickness. Salt [them] and put to one side.

In a dish put some dissolved salt, *murrī*, oil, pepper, cinnamon, crushed garlic, and ginger, and provide yourself with a clean feather. Insert iron skewers through the pieces of fish. Put the fire near it on both sides, and the extremities of the skewers should lie upon the stones. Turn the skewers by hand. Use the feather to baste the pieces of fish with the marinade until they are roasted.

In a bowl put oil and garlic that has been cooked and crushed. Remove the pieces of fish from the skewers and cut them into smaller pieces, mixing them with the oil and garlic marinade. Eat, with God's blessing.

60. GRILLED SARDINES [R]

If you wish to roast small fish—such as sardines, which appear in the months of May and October, or *jorkom* [unidentified], which come out in September, or other small fish on their first appearance—over a bed of embers, then prepare a fire without either flame or smoke and lay the fish over it after having salted them. Turn them when they are well roasted.

Then season them with a sauce of oil and garlic, or [serve them] without any sauce. Do as you please.

61. SHAD COOKED IN SALT [R]

Shad is related to sardines and herrings, and swims upriver in the spring in order to spawn. It was greatly valued in Andalusian cuisine, as well as in Morocco, though not at all in the neighboring lands of the Maghreb.

Put a layer of salt on a new [terra-cotta] tile, lay the fish on top, and cover it with another [layer of] salt. Put it in the oven. When you see that the salt has formed a crust and begun to brown, then remove the tile from the oven and scrape the salt off the fish.

In the meantime you will have prepared
—a sauce, in a bowl, with salt, pepper, ginger, cinnamon, and other flavorings of the same kind;
—oil and garlic, in a second bowl;
—infused *murrī*, in a third [bowl]; and finally,
—a bowl containing a sauce prepared as [indicated] in the fifth chapter of the second part of this book [where various rather sophisticated sauces to accompany rabbit are described; which one the author has in mind here is unclear].

62. SARDINE TIMBALE WITH FRESH HERBS [R]

Take some small sardines, wash them, and salt them.

Chop as finely as possible fresh coriander [cilantro], fresh mint, fresh fennel [fronds], and onion. Spread out a layer of these chopped ingredients on the bottom of a pot, then a layer of sardines. Alternate [the layers] until the pot is full. Sprinkle cinnamon, ginger, and a little mastic, and bring to the oven. Take out when it is cooked and roasted.

63. FISH RISSOLE IN THE SHAPE OF SARDINES, WITH ALMONDS AND PINE NUTS [R]

Take some sardines of any variety. Clean them, wash them, and drain them.

Take the soft white part of bread and salt [it], if the bread is not salted, [and add] a mixture of pepper, ginger, cinnamon, spikenard, some cloves, a little powdered saffron, dry coriander and cumin [seeds], and enough egg—not too much—to hold the flesh [of the fish] together.

Take the flesh with a fork [after having mixed it with the spices and the egg] and give it once again the shape of the fish. Arrange the fish obtained in this way in a single cooking dish, one next to the other. With a part of the mixture that remains, form round balls into which peeled almonds and pine nuts have been incorporated. Moisten the rest with coriander [cilantro] water and put it between the fish; lubricate with much oil, and put [the cooking dish] in the oven. It is cooked when the sauce is reduced and the fish balls are golden brown.

64. FILLETS OF FISH WITH CUMIN AND SAFFRON [R]

. . . Use fish without scales. Cut [them] open at the level of the dorsal gills, remove the head and bones, leave the fillets whole without cutting them into pieces, and wash them. Put [them] in a frying pan with a little water, oil, pepper, dry coriander [seeds], powdered coriander, crushed whole garlic, saffron, and *murrī*. Leave the fish in this marinade for as long as you like. Then cook it over the fire until the water has evaporated and the fillets are done. Then remove them from the heat and wait until they have cooled. And may you enjoy your meal, should God will it.

65. *BASBĀSIYYA*: FISH WITH FENNEL [R]

You need large fish. Scale them, wash them, cut them into pieces, and lightly blanch them in salted water. Take them out and put them in a frying pan. Crush some [fresh] green fennel to extract its juice. Cover the fish with fennel juice, generously coat with oil, and add pepper, dry coriander [seeds], ginger, salt, and onion juice, then a bit of must. Put [the pan] in the oven.

When [the fish] is golden brown on the outside and the sauce has evaporated, take it out and eat.

66. FRIED SARDINE BALLS [R]

Compare to recipe 157.

Take sardines or similar fish. Scale them, wash them, blanch them in salted water, remove the bones, and crush the flesh in order to obtain a paste similar to the one that is used to make fish balls. Incorporate into it black pepper, dry coriander [seeds], cinnamon, ginger, spikenard, mint juice, and fresh coriander [cilantro]. Sprinkle with a little extra-fine flour and mix well. Make balls and flatten [them] into the shape of sardines or some other shape that pleases you. Sprinkle with flour and fry the [flattened] balls in a skillet that contains hot oil. Prepare a sauce with vinegar, oil, and crushed garlic, and bring it to a boil in an earthenware pan. Pour it over the fried fish balls.

67. FISH CAKE IN THE MANNER OF AL-JUMLĪ [R]

This is practically the same as the Tunisian maʾqūda *with herrings (see recipe 156).*

Select the fish from among the best varieties. Scale it and blanch it in salted water after having cut it into pieces. If [the fish] is large, cut it open lengthwise and extract the bones. Fry it to impart a golden brown color.

In a skillet, break a few eggs, adding the soft white part from a loaf of bread, pepper, saffron, cinnamon, spikenard, ginger, and dry coriander [seeds]—all of this crushed in the mortar—along with much oil and infused *murrī.* Sprinkle with cracked almonds and mix in the pieces of fish.

Put [the mixture] in the oven, and when it has thickened and the outside is well browned, take it out.

A marvelous dish!

68. FISH STUFFED INTO ITS OWN SKIN [R]

Take a *kahla* [thick-lipped gray mullet]. Clean it inside and out. Rinse it and remove the skin, pulling gently from the head to the tail while leaving it attached to the tail. Remove the flesh and throw away the central bone.

Pound the flesh and add to it salt, a little pepper, dry coriander [seeds], cumin, cinnamon, ginger, spikenard, cloves, and mastic. Mix with an egg white and stuff the skin of the fish [with it].

Fry [the stuffed skin] in oil in a skillet until it has become golden brown. Delicately remove it from the skillet so that it does not break apart and place it on a serving dish.

69. CALZONES STUFFED WITH FISH [R]

Make a dough with flour, yeast, salt, and water. Knead it well and let it rise. Season the flesh of the fish with saffron and coriander [cilantro] water to color it.

Roll out the dough to make thin layers that are to be filled with stuffing. Cover them with another layer [of dough] of smaller dimensions. Close by pulling the edges of the bottom layer back over the edges of the top layer. Press down [to seal] and cook in the oven.

70. SHRIMP [R]

The Arabic word for shrimp, qamrūn, *derives from the Greek* kammoron, *source also of the Latin* cambarus *and the Italian* gambero (*crayfish*). *This recipe appears in M. Benchecroun's edition of Ibn Razīn published at Rabat in 1981 (p. 185).*

These are cooked in a pot filled with water over a slow fire for three hours [*sic*]. Then they are taken out of the water, and once they have been sprinkled with fine salt they are ready to eat.

Others fry them in oil with some *murrī*, thyme, salt, pepper, and cinnamon.

Shrimp are found in great quantities in large rivers and in particular in the region of Seville as well as in the river of Bougie. They have the effect of loosening [kidney] stones.

71. LITTLE FISH BALLS [K]

You need fresh fish, pepper, sesame oil, coriander seeds, a little oil of good quality, and one onion. Wash the fish, separate [the flesh] from the bones, and crush it carefully in a mortar. Crush the pepper and coriander seeds and add [them] to the fish with a little oil of good quality. Mix together while crushing everything in the mortar and [from this mixture] make little balls, larger ones with holes in the middle, and flattened ones. Put these in the *sahnā* [a condiment described later in the original text; see recipe 118], sprinkle with coriander seeds and powdered salt, and serve.

---

72. MUJABBANA COOKED IN A PAN [R]

Both styles of eating this little fried dumpling of semolina and cheese—moistened with butter and honey in the Andalusian manner, or dipped in honey in the "eastern" or "Berber" manner—are still common today. The first is better suited to children; the second is preferable for adults, because they can decide how sweet they want their dumplings to be. This dish is to be served for breakfast.

Soak the semolina with cold water, if it is summer, or hot water, if winter. Knead as if one is making dough for dumplings and let rest.

Take fresh, soft cheese, rinse with water, and crush by hand in a bowl until it has the consistency of marrow. If the cheese is dry and salty, cut it into pieces, leave it to soak in water to desalt and soften it, then rinse it with water and rub it by hand until it has the desired consistency.

Taste. If it lacks salt, add some; if it is too salty, add some fresh milk or, if milk is lacking, hot water. Put in as much as necessary.

Take an amount of dough equal to a quarter of the cheese. Add to it a bit of aniseed, mint water, and coriander [cilantro] water, and then knead in order to obtain a homogeneous dough.

Place on the fire a tin-plated frying pan containing quite a lot of oil. While waiting for the oil to become very hot, your assistant should wash his hands and take with the left hand a piece of the dough and spread it out a little on the palm, and then, with the right hand, take a little of the cheese and put it in the center of the dough spread out on the left hand. At this point he will make a fist and remove the excess dough that comes out between the thumb and index finger. Then he will give a flat and rounded shape to the dough remaining in the hand and make a round hole in the middle of it. He will then place these cakes [*mujabbana*] next to one another in the pan until it is filled. One needs to stir them continually with an iron fork so that they are cooked and well browned. If a *mujabbana* is not thoroughly immersed in the oil, it is necessary to place a well-cooked one on top of it in order to assure that the cooking is uniform throughout. Remove them at the end from the frying oil and let them rest for an hour in a dish before moving them to a *mithrad*. Moisten them with fresh filtered butter and melted honey, and sprinkle them with sugar and cinnamon. Eat them, God willing, and may good health be yours.

Whoever prefers [to eat] them dry, without moistening them in the Andalusian manner, puts them in a *tayfūra*. You sprinkle them with cinnamon, ground aniseed, and sugar. In the middle of the *tayfūra* put a dish filled with honey and the cakes are eaten [after dipping them] a little in the honey.

As for the preparation of the dough, eggs may be mixed with the semolina: seven or eight for a pound of semolina. Do this, because they will be still better and more delicious.

73. FRIED *MUJABBANA* IN THE TOLEDO STYLE [R]

This recipe calls to mind a modern Tunisian dish (similar to Italian cheese ravioli) called brīk dannūni *that is eaten during the month of Ramadan. The Tunisian version is eaten without honey, however (see recipe 152).*[1]

A dough is prepared using extra-fine flour and water, salt, and oil as indicated in the recipe for oven-baked *mujabbana* [see recipe 74]. An amount of fresh cheese equal to three-quarters of the amount of flour is grated. It is mixed with aniseed and mint juice and fresh coriander [cilantro], as already indicated. The dough is rolled out with a rolling pin to make [small] round leaves. Place the necessary quantity of grated cheese in the middle of each piece of dough, and pull back the edges toward the center, pressing down lightly. The little packets one obtains in this way are placed in a copper or ceramic pan and cooked in the oven that is used for cooking biscuits and such things.

When these little packets begin to brown, they are taken out of the oven and arranged on a ceramic or wooden serving dish, one on top of the other. They are then covered with honey and fresh melted butter. After they are sprinkled with sugar and cinnamon, they can be eaten, God willing.

74. LAYERED CAKE [R]

This oven-baked mujabbana *is another Andalusian specialty that combines cheese and honey, and resembles a sort of quiche or cheese pasty. I suggest making it with ricotta.*

Prepare a dough with extra-fine flour, [kneading] first with water and then with oil, and add the yeast and milk in order to obtain the consistency of pancake dough. Let rise. When you see that it has risen, oil a large ceramic pan and in it spread out a thin layer of dough, then a piece of cheese, alternating as you did before. Cook in the oven, then drizzle honey over it and dust with cinnamon and pepper. Then serve.

75. PANCAKES WITH PISTACHIOS AND PINE NUTS [R]

Knead a pound of extra-fine flour and a pound and a half of fresh cheese so that they are well mixed together, then work [the mixture] some more with five eggs, salt to taste, and add a little water if necessary. Make some very thin layers of dough. Fry in a pan with a large amount of oil; they must remain white. Next, boil honey together with some crushed walnuts and pour [the mixture] on top [of the layers of dough]; also crumble over them some pine nuts and pistachios, sprinkle some sugar, and it will be ready to serve, may it please God.

76. ANOTHER *MUJABBANA* [R]

This mujabbana *with eggs is the ancestor of the contemporary Tunisian turnovers known as* brīk, *which are typically fried in oil, as in the version I have included later in the book (see recipe 152). They can perfectly well be cooked in the oven, however.*

Crumble the cheese as finely as you can and mix it with eggs, then with mint water and coriander [cilantro] water, and finally with whatever common spices are at hand. Spread [the mixture] over a thin layer of dough and cover with another layer. Cook in the oven. Learn to do this, in accordance with the will of God!

77. CHEESE AND EGG CAKE [R]

Some culinary authorities trace the original version back to Sicily (along with other regions of Italy, the source of a substantial wave of immigration to Tunisia between the middle of the nineteenth century and the middle of the twentieth), just as brīk are attributed to Ottoman influence; but it is clear from medieval sources that such cakes were known considerably earlier.

Take as much cheese as you like, rinse it, and crumble it in a bowl. Into this break as many eggs as are needed for the cheese. Add some salt if the cheese is not salty, some ground saffron, pepper, coriander [seeds], water in which coriander [cilantro] leaves have been soaked, mint, and cloves. Mix by hand so that everything is well blended together. Take a baking pan, moisten it with a little oil, and pour in the mixture of cheese and egg; mold [the mixture] with the hands and add enough egg yolk and oil to cover the surface. Sprinkle some saffron [on top] and put the baking pan in the oven, taking care to place it far from the flame. It is cooked when it has thickened and the cake is golden brown. Remove it from the oven and eat it when it has cooled, may it please God.

78. DRY CHEESE ROASTED ON SKEWERS [R]

Cut [dry cheese] into small pieces and insert a thin wooden skewer through them. Roast on all sides until they are golden brown and eat.

79. CONDIMENT WITH DRY CHEESE [R]

Take as much cheese as you like. Cut off the rind and, using a grater [*iskirfāj*], reduce the cheese to powder. Next, put it in the mortar with garlic and salt, then dissolve it in hot water and mix well. Finally, pour some good olive oil on it. Eat with the blessing of God. Then, with the will of God, add walnuts that have been shelled and ground up in the mortar.

80. CURDLED MILK WITH HONEY [R]

Strain fresh milk and make it curdle as indicated before [in the original text] or with thistle flowers, which we call *lasīf,* and which are quite efficacious. While the milk curdles, dilute some honey in the milk in an amount that depends on how sweet you wish it to be. When the honey and milk are well blended, drink, God willing, as much as you like. The curdled milk may be accompanied, without adding sugar, by good figs.

81. *BIRĀF* [K]

Wide ceramic containers are used that have the capacity of a large skillet. One draws the milk, strains it at once while it is still warm, and then puts it in these pans. This should be done in the evening when the herd comes back from the pastures. The pans are placed outside, exposed to the air and the damp, but covered by a large cage. The next morning at dawn, before sunrise, with the aid of a long shell, one collects whatever has risen to the surface and transfers it to another ceramic container that is new and clean. One continues [to do this] until nothing is left on top. Then the containers are covered and let be. If one fears that the sun may fall upon them, move them to a cool place. During the day one may draw out whatever has risen to the surface and serve it.

Many people prefer to eat *birāf,* which is one of the best kinds of nourishment, without anything added. Others eat it with honey, others still with powdered sugar. As for Ahmad al-Safasī, he prefers to eat it with syrup and rose water because this way, according to him, is the best. I told a group of friends about this way [of eating it], and they liked it because, with rose water, not only is it delicious but it has beneficial properties that offset the undesirable effects. If one fears indigestion after having eaten *birāf* without taking anything with it, drink *sikanjubīn,*[2] which is made from quinces, or eat a quince, a pear, or some figs. I saw someone eat *zulābiyya* with *birāf!* I tried it, and it was good.

soups

82. SOUP OF WHEAT WITH MEAT [W]

The original name of this dish was kushkāt.

I recommend using a large pot [for cooking] so that the ingredients altogether occupy half of it. Cook the meat in boiling water until it is half done, then remove it from the pot. Rinse the threshed grain and put it in the pot. The quantity of wheat must be equal to a third of that of the meat. When it is almost cooked, add small pieces of Chinese cinnamon and mastic, add salt and water if necessary, and arrange the meat over the wheat. It is necessary to keep the fire hot continually for an hour. Then cover the pot and leave it over a low fire until morning. When it is uncovered, add fat from the sheep tail, mastic, cinnamon, and sesame oil. Then one eats.

83. CHICKEN BROTH WITH BREAD CRUMBS [R]

This Andalusian hasu *is made from chicken broth and thickened with the same bread crumbs that are used to make* tharīd. Hasu *is a simple dish, generally thickened instead with flour or semolina. This recipe departs from traditional principles in calling for unusual ingredients (in addition to meat and bread crumbs there are costly spices) and represents a superior version of the customary dish, which is still made today in the countries of the Maghreb.*

Take a fat hen, or pullets. Open up the belly, remove the insides, and clean the outside. Break the bones and all the joints, leaving it outwardly intact. [Next] put it in a ceramic pot with salt and oil, sticks of cinnamon, mastic, ginger, coriander [seeds], a bit of onion, and enough water. Put the pot on the fire. Then take crumbled bread, made from semolina or flour with yeast.

Rub it gently to reduce it to bread crumbs [*futāt*], then push it through a sieve, still rubbing it between the hands so that all of it is equally fine, and put it in a copper vessel. [Returning to the pot that was left on the fire,] slowly pour into the boiling broth the *futāt* with one hand, while with the other mix it with a spoon until the *futāt* is used up. Do not cease stirring [the mixture] until it seems homogeneous and well cooked. Then remove it from the fire and empty it onto a serving dish, sprinkling cinnamon over it. One may add vinegar and verjuice to it [as well]. Eat it in good health, may God be willing.

84. CREAM OF FARINA [R]

This rather flavorless Andalusian recipe for hasu, made without spices, is found in Tunisia under the same name. It is probably improved by the addition of toasted bread crumbs and a bit of olive oil. In Tunisia a teaspoon of vinegar is added at the end.

Pour into a new pot a sufficient quantity of water, add salt, and place over the fire. In a *mithrad* put wheat meal, moisten it with water, and mix with a spoon to dilute it, taking care to eliminate any lumps. When the water boils, pour into it the diluted farina and stir gently to keep it from sticking to the bottom of the pot. Cook until it is quite thick, then remove from the fire. Wait until it ceases to boil and pour the *hasu* into a dish to serve it. Whoever wishes to add bread crumbs should take some bread, cut it with a knife, and place it over the fire until it is browned, then break it into crumbs. Moisten with oil and eat.

85. SOURDOUGH SOUP [R]

This is another version of an Andalusian hasu that is still current in Tunisia today, although there it is enlivened by red chiles.

Pour enough water into a new pot, salt, and add a little wild fennel, coriander [seeds], and an unpeeled clove of garlic. Keep the pot over a low fire. Take the necessary quantity of yeast, which should be at a very advanced stage of maturation, and dilute it with hot water in the *mithrad* with the help of a spoon. When the garlic is almost cooked, pour the dissolved leaven into the pot and mix continually with the spoon until it is cooked just enough, not more, because it is better that the dish be light. Then pour [the food] onto a serving dish and present it. Whoever wishes to remove the garlic may do so; whoever wishes to eat [the garlic] should keep it.

86. ANDALUSIAN PUREE OF WHEAT WITH FENUGREEK [R]

Jashīsh is a coarsely milled semolina comparable to the dashīsh *or* dashīsha *popular in North Africa. Frequently obtained by grinding barley, it is used to make various more or less rich winter soups. The one eaten during Ramadan is made with mutton, chickpeas, and celery leaves or fresh coriander [cilantro]. A particularly unusual* dashīsh *(a specialty of the Qarqannah [Kerkennah] Islands, off the Tunisian coast from Sfax) is cooked in broth made from dried octopus tentacles that have been cut into small pieces.*

Clean some wheat of good quality and coarsely grind to reduce it to *jashīsh,* then push the *jashīsh* through a sieve and separate the semolina from the bran. Rinse it and put it in a new pot. Add some tanned fenugreek [seeds], equal to an eighth of the quantity of *jashīsh.* Add much water and place over the fire until it is cooked. Then pour into a tureen and sprinkle with seasonings ground by hand, and it is ready to be consumed.

Whoever wishes [to eat it] with milk should not use fenugreek. [In this case it is necessary to] reduce the quantity of water that will be substituted for by the milk, so that the *jashīsh* cooks in the milk until it is completely absorbed.

87. QAMHIYYA: PUREE OF WHOLE WHEAT [W]

The author of Wusla *mentions the existence of two recipes for purees of wheat. "Of the first I do not speak because it is famous, and therefore well known!" This is not much help—and not the first time that this author has left us guessing. The term* qamhiyya *refers simply to wheat that has been cooked in milk after being rinsed in rose water. The author seems to consider the prior cooking of the wheat in water not as part of the recipe but as a preliminary step, which calls to mind the procedure followed in making* burghul. *In this recipe the wheat is not cracked, however, as in the case of* burghul, *but conserved whole, as is still done today in certain parts of North Africa, for example at Sfax, where the whole wheat is precooked and dried (in one of many versions still current).*

Although it is said to have been introduced by the Turks, burghul *seems always to have existed in the Mediterranean area, as the historian Ernest-Gustave Gobert suggested in an essay on historical accounts of foods, comparing it to a dish of classical antiquity that the Romans called* alica *(which was made with spelt).*[1] Burghul *is made by boiling grains of wheat that have been thoroughly rinsed with salted water, then dried in the sun for many days, and finally passed under the grindstone or crushed in a mortar to separate out any impurities. Treated in this fashion, semicooked and lightly salted wheat can be preserved for long periods of time without loss of nutritional value. The basic procedure has been known since ancient times: it is mentioned by Pliny the Elder in his* Natural History, *where he cites the method of Mago of Carthage.*

The precooked wheat is moistened with warm milk instead of cold water. One leaves it on the fire until the preparation has thickened. But having been half cooked beforehand, then rinsed several times in rose water, the wheat is cooked as indicated only afterward.

88. CRACKED RICE [R]

This type of *jashīsh* is rare, except in Murcia, my city, and in Valencia, may God restore it to us! Murcia and Valencia specialize in the cultivation of rice, which grows well there, unlike in the rest of Andalusia.

When the rice is beaten to separate it from the chaff, a certain amount of rice is broken, and these pieces are used to make the *jashīsh*. They are pushed through a large sieve and preserved for use as needed.

Method of cooking: Wash well with fresh water and, in a casserole, put six pounds of water for each pound of *jashīsh*. Cook over a medium fire until just cooked, then add the necessary quantity of fine salt and serve.

PASTA

The recommendations of Ishāq ibn Sulaymān (Isaac ben Solomon), the Jewish physician from Qayrawan, with regard to the consumption of the pasta known as *itriya* (or *itriyya*) are curious to say the least; on the other hand, they are almost identical to ones found in Ibn Sīnā's *Canon of Medicine* about a century later. Although he does not describe the shape of *itriya* (Ibn Sīnā notes that they have the form of very fine threads and that in Iran they are called *rishtā*), Ibn Sulaymān says they are sticky, being made with unleavened and unsalted dough—an unpromising choice in view of the fact that all dietary experts of the period were agreed that any kind of unleavened dough was bad for the digestion. *Itriya* were cooked in water over a low fire. According to Ibn Sulaymān, this kind of pasta is improved if it is cooked with purslane or sugar, for example, because in that case it counteracts hemophilia; and it is better still cooked with almond oil or oil extracted from olives harvested before they ripen, along with salt, pepper, and chicken, because this way it is more rapidly digested than if it were cooked with the chicken alone. A glass of wine at the end of the meal is said to aid digestion as well. Not such bad recommendations, one might conclude.

It should be noted in passing that official statistics for the per capita consumption of pasta today, which may or may not be accurate, put Tunisia in third place behind Italy and Venezuela.

89. *ITRIYA:* NOODLES [R]

In Andalusia this type of pasta was cooked after having been dried and apparently could be kept for a long time. It seems to have been made at home in great quanti-

ties, or else purchased at the market. Itriya *were made by pressing and twisting* (fa-
tala) *small pieces of thin pasta in order to produce strands that were as slender as
possible. The dimensions are not indicated, but one may imagine something similar to the modern Egyptian* treyya, *which is likewise made by twisting little pieces
of dough.*

Follow the same procedure for cooking as described earlier [in the original
text], with a meat of one's choosing, adding fat if one likes, and frying the
meat or not. If *itriya* are not already available, make a dough of semolina or
flour with water and salt. Vigorously knead [the dough] and stretch [it] out
with a rolling pin on a table or a rectangular ledge. Shape [small pieces of
dough] with the hands so that they are as thin as possible, then dry them
in the sun and cook them as already indicated.

90. COOKING *ITRIYA* [K]

No mention is made in Kanz *either of the preparation of the* itriya *or of their
shape, as though this were an ingredient that one did not make at home, but rather
bought at a market—which would run counter to the implication of the previous
recipe from Ibn Razīn.*

You need some meat, *itriya*, pepper, and a little coriander seed for the meatballs. Make the balls with a little meat, pepper, coriander, and grilled onion.
Blanch the rest of the meat, then cook it with a little oil, ground pepper, and
fresh coriander [cilantro]. Add water and, when it boils, put in the meatballs. When they are ready, add the *itriya*, aniseed, and some chickpeas that
have been soaked the night before [and precooked]. Let [everything] rest
[after the pasta is cooked], then serve.

91. FIDĀWISH: TROFIE [R]

It is probable that the Andalusian term fidāwish *gave Italian its word* fedeli, *or vice
versa. We know that Genoa in the fourteenth century specialized in its production,
to the point that the artisanal producers of* fedeli *had incorporated themselves as
the Fidei. Fidāwish are similar to the* trofie *that today in Liguria are usually
served with pesto (fedeli having become in the interval a thin cylindrical-shaped*

pasta similar to vermicelli), and in North Africa they are used in soups made with vegetables and dried meat. Making it still occupies the winter days of elderly women in our own time.

Preparation of the pasta: Mix well a quarter-pound of semolina with water and knead vigorously, then put the dough in a covered dish. Gently roll up a little piece between one's fingers, giving it the dimensions of a grain of wheat; each grain should have a slender body, with the extremities thinner than the center. Put the *fidāwish* [thus] obtained on a tray; . . . when the dough is used up, put the tray out to dry in the sun and knead another quantity of dough to obtain the necessary quantity of *fidāwish*.

92. SHA'IRIYYA: FRESH SHORT PASTA [K]

This is a pasta that is cooked fresh, the moment it is made (unless this author has once again left out a step in which the pasta is dried). The instructions for cooking indicate that it was cooked as in a soup. Compare recipes 163 and 164.

You need flour, meat, sheep tail fat, mastic, and cinnamon. Crush the fat and clarify it with an onion, then brown the meat in the [heated] fat with the mastic and, finally, add a little broth. Knead a hard dough and make little elongated balls in the form of barley grains. When you have finished, cook [them] in the broth with the meat. The moment the dish is cooked, moisten with the sheep tail fat. The pasta is done when it floats [to the surface].

93. SHA'IRIYYA: DRY SHORT PASTA [W]

This is practically the same as the recipe for pasta asciutta, or dry pasta, which is cooked in broth, strained, and seasoned with fat.[1]

Make a dough with yeast and give it the form of barley grains. Cover them with meat [and] broth and let them cook until they are done, then strain and add sheep tail fat and cook over a low fire. Serve, cutting the meat into small pieces and arranging it on top [of the pasta] with other things. The pasta should not stick together, being cooked in the same manner as *rishtā*. One can also put chickpeas [in the broth].

94. *TILTĪN*: SMALL PASTA SQUARES [R]

Ibn Razīn mentions two methods for cooking this dry pasta. In winter it is used in a kind of soup of cabbage and onions that is seasoned with pepper and coriander seeds. The tiltīn *are added to the broth when the vegetables are cooked ("stir the* tiltīn *with the tip of the spoon to keep them from sticking together"). When they are cooked, the contents of the pot are poured into a* mithrad *and the dish is moistened with butter or* samn *or oil.*

In summer and autumn, he suggests combining them with squash that has been cut into small pieces, cooked in milk, and sprinkled, after cooking, with sugar, then moistened with butter. The recipe is incomplete, however, and it does not indicate whether the tiltīn *are to be cooked separately or with the pieces of squash.*

These recipes may also be made with rishtā, nuwāsir, tlitlu, graytla, *and the like, all of which are still made in North Africa today using a very thin dough that has been stretched out with a rolling pin, cut into squares or rolled up to form very thin strands, dried in the sun, and finally steamed (see recipe 165).*

Make a dough with flour, water, salt, and a little yeast. Knead energetically and stretch it out on a table; the layer of dough should be extremely thin. Using a knife, cut squares the size of two fingers and dry [them] in the sun. Keep to be used as needed.

95. *MUHAMMAS:* BULLETS [R]

Today the pasta bearing this name is obtained instead by following the same procedure for making couscous, using a large-mesh sieve, which saves a great deal of time.[2]

One prepares a dough like that of *fidāwish* and rolls it up with the fingers so as to obtain small pieces in the shape of a peppercorn. They are dried in the sun and cooked like *fidāwish*, whether with beef or mutton or with chicken, and eaten thus.

96. *HASU:* LARGE BULLETS [R]

Ibn Razīn says that this pasta, hasu, *was called "*zabzīn *by the Andalusians and* barkūs *by the ones from the other shore." By the latter people he meant the Berbers, who had come to conquer Andalusia in the twelfth century. In the*

Maghreb this large type of couscous is still called barkūkish *and is available at retail markets. It is made according to the same procedure as the one followed for making couscous and* muhammas *(whose name derives from* hummus, *or chickpeas, on account of their size and shape). The North African* barkūkish *is cooked in two stages, being first steamed in the same way as couscous, then cooked in broth. Among the peoples of the Tunisian oases, there is a holiday dish that calls for* barkūkish *to be steamed with dried octopus and small fish, also dried, known as* wuzaff (Engraulis meletta), *and served in a vegetable broth.*

Put some semolina in a special bowl to make the dough. Sprinkle it with water in which salt has been dissolved. Stir it by hand until [the grains] agglutinate and are joined to one another. Turn [the dough] over gently in the palm of the hand, [shaping it] to form small chickpeas [large bullets], and then toss them in a light sieve in order to remove any remnants of the semolina, and let dry on a tray.

Pour enough water into a new casserole dish; add salt, a little oil, pepper, coriander [seeds], and a piece of sliced onion, and place over the fire. Once it has come to a boil, gently pour the contents of the tray [into the pot] and stir so that the water begins to reduce, then add fragrant dry cheese cut into small pieces, and very finely chopped fresh coriander [cilantro]. After it has come to a boil once more, pour [into a tureen] and partake, may it please God!

97. *NABATIYYA:* CHICKEN BROTH WITH *ITRIYA* [S]

This recipe for chicken broth and itriya *is the oldest one known that mentions pasta cooked in a soup, dating back to the second half of the tenth century. Itriya was the first type of hard-grain pasta known in the history of Arab—indeed, Mediterranean—cooking (see recipe 89).*

Take two magnificent chickens, clean them, dismember them, and put them in a pot with finely chopped white onion, olive oil, chickpeas that have been soaked and crushed, and a stick of Chinese cinnamon. Cook for about an hour, then pour in enough water to cover all the ingredients. Cook for the time it takes to boil twice, then add a good piece of cheese and salt to taste, and season with spices—dry ground coriander [seeds], ground pepper,

Chinese cinnamon, galangal, spikenard, cloves, nutmeg, long pepper, and ginger—all crushed in the mortar. After a pair of boilings, throw into the broth three handfuls of *itriya* made with a dough of white flour, pour ten *dirham* of rose water on it, and let the *itriya* cook over a low fire.

Next add five peeled [hard-cooked] eggs and, from the moment [the broth] ceases to simmer, stir with a spoon, remove the cheese and eggs, cut them into pieces, and arrange these all around [the *itriya* and chicken, served on a platter].

One may also substitute [for the pasta] a handful of rice and [for the chicken] two scallops of smoked meat.

couscous

The origins of couscous are wrapped in mystery. Did it come from the Berbers? If so, from which region of the vast Berber world? If its introduction in Andalusia was due to the last Berbers who came as conquerors, they would have been people from the south of Morocco and, in the later stages, Mauritania. Ibn Battūta remarked that in the neighboring villages of Mali, couscous was made from white *fonio* (the smallest of all species of millet).[1] However this may be, it matters little to whom credit for this brilliant invention is to be ascribed. The fact remains that in the popular mind couscous comes from North Africa. In the Middle East it has been considered thus since the time of *Wusla*, where it is called "the North African dish" (*moghrabiye* or *maghribiyya*).[2]

98. CLASSIC COUSCOUS [R]

This is the typical couscous with meat—in this case, veal—and vegetables. The fact that Ibn Razīn mentions tapping the couscous once the grains have swollen up and the hissing with which it answers—a gesture that I myself have made so many times, without thinking about it—is proof that he had personal experience preparing this dish or else that he was a very sharp observer (cf. recipe 166).

Confection of the pasta: Take semolina of good quality, put it in a pot, and moisten it with water in which a little salt has been dissolved. Mix with the tip of the finger until the grains are agglutinated and stick to one another. Rub them gently between the hands until they are the size of an ant's head. Then shake [them] in a fine sieve to eliminate any excess wheat. Cover [with a cloth] and leave in a ventilated room.

The cooking: Take the finest meat of young, fat calves and the biggest bones; put everything in a large pot and add salt, oil, pepper, dry coriander [seeds], and a little chopped onion. Cover with an ample amount of water, and put the pot over the fire. When the meat begins to cook, add the vegetables of the season, such as cabbage, turnips, carrots, lettuce, fennel, green broad beans, squash, and eggplant. While the meat and vegetables cook together, take the pot specially made for couscous, the bottom of which is pierced with holes; carefully fill it with couscous and place it over the large pot containing the meat and vegetables. All along the line of contact between the two pots stick a little dough to keep the steam from escaping. Cover the top of the couscous pot with a thick napkin or cloth towel to keep the steam inside in order to assure the best cooking. The signs indicating [that] the end of cooking [is near] are the very dense steam that seeps out from the pot and the echo emitted by the couscous when one taps [the grains] with the hand.

When the couscous is cooked, pour it into a deep platter, incorporate in it some good *samn,* cinnamon, mastic, and spikenard, and rub it between your hands to separate the grains from one another.

Then put the couscous grains in a *mithrad,* taking care not to fill it completely [so that the grains do not touch the sides] since the [need to add broth] must be taken into account. Check to see that there is enough broth; if not, add water and bring again to a boil. Once this has been done, remove [the pot] from the fire and wait until the boiling stops. Then moisten the couscous with moderation, starting in the middle [and moving] toward the sides. Cover. Let sit for an hour, the time it takes for the couscous to absorb the broth. Taking some [couscous] on your finger, check to see that it has [absorbed] the right amount of broth; if not, add some more. Now remove the bones and put them in the center of the *mithrad* [inserting them into the couscous], and arrange the pieces of meat and the vegetables on top all around, sprinkling ground cinnamon, cloves, and ginger. Eat, and [may] good health [be yours], God willing!

One can also make the couscous with lamb or chicken according to the recipe given, if God wills it.

99. COUSCOUS WITH WALNUTS [R]

This is an unusual recipe, calling for walnut butter rather than samn, *the eggplant being cooked separately so as not to darken the couscous (cf. recipe 167).*

This is a delicious dish. Take the necessary amount of veal, lamb, and fattened chickens. Cook [them] with the [usual] spices and with eggplant cooked in salted water, peeled but not chopped, rinsed in hot water, and dried. When the meats and vegetable are almost cooked, cook the couscous as indicated earlier, then pour the couscous into a serving dish, rub it with butter made from blanched walnuts that have been peeled and crushed in the mortar with cinnamon, spikenard, and a little mastic, and then moisten it well several times. Arrange the meats and vegetable, sprinkle cinnamon and spikenard [over them], and eat, God willing!

100. COUSCOUS COOKED IN BROTH [R]

This is nothing other than what is marketed today as "quick couscous," for it saved the cook the time and effort of steaming it. The recipe given here certainly involves couscous that has been preserved and precooked.

One must extract the cooked meat and vegetables, strain the broth while removing the bones and everything else, and then put [the broth] over the couscous. One waits until the broth is absorbed, then turns [the couscous] over onto a serving dish and arranges the meat and vegetables on top. Then one eats. This dish is called "the Ghassanid."

It may also be made with a broth of meat cooked with vinegar and saffron according to the recipe for *tharīd* with vinegar, and the vegetables will be eggplant and zucchini.

101. MUTTON STUFFED WITH COUSCOUS [R]

In Mauritania, mutton stuffed with couscous is considered the finest dish that can be offered to a guest.

Take a fat sheep, remove the hide, open up the belly, and remove the viscera. Clean the inside and grease it with fat that has been crushed with the spices that are used to make meatballs.

When the couscous is cooked, season it with *samn,* spikenard, cinnamon, and a little mastic and stuff the belly of the sheep with it. Sew up the belly of the sheep and then put it in the bell-shaped oven [*tannūr*]. Cook it until it is well roasted.

Transfer the couscous to a *mithrad,* remove the mutton [from the bones], and arrange it on the couscous. Sprinkle cinnamon and spikenard [over it], and, God willing, eat.

102. MOROCCAN COUSCOUS [W]

The author of Wusla *gives a second recipe in which the couscous is cooked in a meat broth, then drained and mixed with sheep tail fat. In the Maghreb, yogurt is considered the ideal accompaniment for mutton couscous, either as a beverage to be consumed during the meal or as a complement to the broth, poured directly on the couscous.*

Sprinkle the flour with water and rub between your hands as one does to make lumps of dough, and shake in a sieve to produce grains that you will remove with your fingers until you have the amount you need. Cook the meatballs (*kubāb*) and chicken in a pot and put what you have extracted from the sieve in another pot, pierced [with holes], on top of which you will place a cover. Seal the line of contact between the two pots with a piece of dough so that the steam will not escape. Steam [the couscous] in this manner. Then moisten it with oil and *samn,* rub between your hands, moisten [again] with the broth, and serve on a platter, arranging the meat, *kubāb,* and chicken on top of the couscous. Decorate and present [the dish].

A good rice should be *mufalfal;* that is, its grains should be well separated when they are done, which requires a particular method of cooking that the author of *Wusla* is supposed by some to attribute to India.[1] Most rice dishes were very sweet, and flavored primarily with cinnamon and rose water.

103. *DAKBARYĀN:* STEAMED MEAT AND RICE IN MEAT BROTH [S]

The principle underlying this dish is the opposite of the one involved in cooking couscous. In the course of steaming, the meat loses its fat, which falls into the water; and this in turn is used as a broth for cooking the rice. It is for this reason that Ibn Sayyār compares this way of cooking to the one used to make jūdhāba *(a pudding that is cooked under a fatty hen or other meat and thus receives the grease that drips from it during roasting). The author explains how to outfit the pot for steaming, either because this particular piece of equipment was his own invention or perhaps because it was not widely available at markets.*

Today in Afghanistan, pots called deg *(similar to* dak*) are specially made in different sizes for cooking rice. The* deg-e-yak *is used to cook one ser (equal to seven kilograms, or a little more than fifteen pounds). The smallest,* deg-e yak pao, *has a capacity of 438 grams (about a pound), and the largest,* deg-e dah, *a capacity of 70 kilograms (a little more than 150 pounds). There is also a steamer called* deg-e bokhar, *introduced by the Uzbeks, that is used to cook a kind of ravioli known as* mantù.

This name is in Persian, and its interpretation in Arabic is "pot roast." Take a stone pot that is high enough and bore six holes halfway up [the side], one after the other all around the pot, like a necklace. Insert a scraped willow wand from one hole to the other [across from it]—three stalks, then—and plug the holes from the outside of the pot with a piece of dough.

Pour some water into the pot, without letting it reach the level of the slats, and throw in a piece of galangal root and a stick of cinnamon. Take a good shoulder of mutton together with the ribs. Wash, salt, and moisten [it] with oil, and place it on the slats that are above the water. Cover the pot and seal the cover with clay. Light a medium fire underneath the pot. When you know that the meat is cooked, open the pot, take out the meat, and set it aside. Throw some rice in the water. This is a dish that is prepared like *jūdhāba*.

If you wish to put honey or saffron or something else in the water, do as one does in the case of the various *jūdhāba*, God willing.

104. INDIAN RICE [W]

Rinse the rice in boiling water and cook it immediately in a copper pot [*dast*]. The quantity of water must be equal to two and a half times that of the rice. Once it has absorbed all the water, add *samn*, cover it, and cook it for an hour. In this way it will become *mufalfal*; that is, the grains of rice do not stick together. Add some powdered sugar and remove [the pot] from the fire. The secret of cooking rice well lies in not rinsing it until the very moment of cooking.

105. *MUFALFAL* RICE (WITH MEAT AND CHICKPEAS) [W]

Cook the meat in water, then [take it out and] braise it in sheep tail fat, and finally put it back in its broth. Some whole chickpeas soaked in water will have been cooked together with the meat [during the first cooking]. Add next some rice that has been cleaned and rinsed and cook it; then drain off the excess water and put in some melted sheep [tail] fat. Cover the pot and let an hour go by. In place of chickpeas, one can use blanched green pistachios. Sprinkle with sugar and rose water and serve.

106. *RUKHĀMIYYA*: MARBLED RICE [W]

Cook the meat in a little water. When it is cooked, remove it from the fire and pour fresh milk into the broth in an amount equal to three times that of the broth itself. Bring it to a boil and throw in the cleaned and rinsed rice together with some sheep tail fat. When the rice is cooked and its grains are well separated, incorporate the meat and some pure white sugar, add a generous amount of fat, and serve.

107. YELLOW AND WHITE RICE [W]

Cook the meat following the recipe for *mufalfal* rice. Then cook the white rice separately, and some yellow rice [white rice colored with saffron] in another pot, and strain both. Put the yellow rice over the meat, mix the fat in with it, and let it sit for a moment; then add the white rice and leave that for a moment. Instead of chickpeas, pistachios will have been blanched and peeled [and added as a garnish]. Then [the dish] is served.

108. *KHĀTŪNĪ*: RICE WITH PISTACHIOS [W]

Boil some water and add the fat of the sheep tail and some fat of the hen, after having melted them without salt. [Then] throw in the rice. When it is half cooked, strain the water and add some fat. Then take pistachios that have been peeled, toasted in sesame oil, crumbled, and mixed with powdered sugar, and add an abundance of them to the rice. Sprinkle drops of rose water and musk. Eat. It is a marvel.

109. RICE WITH YOGURT [W]

The reputation [of this dish] makes up for its appearance. But if one puts [in] a little toasted cumin from Kerman [a province in southern Persia] and some Chinese cinnamon, cracked rather than crushed, this will give it an extraordinary taste.

110. *ARUZZIYYA* [K]

You need meat, rice, pepper, coriander seed, and aniseed.

Blanch the meat and drain it. Then crush it in the mortar and add pepper, coriander, and a little salt, all crushed together. Next add a little rice and make some meatballs. Cook the rest of the meat and add to it the broth and the meatballs; when it is ready, wash the rice and cook it in the broth [together with the meat, cut into pieces, and the meatballs] with a little aniseed. Let [it] rest and then serve.

111. RICE WITH SPINACH [W]

Cut the meat into big pieces and boil it together with chickpeas. When the meat is cooked, remove it and braise it in fat [*duhn*] and olive oil, then moisten it with its broth. Wash the rice and pour it into this broth. Cook [the rice and broth] with much garlic in whole cloves. Separately, boil all of the spinach in water, then put it over the rice, where it is left alone until the liquid has evaporated and the whole mixture has thickened.

One may make the same thing with *rishtā*, over which eggs are broken [at the end of cooking].

There are innumerable recipes for omelets (ʿujja). Only Ibn Sayyār gives ones that are novel, several of them very sophisticated, calling for game birds, truffles, almonds, nuts, and so on. Here are two of the simplest recipes.

112. WHITE ʿUJJA [S]

Brown fresh coriander [cilantro] in a little oil with sliced leek and onion, and add a teaspoon of *murrī* and a teaspoon of vinegar. In a jar break ten eggs and sprinkle them with pepper and leaves of rue from the garden. Beat [the eggs] in the jar [and pour them into the pan]; turn over the ʿujja [and then turn it over again onto the] serving dish.

113. ANOTHER ʿUJJA [S]

Beat egg whites well with a little honey and chopped rue, tarragon, mint, and parsley. Pour into a pot and place over a lively fire. When [the ʿujja] has thickened, sprinkle with a little cumin and a little cinnamon, and [add] some *murrī* and oil. Then turn over everything into a serving dish [*jām*] in which [you will already have put] the yolks, separated [from the whites] and beaten with sugar. Serve, if God wills it.

SAUCES

Sauces (*sibāgh*) occupy a place of the first rank in classical Islamic cuisine. They serve to bring out the flavor of cooked dishes and to enliven cold foods such as salted fish and dry dishes such as roast chicken. They were presented at table in small bowls (*uskurruja*) along with bowls of the same type containing seasoned salt, vinegar, and *murrī*.

The Alexandrian sauce taken from *Kanz* (recipe 118) has the same base as the modern Italian *salmoriglio* used to flavor swordfish: oil, lemon juice, and garlic. In the *Kanz* recipe, the sauce is sharpened by the addition of hot spices, whereas Italian versions are flavored with parsley, mint, and oregano. The Sicilians add slivered almonds to this combination.

The recipes that follow are still current in rural Arab communities that have not yet given up their traditional condiments for modern sauces imported from Europe and the United States (vinaigrette, béarnaise, mayonnaise, ketchup, and so on).

Iraqis during the ʿAbbasid period invented a special sauce for long-distance travel (recipe 115), a dehydrated preparation similar to the powdered soups—Maggi and Knorr tablets—we know today; it was a forerunner of Liebig's famous extracts in the nineteenth century.

114. SAUCE OF CHICKEN FAT WITH POMEGRANATE JUICE [S]

Take an excellent hen, blanch it, and wash it. Take ten pomegranates, half of them sour and half sweet. Press all of them to extract the juice, which is then put in a dish with one *ūqiya* of aged *murrī*. Sprinkle the hen with oil, then with [fine] salt and thyme, and roast it on a spit over a fire of wood coals. Little by little as its fat melts, collect it and pour it into the pan that contains the pomegranate juice and the *murrī* until the cooking is done. Then take twenty walnuts, remove the pits, carefully crush them in a mortar, and mix them into the sauce [*sibāgh*]. It is delicious.

115. *SIBĀGH* FOR LONG-DISTANCE TRAVEL [S]

Take one part pomegranate seeds and one part raisins, crush them, add pepper and cumin, mix, and make into flattened disks. If need be, dissolve in vinegar and eat.

116. *SIBĀGH* FOR FRESH FISH [S]

Wine vinegar, celery leaves, rue, mint, thyme, pepper, cumin, caraway, cinnamon, sugar, salt.

117. *SIBĀGH* FROM ISFAHAN [S]

Grind up some salt, cheese, walnuts, asafetida, and thyme and [mix] with vinegar and *murrī*.

118. ALEXANDRIAN SAUCE *(SAHNĀ)* [K]

First version: olive oil, lemon juice, hot spices, garlic.

Second version: add some fine sumac [flour], *atrāf tīb*, finely crushed walnuts, and hot spices.[1]

119. A *SAHNĀ* FROM BAGHDAD AND UPPER IRAQ [K]

Take some small fish, salt them without washing, and they are ready. If you wish to eat them in a sauce, put in a mortar green seeds [cardamom] and equal amounts of cumin and aniseed, peeled Syrian apples, and unripe quinces. Grind all of it to make a puree, adding a little oil and a little water from the marinade, and then serve.

PASTRIES AND JAMS

The Muslim world of the Middle Ages was a paradise of sugar, especially in the eastern regions that border on the traditional places of production— Afghanistan, for example—and everywhere that the culture of sugarcane was developed in Yemen and Egypt.

The ʿAbbasids showed great imagination in creating pastries, devising diverse shapes, colors, and flavors for each kind. Cannoli, for example, were made by rolling semolina dough kneaded with oil around reed stalks that were removed after cooking. Decorative patterns were imprinted on the dough using an incised stamp (*minqāsh*) and tinted red, yellow, green, and blue. Molds of different shapes were used to create figurative forms. The cannoli were stuffed with a mixture of walnuts and sugar, crushed in the mortar, and then soaked with syrup made from white sugar and sprinkled with crystals of colored sugar.

A poem quoted by Ibn Sayyār describes the fritter known as *zulābiyya* thus:

> *Zulābiyya* are my favorite cakes,
> round and intertwined,
> yellow and white and colored,
> fried in purified sesame oil;
> soft to the touch, smooth,
> dipped in white honey,
> lined up one after the other like nuggets,
> like incised bars of gold.[1]

120. *ZULĀBIYYA MUSHABBAKA WĀTHIQIYYA* [S]

Ibn Sayyār gives seven versions of this dish. This one, attributed to Caliph al-Wāthiq, is nearest to the present-day version, which the Moroccans call shabkiyya. *It is the only recipe that uses a pierced bowl, as is still done today.* Zulābiyya *are made especially during the month of Ramadan. Men generally go to buy them when they are still warm, in the evening, just after the meal that breaks the day's fast; others buy them on returning home from the mosque. Bakers known as* ftāyrī, *who specialize in* ftāyr (*a sort of cream puff*) *and* maqrūd (*recipe 169*), *devote themselves to the confection of* zulābiyya *during the entire month of Ramadan. It is therefore a male specialty. In the Middle East* zulābiyya *are half red and half yellow, while in North Africa they are entirely yellow, colored with turmeric (compare recipe 171).*

Take a half-pound of semolina flour of excellent quality, mix it little by little with yeast and let it rise overnight. The next morning, take half a pound of starch and knead it with the yeast; then mix everything together and knead, adding water little by little until all of it flows like the batter [used to make] *qatāʾif* and incorporate a little borax.

You will have already prepared a coconut for the dough, a coconut from India, slicing off the rounded end to give it the shape of a glass and then making a hole in the opposite end of such a size that you can plug it with a finger.

During this time let the dough rest.

Take a skillet of medium size, iron or copper, and pour into it enough oil to be able to immerse the *zulābiyya.* Keep a lively fire under the skillet so that the oil begins to boil. Fill a ladle with the dough that you have carefully prepared and pour it into the coconut that you hold in your left hand, plugging up the hole [at the bottom] with a finger. When the coconut is full, still holding it by the [lower] part with the left hand, let the dough drain out from the hole into the skillet while with movements of the [right] hand you form it into interwoven designs [*mushabbak*] in whatever shapes you please, circles, triangles, or squares.[2]

The sign that the dough is well made and perfect is when, falling into the oil, it becomes contorted in [the shape of] empty bracelets [that is, a disk with intricate arabesque patterns].

Next you immerse [the *zulābiyya*] in the honey that you will have previously boiled over the fire, skimmed, and flavored. Allow the honey to be absorbed for as long as necessary, then take it out and put it on the pastry tray. If it is good, serve it. It is good if it is crunchy and hard in the mouth, still warm, and it melts in the mouth. If it is supple like skin, this means that it is not well made, either because it was not allowed to ferment long enough, or because the yeast was of poor quality, or because the honey remained too liquid (because the fire was not hot enough), or, finally, owing to the climate: cold and damp, for example[, are harmful].

If the problem is one of fermentation, let [the dough rest] some more until it has risen enough. If the cause is the mediocre quality of the yeast, improve it with borax. If the honey flows too easily, put it back on the fire and bring it to a boil just once, and only for as long as necessary. In cold and rainy weather, make the *zulābiyya* in a heated room where the air is dry, a room where you have a great deal of fuel [to heat the room]. Make it on days when the wind blows from the north and the west. It is necessary that the yeast be kept next to the fire to protect it from the cold. Avoid facing the south while making [the *zulābiyya*]. Respecting all these conditions, and showing care and perceptiveness, [you will succeed] if God wills it.

121. DATES WITH HONEY [K]

Compare recipe 170.

Take some dates, remove their stems, and dry and decorticate them. Blanch some almonds and substitute one for each pit [that has been removed]. Cook some honey to make a syrup and immerse the dates in it. Leave over a low fire and, when the honey has thickened, add all the flavorings and remove from the fire.

122. FRIED BANANAS [W]

The bananas are fried and immersed in a thick syrup in which there are pistachios.

123. QUINCE *SIKANJUBĪN* [K]

This syrupy preparation was consumed primarily as a beverage, though it was also thought to have medicinal properties, particularly in relation to purgation and the easing of constipation.

One needs the juice from Isfahan quinces or from [quinces] of another delicious and fragrant kind [*barzi*]. Take one part [juice], an equal amount of refined white sugar, and one-quarter of this same amount of strong vinegar, and make a thick syrup from it. If one wishes to add to it thin slices of quince, as the common people do, do this toward the end of the cooking. . . . One may scent it with rose water in which saffron and musk have been dissolved. Some add honey; . . . others do not put in vinegar.

124. QUINCE SYRUP [K]

Compare recipe 174.

Take some quinces, peel them, pit them, and cook them in water. When they have become tender it means that they are half cooked. Take them off the fire and reserve the cooking liquid. Dissolve some sugar in this liquid and add vinegar. Then, the moment it begins to thicken, throw in the quinces and bring them to a boil once or twice. Then take them off the fire, and add the juice from one or two limes, and scent with rose water.

125. CANDIED CITRON PEELS [K]

Take peels of citron, immerse them in salted water to eliminate the bitterness, then rinse them in fresh water and lay them out to dry. Cut them into pieces. Take a pound and a quarter of sugar and as much honey and blend them together in a casserole [*dast*] that one puts on the fire. Skim [the honey mixture] and throw in the peels. Let it thicken. Before taking it off the fire add some ginger, long pepper, Chinese cinnamon, and mastic. If the syrup becomes quite thick it will be very good.

126. CARROT JAM [K]

It is necessary to select fresh, red carrots, to wash them, clean them, and cut them as thinly as possible. Put them in a ceramic pot, add a little bit of honey, and cover them with water. Cook them until they are soft, then strain off the water with a sieve and add a quantity of skimmed honey equal to that of the carrots. Mix in seasonings chosen from among pepper, ginger, cardamom, cinnamon, cubeb, spikenard, mace, galangal, aloe wood [*Aquilaria agallocha*], saffron, and musk. Cook to thicken the carrot jam [*jawārish*]. Pour [it] into a glass jar and consume it as needed.

127. ANOTHER CARROT JAM [K]

Take some carrots, clean them, scrape them, and crush them properly. Take two and a half measures of honey for every measure of carrots. Boil [it] for a little while and take off the fire. Put the crushed carrots in a casserole [*dast*] without water; dry [them] a little bit over the fire, pour over them the filtered honey, and cook until it has thickened. Take it off the fire and season [before serving].

128. SQUASH JAM [K]

Take some sweet green gourds and remove the rind, scraping until the white layer disappears. For every pound of squash take nine *ūqiya* of sugar and half a pound of honey. Put [the pieces of] sugar in a casserole [*dast*], pour over it half of the honey and rose water, and put over a low fire. Stir with a wooden stick. Little by little, as it dries up, add [honey and rose water] until it becomes a jam. Sprinkle over it two *ūqiya* of pistachios with powdered sugar, scented with musk. At the end, add rose water before taking off the fire.

129. CARAMELIZED SEMOLINA [W]

Brown half a pound of coarsely ground semolina in four *ūqiya* of *samn* over a fire of small coals. When the semolina is deep red and its fragrance has been brought out, take the casserole off the fire and sprinkle the semolina with a half-pound of very finely ground sugar. Bang the casserole against the ground. When the ingredients have been well mixed together, turn out the roasted semolina onto the underside of a tray that you have previously cleaned. On top of the mixture [of semolina and sugar] put another tray to crush it and make the surface level. Let [it] cool a bit, then with a large knife cut [it] into pieces of the desired size, and with the knife pry them off the bottom of the tray and arrange them on another tray or on a dish, where they are left to cool. Sprinkle with very fine sugar that has been ground with more or less musk. It is good this way.

The proportions for a pound of semolina are a pound of sugar and eight *ūqiya* of *samn*. It is a delicious meal that one makes in winter.

130. *ISFUNJ AL-QULLA:* SPONGE CAKE COOKED IN A JAR [R]

Knead semolina or extra-fine flour, making a soft, light dough. Take a small new jar and pour into it quite a lot of oil, enough to coat the walls and the bottom. When the dough has risen, fill up the jar [with it], almost as far as the neck, and stick a palm rib inside, or a reed without knots that has been soaked in oil, and take the jar to the oven. Leave it far from the fire until the cooking [is done]. At this point, remove it from the oven and gently shake it to pull out the reed. Into the space occupied by the reed pour some honey and *samn* or melted butter, let it sit for a moment, and then delicately break the jar so that the contents remain perfectly intact. Sprinkle with cinnamon, moisten again with *samn* and honey, and eat, may it please God.

131. *KUNĀFA:* PANCAKES [R]

Moisten good pure sifted semolina with hot water and let sit for an hour. Then knead with yeast, salt, and half a pound of extra-fine flour. When all of it is well mixed and has become homogeneous, pour hot water over it a little at a time, and mix by hand until it dissolves and becomes like silk. Put it in a new pan and let it rise. The sign that fermentation has occurred is that small holes appear in the foam on the surface.

Heat a tin-plated skillet and knot a piece of clean cloth filled with crushed salt and soaked in oil, cleaning the skillet repeatedly with it; then pour in enough batter to cover the bottom of it and shake [the skillet] to the right and the left so that the contents are well distributed. The result is a pancake like *khabīs* [made with starch paste]. One must be careful not to burn [the *kunāfa*]. They are then taken out and placed on a flat surface or on a table. Continue to cook them thus, one after another, until all the batter is used up, wiping [the skillet] again each time with the little pouch soaked in oil.

Put [the *kunāfa*] on a plate, one on top of the other, and cut them cross-wise with a knife. Then moisten [them] with melted honey, butter, or *samn* and sprinkle cinnamon [on top]. Partake, if God wills it.

132. *KUNĀFA*: GRIDDLE CAKES [R]

Put the special griddle for cooking *kunāfa* on a fire of small coals with no flame. When it is very hot, grease [the griddle] using a clean piece of cloth soaked in sweet oil and pour over it a quantity of batter sufficient to cover the griddle. Leave [it] on the fire long enough for the cake to cook, then remove it and put it on a plate. Continue with the rest of the batter, each time greasing the griddle with the oiled piece of fabric and peeling off the cake with a knife.

Then melt a quarter pound of butter or *samn* with two pounds of honey and mix them. One may add some pepper to this mixture of butter and honey, using it to moisten the cakes, which are eaten warm.

For this preparation, *samn* is preferred to butter.

If one wishes to preserve [the *kunāfa*], it is necessary to cut them with scissors into very narrow strips and cook them for a long time in clarified honey in a new pan. When the strips of cake are nearly firm, moisten them with *samn* or oil as one does in the case of a *tharīd*. When [the *samn*] has been fully absorbed, take [the strips] off the fire and remove [them] from the pan so that they will be ready to serve. They are eaten either hot or cold. Before serving, sprinkle [them] with sugar and cinnamon, and eat, if God wills it.

133. *RUQĀQ AL-KHABĪS*: STARCH GRIDDLE CAKES [R]

Take the necessary quantity of starch [*nisha*] and dilute it with water until it has the consistency of melted wax. Put the special griddle for cooking *kunāfa* over a low fire and grease it with a clean piece of cloth soaked in oil. Pour the dissolved starch on the griddle and make cakes exactly as one does in making *kunāfa*. The cakes obtained by this method are stretched out over a rope or a clean stick to dry them in the open air. They are served at the desired moment, if God wills it.

134. CHEESE [S]

Use milk that is just drawn, still warm, incorporating the rennet as it is, with its skin, and whipping the milk while it is warm so that it coagulates. Then pour it into molds made from willow and ʿasr [an unidentified wood], sprinkle salt [over it], and set it aside.

If you wish to eat it right away, it is not necessary to salt it, in which case it is called simple cheese.

135. *SHIRĀZ:* FRESH SALTED CHEESE [R]

Take as much milk curd as you like, and put it in a straw basket that you cover and hang. When the curd has lost all its water, shake it by hand against a [goat-]hair sieve above a *mithrad*. Salt and mix with a spoon to incorporate the salt thoroughly into the cheese [*shirāz*].

You can keep it in a new, well-dried ceramic pot and serve yourself by taking it out with a spoon. If you wish to eat some, take the amount you need, put it in a bowl, and arrange olives and capers around the edges and a lemon coated with salt in the middle. Sprinkle nigella [*Nigella sativa*] seeds [over it] for decoration and drizzle some sweet olive oil. It should be cool, and, remember, it is better the smoother it is. It may also be eaten with fresh onions.

136. DRY CHEESE AGED IN A JAR [R]

Take some cheese made in the second half of the month of March or in the month of April; salt it and put it on a wooden board in a well-ventilated place, high above the ground. You must frequently dry it with a woollen cloth, and coat it with oil and salt until you think that it has absorbed enough salt and that it is thoroughly dry. This should be done during the month of May.

Take now a jar that previously contained oil, clean it simply by wiping it with a cloth, without washing it with boiling water, and fill it with pieces of cheese that have been moistened with oil, placing them next to one another without leaving any space. When the jar is full, close it and seal the cover with clay so that no air can get in. After fifteen days, open [it] to stir the cheese, then close and reseal. You will repeat this procedure ten days later, and repeat it again until the cheese has softened and holes filled with oil appear inside. Eat it with flavored bread and sweet grapes throughout the fall, if God wills it.

137. INSTANT *MURRĪ* [R]

Toast a pound of wheat flour or barley in a ceramic skillet, then add to it two *ūqiya* of salt and of water, mixing vigorously by hand and straining. Cook some honey in a ceramic skillet, and when it is ready and skimmed [of impurities], add the water previously drained [from the mixture]. Fennel, nigella [*Nigella sativa*], coriander, and anise seeds are mixed in along with thyme and cinnamon.

138. FISH *MURRĪ* [R]

Take a pound of *sīr* [small salted fish ground into powdered form by more or less sophisticated methods] and put it in a sieve placed on top of a bowl. Little by little pour five pounds of sweet must on the *sīr*, mixing it by hand to strain the contents of the sieve, and repeat this procedure, adding *sīr* and must until the desired quantity is obtained. You will have flavored it with oregano. Then put everything in a two-handled jug used previously as a container for oil; add quinces and onions that have been chopped but not cut up into pieces, and let sit until [the fermentation subsides] and the contents settle. Next decant the preparation into another such jug and let it be. Cover with a layer of oil and seal with clay until you are ready to use it.

To consume it, pour some into a bowl, add oil and chopped onion, if you wish, fried eggs, fried fish, and olives.

You may also make it with grape wine instead of must.

139. *KĀMAKH* WITH TARRAGON [K]

Take some bread and let it go moldy [while wrapped] in fig leaves. When it has become moldy, [unwrap] it so it can dry out. Then take some sheep's milk; beforehand you will have prepared the tarragon, separating the leaves from the stems. Knead the moldy bread by hand with the milk and the tarragon, with much salt to keep it from fermenting. Transfer [the mixture] to a tin-plated ceramic container and put it out in the sun with a fig branch planted inside, mixing [the contents with the branch] for ten days.

140. LOCUST *SAHNĀ* [S]

Take locusts that have returned from hunting, discard the dead ones, and drown the ones that are alive in water and salt. When they are drowned and dead, put them in a large container. In a mortar crush dry coriander [seeds], fennel, and asafetida in due quantity, and in [another] container alternate a layer of locusts with a layer of spices, adding salt generously in the course of doing this. [Let the preparation macerate for a while.] When the water in which the locusts were drowned has lightened and become clear, pour it little by little [over the locusts] until there is none left and seal the two-handled jug, taking care that you do not let in air, which would ruin the contents. It is necessary to wait for the product to mature; then it may be eaten.

141. GRAPE WINE [S]

Extract the juice from juicy grapes having skins as thin as possible. Put the juice in tarred jugs and cover the openings with vine leaves. Wash the outside of the jugs. Let five days go by, then seal the openings with clay and do not open for a certain time, God willing.

142. HONEY WINE WITH RAISINS [S]

Take fifty pounds of raisins and thirty [pounds] of clarified bees' honey. Put the honey in a pot with a quantity of water equal to half the honey. Boil the honey and water over a strong fire, and when it is cooked add the raisins with twenty pounds of water and boil again. Strain out the grape seeds and add a weight of five *dirham* of saffron, five *dirham* of spikenard, and three [*dirham*] of mace, along with the weight of one *dāniq* of musk. Keep in bottles in the shade and use after forty days. It is a marvel.

143. HONEY WINE WITHOUT RAISINS [S]

What nāfāya *refers to in this recipe is unclear. The term does not figure in Ibn Manzūr's fourteenth-century dictionary* Lisān al-ʿArab.

Take fifty pounds of honey and put it in a pot with fifty pounds of water. Boil until one-third, or thirty-three pounds, has evaporated. Then add two *mithqāl* of saffron, the weight of two *dirham* of mace, and five pounds of cold water, and pour into bottles. Leave in the shade for fifty days; once this time has passed, seal with clay. Consume during the winter, one part *nabīdh* and two parts *nāfāya:* it will be excellent.

PART THREE

—

CONTEMPORARY NORTH AFRICAN CUISINE

CHARACTERISTIC SEASONINGS OF
CONTEMPORARY ARAB CUISINE

The quantity of salt required in the modern recipes that follow—drawn from Tunisia and the neighboring countries of the Maghreb—is difficult to specify for American readers. Even along the Mediterranean there is considerable variability: salt from the salt marshes of Tunisia and Sicily, for example, has a higher degree of salinity than that of Aigues-Mortes on the French coast, in Languedoc; and this in turn is higher than that of the salt from Brittany. The sea salt from the south of France marketed in the United States may be recommended, but ordinary table salt can be substituted in somewhat greater quantities. The precise amount must in any case be left to the judgment of the individual cook.

Much the same thing is to be said with regard to black pepper, of which a great many kinds, more or less finely ground, are readily available, and to the pepper obtained by grinding dried red chiles. In North Africa and elsewhere in the Arab world, ground red pepper is typically very strong; the nearest equivalent in American markets is cayenne pepper, imported from Asia or Africa, though milder alternatives, such as paprika, can be used instead. In the eastern Arab world, red pepper generally plays a rather restricted role, often showing up only in table condiments and on pizzalike flat breads. In northwestern Syria, however, an aromatic, medium-hot chile called Aleppo pepper is heavily used, often taking the place of herbs in dishes.

All the spices used by Arab cooks are available in the United States. Supermarket spices tend to be overpriced, so it's better to shop at Indian or Middle Eastern import shops or to use mail-order spice merchants such as Penzeys Spices.

Spices and Spice Mixtures   Most of the eastern Arab cuisines have their own spice mixtures. The most common is *sabᶜ bahārāt*, "seven spice," typically cinnamon, cloves, cumin, coriander, pepper, ginger, and cardamom or nutmeg. (Many Lebanese and Syrian cooks, however, use allspice instead of *sabᶜ bahārāt*.) In Iran, *sabᶜ bahārāt* is known as *haft adviyeh*.

In Egypt, a mixture of nutmeg, cinnamon, and pepper is sold in markets. A usual *bahārāt* mixture in the Gulf region is equal quantities of coriander, cumin, cinnamon, pepper, cloves, and cardamom. Some mixtures add turmeric, giving a result much like curry powder.

Southern Arabia has a number of spice mixtures. The basic one in Oman is cinnamon, cumin, cardamom, and black pepper. For pit-roasted meat, red pepper and turmeric are added to it, along with vinegar or *khall al-mazza* (an aged paste of dates, red pepper, and garlic). The common stew spice *bizār* adds red pepper, coriander, ginger, and nutmeg to the basic mixture, with the spices fried separately before crushing. For fish dishes, turmeric is added to *bizār*. Spit-roasted meat (*mashakaik*) is rubbed with cinnamon, cardamom, and both red and black pepper.

In Yemen, a cook's favorite choice of compound spice is called *suhūg* (or *sahāwig*; in San'ā' the mixture includes fresh tomatoes and garlic, making it more like a salsa). It nearly always includes Yemen's favorite flavoring, fenugreek. Some specific spice mixtures are *hawāyij sauda* (black spices): pepper, cardamom, salt, cumin, and garlic; *hawāyij al-shāy* (tea spices): coriander, clove, and nutmeg; *hawāyij al-gahwa* (coffee spices): ginger, clove, and *nankhwā* (bishop's weed); and *hawāyij al-shurba* (soup spices): pepper and coriander. *Hawāyij sufra* (yellow spices)—turmeric and cumin—are also added to soup.

Popular spices used in the recipes that follow include:

>   Black pepper, white pepper, cubeb (an Indonesian pepper variety), coriander, caraway, cumin, cinnamon, turmeric, saffron
>
>   Dried herbs and seasonings: mint, bay leaves, orange peel, rosebuds
>
>   *Bharat:* A mixture of equal quantities of cinnamon and rosebuds
>
>   *Offah:* A mixture of eleven ingredients typically found in the cooking of the region of Gabès, in southern Tunisia: coriander, caraway, cumin, green aniseed, cinnamon, gallnuts, rosebuds, turmeric, dried chiles, garlic, and cloves

Ras el-hanut: A seasoning that can range from a simple mixture of finely ground pepper, rose petals, and cinnamon to as many as twenty-five spices

Tabel: A mixture of caraway, coriander seeds, dried red chiles, and a little dried garlic, all ground into powder

Other ingredients:

Brīk (phyllo pastry, sold frozen by the pound, used in pastries such as baklava; it can substitute for the *warka* or *malsouka* used in North African pastries such as *brīk*)

Dried ground *mulūkhiyya* (jute leaves)

Lemons pickled in brine

Tahini: sesame paste

MEAT AND POULTRY

LEMON CHICKEN STEW

MDARBIL: VEAL WITH EGGPLANT

MEAT STEW WITH QUINCE IN THE TUNISIAN MANNER

LAMB STEW WITH FRESH APRICOTS

MAʿĀSIM EL-BEY: KING'S WRISTS

BANĀDIQ: TUNISIAN MEATBALLS

MEAT KOFTA

MERGUEZ AND PICKLED VEGETABLE STEW

BRĪK DANNŪNI

TUNISIAN *MULŪKHIYYA*

BESTILLA: MOROCCAN PIGEON PIE

SQUAB WITH DATES

144. LEMON CHICKEN STEW

1 chicken (about 3 1/2 pounds), cut into pieces
4 tablespoons olive oil
Salt
1/4 teaspoon ground cinnamon
1/2 teaspoon ground turmeric
1/4 teaspoon ground white pepper
2 medium (or 3 small) potatoes, peeled and thinly sliced
1 medium onion, peeled and thinly sliced
2 tomatoes, thinly sliced
2 small lemons, thinly sliced
1 bunch fresh parsley, leaves only, finely chopped

Moisten the best pieces of the chicken (thighs, wings, and breasts) with a tablespoon of the oil and season them with a pinch of salt, the cinnamon, and half the turmeric and white pepper.

Arrange the potato and onion slices in the bottom of a terrine. Sprinkle them with salt and the rest of the turmeric and white pepper, and add enough water to cover them completely. Add the remaining 3 tablespoons of oil and mix well. Arrange the chicken pieces on top along with the tomato and lemon slices.

Put the terrine into a preheated medium oven and cook for about 45 minutes, turning the chicken pieces from time to time. Before serving, sprinkle with the chopped parsley.

145. *MDARBIL:* VEAL WITH EGGPLANT

1 pound veal
Salt and black pepper
6 tablespoons olive oil
2 medium onions, coarsely chopped
2/3 pound fresh tomatoes
1 dried red chile
Handful of chickpeas, soaked overnight in water
Plump purplish eggplant, about 1 pound
Coarse sea salt
2 tablespoons vinegar

Cut the meat into slices, sprinkle with salt and pepper, and brown in the olive oil together with the onions. Peel and seed the tomatoes, crush them into a puree, and add them along with the red chile and the chickpeas. Cover and cook for an hour. Cut the eggplant crosswise into rounds and sprinkle them with coarse sea salt to make them disgorge their water. Rinse the sweated slices and press them. Fry them in a good amount of oil, dry them on paper towels, and add them to the meat. Finally, add the vinegar to the meat and vegetables and continue cooking for 5 to 10 minutes.

146. MEAT STEW WITH QUINCE IN THE TUNISIAN MANNER

In Morocco this dish is called quince tagine (tājin) and is made with lamb, though not vinegar. The chief difference between the two methods of cooking is that in Morocco the meat is cooked first in water, then removed from the heat, and the cooking liquid is used to cook the vegetables and fruit. In a third step, the meat is mixed with the vegetables and fruit in a cooking dish likewise known as a tagine. According to the Tunisian method, the meat is first browned in olive oil and cooked with the onion and spices, everything then being covered with water and the fruit added.

1 pound beef or veal
4 tablespoons olive oil
1 onion, sliced
1/2 teaspoon ground cinnamon
1 teaspoon ground rosebuds
Salt and white pepper
2 pounds quinces, peeled, pitted, and quartered
3 ounces sugar
2 tablespoons vinegar

Brown the meat in the oil with the onion, cinnamon, rosebuds, salt, and white pepper. Halfway through the cooking, add the quinces, along with the sugar. If the mixture sticks to the pan, also add hot water (not quite a cup). Ten minutes before the cooking is done, pour in the vinegar. Serve hot or at room temperature.

147. LAMB STEW WITH FRESH APRICOTS

1 pound lamb
Pinch of salt and black pepper
3 ounces olive oil
Handful of chickpeas, soaked overnight in water
3 ounces sugar
1 pound fresh apricots, pitted
Handful of raisins
1 packet of saffron
1 stick of cinnamon

Cut the meat into pieces and season with salt and pepper. Put it in a pot with the oil and chickpeas, cover completely with water, and cook for an hour. When the meat and chickpeas are cooked and the broth is reduced somewhat, add the sugar, apricots, raisins, saffron, and cinnamon stick. Cook for twenty minutes or so, stirring from time to time. The sauce should be reduced, but not to the point that the ingredients stick to the bottom of the pot.

148. MA'ĀSIM EL-BEY: KING'S WRISTS

¹/₂ pound deboned lamb

Salt

Pinch of ground white pepper

Pinch of ground turmeric

Pinch of ground cinnamon

1¹/₂ tablespoons butter

1 small bunch of flat-leaf parsley, finely chopped

12 sheets of *malsuka* (round phyllo pastry about 12 inches in diameter)

1 egg white, lightly beaten

Vegetable oil, for deep-frying

Juice of 1 lemon

To make the filling: Season the lamb with the salt, pepper, turmeric, and cinnamon. Put it in a casserole, add enough water to cover, and set the casserole over high heat. When the water comes to a boil, reduce the temperature and cook until the water evaporates and the meat is cooked (adding more water during the cooking as necessary). Chop the cooked meat by hand or in a food processor. Heat the butter and parsley for 2 minutes and then mix with the meat.

For assembly: Lay out a sheet of *malsuka* on a flat surface; fold the right and left edges back toward the middle so that the sheet is longer than wide. Fold the lower edge back toward the inside by about an inch and cover it with some of the filling while making sure it does not spill over the sides. Roll like a cigarette. Seal with egg white. Repeat with the remaining 11 sheets.

For cooking: Immerse the stuffed *ma'āsim* in hot oil, rolling them around once or twice so that they are completely browned. Transfer them to absorbent paper towels, then serve while still hot and crispy. A few drops of lemon juice squeezed on the *ma'āsim* just before eating gives them a pleasing note of freshness.

149. *BANĀDIQ:* TUNISIAN MEATBALLS

2 pounds ground beef
$^{1}/_{2}$ teaspoon ground black pepper
1 tablespoon *tabel*
Pinch of ground cubeb
$^{1}/_{2}$ teaspoon ground cinnamon
2 ground rosebuds
Good handful of dried crumbled mint leaves
Salt
10 ounces olive oil

Thoroughly mix the meat by hand with all the spices and dry herbs, and make little balls the size of a hazelnut (the classic size) or of a small nut. Cook them in the oil over low heat for about an hour. These *banādiq* are good whether eaten hot or cold, and the cooking oil, having been permeated with their flavor, makes a good condiment. Covered with this oil, the cooked meatballs keep for quite a few weeks in the freezer.

150. MEAT KOFTA

This dish is called kofta in Egypt, kifta *in Tunisia. Both the pronunciation and the ingredients and spices used vary from one region to another. There are many kinds of kofta: vegetarian (made with potatoes); ones made with fish rather than meat; ones seasoned only with black pepper; and ones with several different spices. The kofta here should be served with a tomato sauce seasoned with garlic and* tabel.

1 medium white onion, finely chopped
1 bunch parsley, leaves only, finely chopped
1/2 pound ground beef
2 tablespoons bread crumbs
Salt and black pepper
1/2 tablespoon *tabel*
1 large egg
Flour
Oil, for frying

Mix the onion and parsley with the ground meat along with the bread crumbs, salt, pepper, *tabel,* and egg. Make large balls from this mixture and flatten them with your hands. Dredge them in flour and fry them in hot oil.

151. *MERGUEZ* AND PICKLED VEGETABLE STEW

This dish should be accompanied by good fresh bread.

1/2 pound deboned mutton
4 tablespoons olive oil
1 cup tomato sauce
3 ounces pickled vegetables
Handful of green and black olives
1/2 tablespoon black pepper
1/2 tablespoon paprika
1/2 tablespoon *tabel*
1/2 pound ground mutton
Salt

Cut the deboned mutton into cubes and put them in a pot with the olive oil and the tomato sauce. Brown them over high heat for several minutes before adding the pickled vegetables, olives, and 1/4 tablespoon each of pepper, paprika, and *tabel*. Cover with water, bring to a boil, and cook over low heat.

In the meantime, mix the ground meat with the salt and the rest of the pepper, paprika, and *tabel,* and shape the mixture into little sausages with pointed ends. Add these *merguez* to the vegetables and cubed meat after they have been cooking for about 30 minutes and let them cook for 20 minutes longer.

152. *BRĪK DANNŪNI*

DOUGH

6 ounces semolina flour
2 tablespoons olive oil
Salt

FILLING

3 ounces ground lamb
Salt and black pepper
$^1/_2$ ounce clarified butter
1 tablespoon water
2 hard-cooked eggs, peeled

BRĪK

3 ounces grated Sardinian pecorino (ewe's milk) cheese
Olive oil, for frying

DOUGH

Make a dough with the semolina, kneading it with the oil, a little salt, and warm water as needed. Let the dough rest for 45 minutes. Then patiently re-work it, roll it out into thin sheets, and cut out round pieces 4 inches in diameter.

FILLING

Season the meat with salt and pepper and cook it in the clarified butter with the water, mixing it together for a few minutes. Chop up the eggs and mix them with the meat.

BRĪK

On each of the round pieces of dough put one or two tablespoons of the filling and sprinkle a bit of cheese over it. Pull back the edges, sticking them together with your fingers, and cook the stuffed *brīk* a few at a time in the boiling oil.

153. TUNISIAN *MULŪKHIYYA*

Some cooks add a few unpeeled cloves of garlic to this preparation.

6 ounces olive oil
6 tablespoons dried ground *mulūkhiyya* (jute leaves)
1 quart boiling water
1 pound stewing beef
Salt and black pepper
¹/₂ teaspoon *tabel*
1 strip dried orange peel (¹/₂ by 2 inches)
3 bay leaves
1 tablespoon ground dried mint leaves

Mix the oil with the *mulūkhiyya* and put it on the stove. Bring to a boil, stirring constantly with a wooden spoon. Add the boiling water, still stirring, and cook over low heat for two hours.

At this point cut the meat into pieces, seasoning it with salt, pepper, and *tabel,* and add it to the pot along with the orange peel and bay leaves. Cook for two hours more. A few moments before turning off the heat, add the mint.

The cooking is done when the water has completely evaporated, leaving only an oily film on top.

154. *BESTILLA*: MOROCCAN PIGEON PIE

2 pigeons
Salt and black pepper
Pinch of saffron
1 small onion, finely chopped
1¹/₂ ounces butter
3 large eggs
1¹/₂ ounces peeled almonds
Vegetable oil
1 teaspoon sugar, plus additional sugar for sprinkling
1 packet of 12 *brīk* (phyllo pastry) sheets
1 egg yolk
Pinch of cinnamon

Clean and gut the pigeons. Season them with salt, pepper, and saffron, and put them in a pot with the onions and enough water to cover. Cook over a low fire for 40 minutes. When the pigeons are cooked, set them aside and let cool. Simmer the broth so that it reduces, adding a little butter. Beat the eggs and pour into the reduced broth. Mix well and turn off the heat. Debone the pigeons and cut into pieces. Fry the almonds in a little oil and crush them coarsely. Mix with 1 teaspoon of the sugar.

Grease the bottom of a cooking dish and spread 3 *brīk* sheets over it, pulling their edges to the sides of the dish. Pour in the broth-egg mixture and cover with a second layer of 3 *brīk* sheets. Arrange the pigeon pieces evenly on top and cover them with a third layer of 3 sheets. Sprinkle with the crushed almond mixture, and cover finally with the remaining *brīk* sheets. Brush the outer surface with the egg yolk and cook in a medium oven for 15 to 20 minutes. When it is golden brown, sprinkle with cinnamon and sugar and serve.

155. SQUAB WITH DATES

4 squab, cleaned and gutted
$1/2$ teaspoon freshly ground cinnamon, plus additional cinnamon for
garnish
Salt and black pepper
Pinch of saffron or safflower, soaked in a little water, for color
4 tablespoons olive oil
1 pound pitted dates

Sprinkle the squab with cinnamon, salt, and pepper, brush with the diluted saffron or safflower, and then brown them in a pot containing the oil. Take care that they are well browned on all sides. Then add enough water to cover and braise for 20 minutes or so. Add the pitted dates to the pot and cook them with the squab for about 15 minutes. Watch over the cooking and, if necessary, add a little hot water. Sprinkle again with cinnamon just before serving.

FISH, SAUCES, AND VEGETABLES

───

MA'QŪDA BIR-RINGA: HERRING AND POTATO PIE

SARDINE *SHIBTIYYA*

TUNA *BRĪK*

TUNA AND EGGPLANT PUREE WITH VINEGAR AND CARAWAY

FRESH FISH IN RAISIN SAUCE (*SHARMŪLA*)

ANOTHER RAISIN SAUCE FOR SALTED FISH

VEGETARIAN *MURŪZIYYA*

156. MA'QŪDA BIR-RINGA: HERRING AND POTATO PIE

1 (5-ounce) salted herring
10 ounces potatoes
Salt
1½ tablespoons finely chopped flat-leaf parsley
Black pepper
4 tablespoons olive oil
6 large eggs, lightly beaten

Blanch the herring, skin it, and clean it, removing the head, and grind up the flesh. Cook the potatoes in water with a bit of salt, then peel. Finely chop the parsley.

In a deep pot, mash the potatoes with a fork (or puree in a food processor), and add to them the ground-up fish, parsley, a little salt (keep in mind that the fish is salty), and pepper to taste. Mix together well. Adjust the salt if necessary, then pour in the olive oil, and add the eggs to the preparation, mixing well with a large wooden spoon.

Butter a pie dish, fill it with the mixture (smoothing out the surface), and put the dish in a medium oven. After about 20 minutes one smells the fragrance of the ma'qūda. Once it has risen and become golden brown, take it out of the oven, let it cool a bit, and eat while it is still warm.

157. SARDINE *SHIBTIYYA*

Accompany these fish cakes with a sauce made from tomato puree, garlic, and ground pepper, and season with coriander seed and caraway.

1¼ pounds sardine fillets
1 teaspoon salt
1 teaspoon *tabel*
1 teaspoon black pepper
1½ tablespoons finely chopped flat-leaf parsley
1 onion
2 large eggs, lightly beaten
2 to 3 tablespoons bread crumbs
Flour
Vegetable oil, for frying

Crush the sardine fillets in a mortar with the salt and mix with the *tabel* and pepper. Finely chop the parsley and onion, add them to the sardines, and incorporate the eggs and bread crumbs little by little to obtain a homogeneous mixture. Shape it into flattened balls about 2 inches in diameter and ½ inch thick. Dredge them in flour and fry them in oil on both sides.

158. TUNA *BRĪK*

1 potato
1 teaspoon salt
Pinch of black pepper
Pinch of *tabel*
1 to 2 large eggs, lightly beaten
1 packet of 6 *brīk* (phyllo pastry) sheets
4 ounces tuna in oil
2 teaspoons small capers, drained
1 tablespoon finely chopped parsley
Vegetable oil, for frying
Juice of ¹/₂ lemon

Boil the potato in water until tender, and drain. Mash the potato with a fork, incorporating into it the salt, pepper, and *tabel*. Thicken at once with 1 egg, and if it is not sufficient, add another egg. Roll out a sheet of *brīk* on a table; fold the edges to obtain a square and put a little filling in the middle, adding a bit of the tuna, capers, and chopped parsley. Fold again, this time to obtain a triangle. Heat a good quantity of oil in a skillet, put the *brīk* in it one or two at a time, depending on the size of the skillet, and fry them on both sides. Transfer them to paper towels to drain when they begin to turn golden brown. Serve while they are hot. Squeeze a few drops of lemon on the *brīk* just before eating.

159. TUNA AND EGGPLANT PUREE WITH VINEGAR AND CARAWAY

3 plump eggplants
1 teaspoon salt
1 teaspoon ground caraway seed
2 cloves garlic, crushed
2 tablespoons olive oil
1 tablespoon vinegar
1 whole piece of tuna ($1/4$ pound) in olive oil
Olives
1 tablespoon capers, drained

Roast the eggplants over a fire until they are quite soft, or roast them in the oven for about 30 minutes. Then peel them and crush the flesh in a mortar or with a fork, mixing in the salt, caraway, and garlic. Put in a serving dish, moisten with olive oil and vinegar, place the tuna in the middle, and garnish with the olives and capers.

160. FRESH FISH IN RAISIN SAUCE (*SHARMŪLA*)

This version of sharmūla *is a specialty of the Tunisian port city of Bizerte.*

1 whole fish of good quality (sea bream, red snapper, or
gray mullet), about 1¹/₂ pounds
Salt and black pepper
¹/₂ cup olive oil
1 cup onion slices
1 teaspoon ground cinnamon
1 teaspoon powdered rosebuds
¹/₂ cup raisins, carefully cleaned
1 cup water
2 tablespoons good-quality vinegar

Clean, scale, and gut the fish, cut it into slices, rub with salt and pepper, and fry in the olive oil. Transfer to paper towels to drain, maintaining the heat under the oil.

Add the onion slices to the oil and sauté. When they are nicely browned, add the cinnamon and rosebuds, a pinch of salt, and the raisins. Pour in the water and let simmer for 20 to 25 minutes.

Adjust the salt, add the vinegar, mix, and remove from the heat. Put the fried slices of fish in the sauce and serve.

161. ANOTHER RAISIN SAUCE FOR SALTED FISH

This version of sharmūla—*a specialty of the Tunisian city of Sfax and of the Qar-qannah (Kerkennah) Islands, where it is made on the occasion of the concluding feast of Ramadan,* ʿīd al-fiṭr, *as an accompaniment for salted fish—will keep for three to four months. Dried salt-cured cod may be substituted for the various Mediterranean fish that the Tunisians customarily eat with this sauce. This recipe makes enough for a fish weighing about 1½ pounds.*

1 cup olive oil
2 pounds onions, sliced
2 pounds raisins
1 to 2 pinches of salt
1 teaspoon *ras el-hanut*
Pinch of black pepper

Heat the oil over high heat and brown the onions. Meanwhile, carefully wash the raisins and crush them in a mortar in the traditional manner; rinse them at length in a colander and extract the juice by pressing them against the sides of the colander by hand. Add the raisin juice to the onions when they are browned. Add the salt, the *ras el-hanut,* and the pepper to the onions and raisin juice, and cook over low heat until all the liquid has evaporated. Take off the fire and let cool.

162. VEGETARIAN *MURŪZIYYA*

1 pound winter squash
2 tablespoons olive oil
1 onion, sliced
2 heaping tablespoons sugar
Salt and black pepper
Handful of raisins, soaked in water 1 hour and drained
1 tablespoon red wine vinegar

In a skillet, fry pieces of the peeled squash in the oil for 5 to 10 minutes along with the onion and sugar. Add enough water to cover along with salt and pepper to taste. Put a lid on the pan and let simmer over a low fire until the squash is cooked and the liquid reduced. At this point, add the raisins and vinegar. After 4 to 5 minutes, remove from the heat. The dish may be eaten either hot or at room temperature. Refrigerated, it keeps for a number of days.

soups, pasta, and couscous

SOUP WITH SPARROWS' TONGUES AND LAMB

DUWĪDA: ANGEL-HAIR PASTA WITH LAMB AND SAFFRON

NUWĀSIR: STEAMED PASTA SQUARES

LAMB COUSCOUS

BAZERGĀN COUSCOUS

163. SOUP WITH SPARROWS' TONGUES AND LAMB

10 ounces boneless lamb
Salt and black pepper
Pinch of turmeric
1 small onion, chopped
3 tablespoons olive oil
7 cups water
1 bunch parsley
1 stalk celery
1½ ounces "sparrows' tongues" (pasta resembling grains of long rice,
such as orzo)
Juice of ½ lemon

Cut the meat into cubes. Season it with salt, pepper, and turmeric and fry it in a large, deep pot with the onion in the oil. Add the water and cook for an hour and a half over medium heat. Add a teaspoon of salt, the parsley, and the celery. Remove the parsley and celery after 10 minutes and add the pasta. Squeeze the lemon juice on the dish when you are ready to eat.

164. *DUWĪDA:* ANGEL-HAIR PASTA WITH LAMB AND SAFFRON

1 pound boneless lamb
Salt and black pepper
4 tablespoons olive oil
Pinch of powdered saffron or 1 teaspoon safflower
1 small onion, chopped
12 ounces angel-hair pasta or capellini
1 teaspoon clarified butter

Cut the meat into pieces, season with salt and pepper, and brown in a large, deep pot in the oil with part of the saffron and all of the onion. Then add enough water to cover and cook over moderate heat for about 40 minutes. Add the pasta and the rest of the saffron, dissolved in a tablespoon of the cooking liquid. Bring to a boil and turn off the heat. The broth should be quite reduced, but there should yet be enough to flavor the pasta. Add the clarified butter.

165. *NUWĀSIR*: STEAMED PASTA SQUARES

DOUGH

1 pound semolina flour
1 tablespoon salt
Cornstarch

CHICKEN AND BROTH

4 tablespoons olive oil
2 chopped onions
1 chicken, cut into pieces
Salt
Pinch of cinnamon
Black pepper
Handful of chickpeas, soaked in water overnight

ASSEMBLY AND FINAL PREPARATION

Olive oil
1 teaspoon butter

DOUGH

Knead the semolina flour with a little warm water and the salt until the dough is quite firm. Divide up the dough into four more-or-less equal portions and sprinkle them with cornstarch, then flatten them with a rolling pin, one after another, to obtain rather thin layers of dough. Let these rest for a while. Then cut them first into long strips about half an inch wide, and next into strips of the same width in the opposite direction, so that you end up with small squares. Let them dry in a sieve.

CHICKEN AND BROTH

Pour the oil into the lower pot of a couscous steamer (see recipe 166) along with the onions and chicken pieces. Sprinkle with the salt, cinnamon, and pepper. Cook for about 5 minutes, and then add the chickpeas and enough water to cover.

Brush the dough pieces with oil before putting them in the upper pot of the couscous steamer, on top of the pot in which the chicken is cooking in its broth. The cooking takes place in four stages at intervals of about 5 minutes. Once the steam has reached the pasta squares, transfer them to a large casserole and stir them with a wooden spoon, letting them breathe a bit before putting them back in the steamer. Repeat three more times. When the squares are cooked, return them to the casserole and toss them in the butter. Then moisten them with some of the broth according to the same method as couscous, little by little, placing the casserole over diffuse but very low heat (either on a grill or across two burners turned down very low), gently stirring them every now and again. Garnish the pasta with the chickpeas and chicken and serve hot.

166. LAMB COUSCOUS

Precooked couscous with medium or large granules is available at supermarkets around the world, but fine (or ultrafine) couscous is available only at a few North African (especially Tunisian) foods stores. Whole-grain couscous, which is sold at health-foods stores, requires longer cooking and has a more rustic taste, in particular Kamut couscous.

The couscous steamer is a sort of double boiler. The lower part is a large deep pot, whereas the upper one is a low pot whose bottom is pierced with holes. It is this upper pot that is properly called a couscous steamer (kiskas).

A few minutes before cooking, pour the couscous granules onto a large plate and moisten them with a quarter of a cup of salted water per pound of couscous. Delicately mix the couscous by hand so that the water is thoroughly absorbed.

Turnips and cabbage are the best additions to this recipe (parboiling the cabbage first and adding both to the broth after the other vegetables, which will take longer to cook). In spring, fava beans may be substituted for the chickpeas.

3 to 4 zucchini or winter squash

2 small potatoes

3 carrots

A few chard stalks

1 large onion

3 to 4 pearl onions

Hot or mild green chiles

1 teaspoon crushed caraway seeds

1 teaspoon *tabel*

Salt

5 teaspoons olive oil

1 teaspoon tomato paste, diluted with a small amount of water

1¹/₂ pounds boneless lamb, cut into 1-inch cubes

Handful of chickpeas, soaked in water overnight

Cayenne pepper or paprika

Pinch of cinnamon

1 to 2 ground rosebuds

Black pepper

2 quarts water

1 pound medium-granule precooked couscous, presoaked (see headnote)
Small knob of *samn* or good butter (optional)

Clean the zucchini, potatoes, carrots, and chard. Cut the zucchini and carrots into two or three pieces (if the pieces are too small, they risk breaking up in the broth); cut the chard stalks into thin slices the length of a finger; leave the potatoes whole. Slice the large onion and leave the small ones whole. Make an incision in the green chiles and stuff them with the caraway, *tabel*, and salt to taste.

Heat the oil in the lower pot of a couscous steamer over low heat and fry the green chiles and sliced onions with the diluted tomato paste. Mix well so that the chiles are cooked on all sides, then take them out and set them aside in a covered dish. Now add the meat and cook for a few minutes, stirring every now and then. When the meat is well browned, add the chickpeas, carrots, cayenne to taste, cinnamon, rosebuds, and pepper. Cover completely with the water and cook over medium heat for 20 minutes. Add the zucchini and the small whole onions together with additional salt to taste. Bring to a boil and place the steamer on top of the lower pot. Seal the point of contact between the two pots all around with a strip of dough if any steam escapes. When the steam begins to rise up through the holes in the bottom of the upper pot, add a handful of presoaked couscous (as indicated above) and then, once the steam has penetrated this thin layer, delicately add the rest of the couscous. Cook for another 20 to 25 minutes.

Transfer the couscous to a large platter (and, if you like, add some *samn* to it). Cover with a clean cloth and let it rest for a few minutes before gently and thoroughly mixing, either by hand or with a wooden spoon, in order to break up any lumps. Little by little add in the broth from the meat and vegetables, using the couscous steamer as a sieve. Let the grains slowly absorb the broth, mix again, and add some more broth. Repeat this step until each grain is saturated, but not floating in broth. Between steps, be sure to keep the couscous covered with a thick cloth so that the heat is retained.

On top of the couscous arrange the meat, chickpeas, vegetables, and fried chiles, presenting whatever will not fit on the serving dish on a separate platter.

167. *BAZERGĀN* COUSCOUS

1 pound boneless mutton or lamb, cut into very small pieces
Salt and black pepper
1 teaspoon cinnamon
1 bunch rosemary
2 pounds fine-granule uncooked couscous
1 onion, thinly sliced
1½ ounces butter
1 pint milk
5 hard-cooked eggs
3 ounces raisins, soaked in water and drained
1½ ounces peeled almonds, lightly toasted
1½ ounces hazelnuts, lightly toasted
1½ ounces walnuts, lightly toasted
½ ounce pistachios
1 tablespoon honey (optional)

Season the pieces of meat liberally with salt and pepper, sprinkle them with half the cinnamon, and steam them on top of a pot filled with water and the rosemary for about 45 minutes. In a steamer on top of another pot filled with about a quart of water, steam the couscous granules three times, each time for about 20 minutes. After each cooking, pour the couscous onto a large platter and, once it has cooled, stir it with your hands or a spatula, then put it back in the steamer. In a skillet, slowly fry the onion in the butter together with a bit of salt and pepper and the remaining cinnamon, without letting it take on the color of the spices. Add the milk and check the seasoning. When the milk boils, add the couscous and decorate with the pieces of meat, hard-cooked eggs, raisins, almonds, hazelnuts, walnuts, and pistachios. Drizzle with honey if you like and serve.

DESSERTS AND CONDIMENTS

―――

CANDIED PEARS

MAQRŪD: SEMOLINA CAKES WITH DATE PASTE

STUFFED DATES

ZULĀBIYYA

QATĀʾIF

SESAME AND HAZELNUT *ZRĪR*

QUINCE JELLY

168. CANDIED PEARS

Serve as an accompaniment to boiled meat or a tagine.

2 pounds small pears
2 quarts white wine vinegar
6 cinnamon sticks (each a finger in length)
12 whole cloves
2 pounds sugar

Peel, quarter, and core the pears, then put them in a large pot of boiling water; take them out when they have become soft to the touch. Drain them well and put them in a glass jar. Boil the vinegar with the cinnamon, cloves, and sugar, then pour the boiling liquid over the pears and let them macerate for 24 hours (let cool before sealing the jar).

Decant the liquid, bring it to a boil, and pour it over the fruit once again. Repeat this step a third time 24 hours later.

169. *MAQRŪD*: SEMOLINA CAKES WITH DATE PASTE

[The stuffed pieces of dough used for this dish are decorated with a qawalib, *a stamp with incised geometrical patterns that can be purchased at Middle Eastern import shops in the United States.—Trans.]*

2 pounds refined sugar
1 small lemon
5½ pounds hard grain semolina, not too fine
1 quart olive oil, for frying
Pinch of baking soda
1 teaspoon salt
3 pounds dates
1 teaspoon ground cinnamon
1 teaspoon ground orange peel
1 teaspoon ground rosebuds
Handful of sesame seeds, lightly toasted

Make a thick sugar syrup with lemon; set aside and let cool. Put the semolina in a large bowl. Heat a bit of the oil (traditionally olive oil is used for frying cakes) and add this to the semolina with the baking soda and salt; and mix well. Then add enough hot water to yield a consistent dough, mixing with a wooden spoon. Let cool and work the dough for some time. Let rest for a few hours or overnight.

Pit the dates, ridding them of all impurities, and crush them to make a thick paste, mixing it with the cinnamon, orange peel, and rosebuds, all ground by hand. Put the dough on a table and roll it out to a thickness of about an inch; then, with a knife, cut it into strips about 2 inches wide. Along the center part of each strip put a line of date paste the size of a finger and pull up the edges of the strip to enclose the filling. Using a *qawalib*, flatten to a thickness of about an inch and, holding the stamp in place, scrape away any filling that spills out of either end. Cut the stuffed dough into diamond-shaped pieces and fry in the remaining olive oil. Drain, then immerse the *maqrūd* for one or two minutes in the sugar and lemon syrup. At the end sprinkle with the sesame seeds.

Another method: Proceed as before, but mix the date pulp with a cup of olive oil. Continue as in the previous recipe, but instead of frying the *maqrūd,* arrange them in a metal pan and cook in a hot oven for 20 to 25 minutes.

At the end, douse with the syrup and sprinkle with the sesame seeds.

170. STUFFED DATES

The dates typically sold in pastry shops in the Arab world are stuffed with almond paste flavored with sugar and green-colored rose water.

Dates
Walnut kernels or whole lightly toasted almonds
Thick sugar syrup
Crystallized sugar

Open the dates, remove the pits, and substitute walnuts or almonds. Immerse the stuffed dates in thick sugar syrup, sprinkle them with crystallized sugar, and let them dry until the next day. Shake them to eliminate any excess sugar and arrange them on an elegant tray.

They can also be stuffed with walnuts and butter, without dipping them in syrup.

171. *ZULĀBIYYA*

2 pounds flour
1 teaspoon salt
1/4 ounce baking powder (in Tunisia, a mixture of sodium bicarbonate,
potassium bitartrate, and wheat starch)
1 1/2 ounces cornstarch
Pinch of turmeric
Vegetable oil, for deep-frying
32 ounces honey or sugar syrup

Put the flour in a pot or some other sufficiently large receptacle, with the salt and baking powder. Knead at length with warm water until you have a flowing batter with no lumps. Cover the pot and let the dough rise for 34 to 36 hours. Incorporate the starch and work the dough again for quite a while, coloring it with the turmeric.

Heat the oil until very hot. Warm the honey in another pan. Put the dough in a small funnel or a container with a pierced bottom and drip it into the oil, rapidly guiding the funnel to make round interwoven cakes about 5 to 6 inches in diameter. Take them out of the oil a few at a time as they are cooked, and immediately dip them in the hot honey; eat once they have cooled sufficiently.

172. QATĀʾIF

50 *brīk* [phyllo pastry] sheets (5 packets of 10 sheets)
5 ounces butter, melted
5 ounces almonds, toasted and coarsely chopped
3 ounces hazelnuts, toasted and coarsely chopped
1¹/₂ ounces pistachios, toasted and coarsely chopped
1 cup sugar syrup
1 tablespoon water infused with geranium or orange blossoms

Cut the *brīk* sheets with scissors into thin strips, brush them with the butter, and brown them on a rimmed baking sheet for 10 minutes in a preheated medium oven; then add the nuts. Add the syrup with the scented water and put back in the oven for about 10 minutes. Take the *qatāʾif* out of the oven when they have absorbed the syrup. Arrange on a serving dish and eat them either warm or at room temperature.

173. SESAME AND HAZELNUT *ZRĪR*

16 ounces honey or 1 cup sugar syrup
3 ounces butter
6 ounces sesame seeds, toasted and crushed
3 ounces hazelnuts, toasted and crushed
1 tablespoon rose water

Heat the honey or use syrup that has just been made, adding to it the butter and the sesame seeds and hazelnuts. Cook for 5 minutes over high heat and add the rose water at the last moment. Mix well, remove from the burner, and serve in little cups or bowls.

174. QUINCE JELLY

2 pounds quinces
1 quart boiling water
12 ounces sugar

Soak the quinces in water, wash them well, and cut them into quarters, removing the pits. Cook them in the water for 15 minutes or so. Drain in a
colander, pressing on the pulp in order to remove as much syrup as possible.
Puree the pulp in a food mill or food processor, and push it through a fine
sieve into the syrup. Add the sugar to the enriched syrup and put it back on
the stove over low heat. When the preparation begins to thicken, remove it
from the heat and let it cool. Put the jelly in jars.

NOTES

CROSSROADS OF THE WORLD'S CUISINES

1. *Sikbāj* derives from the Persian *sikba: sik*, "vinegar," *ba*, "food."

2. See Ibn Sayyār al-Warrāq, *Kitāb al-tabīkh*, ed. Kaj Öhrnberg and Sahban Mroueh, *Studia Orientalia* 60 (1987): 1–343 at p. 9.

3. Founded by Caliph al-Maʾmūn contemporaneously with an astronomical observatory.

4. Ibn Razīn al-Tujībī, *Fadālat al-khiwān fī tayyibāt al taʿām wa-l-alwān*, ed. Mohamed Benchecroun (Beirut: Dār al-Gharb al-Islāmī, 1984); first edition published in Rabat in 1981 and separately the same year in Beirut in conjunction with Franz Steiner Verlag, Stuttgart.

5. See in this connection Geert Jan van Gelder, *Of Dishes and Discourse: Classical Arabic Literary Representations of Food* (Richmond, Surrey: Curzon, 2000).

6. Ibn Sayyār al-Warrāq, *Kitāb al-tabīkh*.

7. Exactly where Ibn Sayyār composed his work is unknown.

8. See Muhammad ibn al-Karīm al-Kātib al-Baghdādī, *Kitāb al-tabīkh*, ed. Daud Chelebi (Mosul: Umm al-Rabiʾ ain Press, 1934); A. J. Arberry, "A Baghdad Cookery Book," *Islamic Culture* 13 (1939): 21–37, 189–214; and Charles Perry's edition (including Arberry's translation) in Maxime Rodinson, A. J. Arberry, and Charles Perry, eds., *Medieval Arab Cookery: Essays and Translations* (Totnes, Devon: Prospect Books, 2001), pp. 20–89. In the meantime Perry has produced a fresh translation, not from the faulty Arabic text used by Arberry, but directly from the original manuscript in the Süleymaniye Library in Istanbul, *A Baghdad Cookery Book, Newly Translated* (London: Prospect Books, 2005). See also David Waines, *In a Caliph's Kitchen* (London: Riad El-Rayyes Books, 1989).

9. The integral translation by Ambrosio Huici Miranda, *Traducción española de un manuscrito anónimo de siglo XIII sobre la cocina hispano-magribi* (Madrid:

Maestre, 1966), was preceded by the publication of an extract in Fernando de la Granja Santamaría, *La cocina arabigo-andaluza según un manuscrito inédito* (doctoral thesis, Facultad de Filosofía y Letras, Madrid, 1960).

10. This name further suggests an aristocratic background. Ibn Sayyār was descended from a seventh-century governor of Khorasan (in eastern Iran), which probably explains his access to recipe collections of the caliphs and others in the court of Baghdad.—*Trans.*

11. Ibn Sayyār al-Warrāq, *Kitāb al-tabīkh*, pp. 1–2.

12. The Buyids controlled Baghdad for a little more than a century, from 945 to 1055. Although Ibn Sayyār makes no reference to them, he mentions a great many recipes from Iraqi cooks of the period.

13. This dating is argued for by Manuela Marín and David Waines in the introduction to their edition of *Kanz*, published in *Al-nasharāt al-islāmiyya* 40 (1993).

14. See the introduction to Sulayma Mahjūb and Durriyya al-Khatīb's edition of *al-Wusla ilā l-habīb fī wasf al-tayyibāt wa-l-tīb*, 2 vols. (Aleppo: Manshūrāt Jāmiʿat Halab, 1986–1988). [In addition to Ibn al-ʿAdīm, three others have been credited as the author of *Wusla*: al-Jazzār, an unnamed grandnephew of Saladin, and "the very erudite chief shaykh of Hama."—*Trans.*]

15. See Lucie Bolens, *La cuisine andalouse, un art de vivre: XIe–XIIIe siècle* (Paris: Albin Michel, 1990).

16. Ibn Jazla's twelfth-century medical encyclopedia, *Minhāj al-bayān*, contained a great many recipes that were immediately extracted and circulated as a cookbook. By the early fourteenth century it had been translated into Latin by Giambonino da Cremona as *Liber de ferculis et condimentis* (Book of Dishes and Seasonings).—*Trans.*

17. See Jean Sauvaget, ed. and trans., *Akhbār as-Sīn wa-l-Hind (851), ou Relation de la Chine et de l'Inde* (Paris: Les Belles Lettres, 1948).

18. My translation.

19. From the *Dīwān* of Bashshār ibn Burd; see also van Gelder, *Of Dishes and Discourse*, p. 30.

20. Al-Jāhiz, *al-Bukhalā'*, ed. Taha al-Hajari, 7th ed. (Cairo: Dar al-Maarif [n.d.]).

21. Ibid., pp. 121–122.

22. Quoted by Ibn Sayyār, *Kitāb al-tabīkh*, p. 338.

23. Van Gelder, *Of Dishes and Discourse*, p. 88.

24. Al-Jāhiz, *al-Bukhalā'*, p. 374.

25. Apicius, *De re coquinaria*, 6.240.4; see too Jacques André's edition, *De l'art culinaire* (Paris: Les Belles Lettres, 1987).

26. See, for example, recipes 1 and 2 in part two of this book.
27. Jean Bottéro, *Textes culinaires mésopotamiens* (Winona Lake, Ind.: Eisenbrauns, 1995).
28. Al-Jāhiz, *al-Bukhalāʾ*, p. 429 (editor's note).
29. Van Gelder, *Of Dishes and Discourse*, p. 25.
30. See al-Bukhārī, *L'authentique tradition musulmane: Choix de hadiths*, ed. and trans. G. H. Bousquet (Paris: Sindbad, 1991); also Sergio Noja, Virginia Vacca, and Michele Vallaro, eds., *Detti e fatti del Profeta dell'Islam* (Turin: UTET, 1982).
31. Qurʾan 6:145. This verse and the ones that follow are taken from *The Qurʾan*, trans. M. A. S. Abdel Haleem (Oxford: Oxford University Press, 2004).—*Trans.*
32. Ibid., 5:3.
33. Ibid., 5:4.
34. Ibid., 6:146.
35. Ethiopian Christians continue to observe the ban on pork.—*Trans.*
36. Ibid., 5:87–88.
37. Ibid., 47:15.
38. Ibid., 2:219.
39. Ibid., 83:22–28.
40. Wine was only very occasionally used in cooking during the medieval period.—*Trans.*
41. Vincent Lagardère, "Cépages, raisins et vin," *Médiévales* (Cultures et nourritures de l'Occident musulman) 33 (1997): 86.
42. Ibn Sayyār, *Kitāb al-tabīkh*, pp. 341–342.
43. Al-Rāzī, *Le guide du médecin nomade: Aphorismes*, ed. and trans. El-Arbi Moubachir (Arles: Actes Sud, 1996), p. 90.
44. Nizām al-Mulk, *Traité de gouvernement*, ed. and trans. Charles Scheffer (Paris: Sindbad, 1984), pp. 198–199.
45. Qurʾan, 97:3–4.
46. Ibid., 2:187.
47. Quoted in Ibn Sayyār, *Kitāb al-tabīkh*, p. 133.
48. Thus the definition given by the fourteenth-century dictionary *Lisān al-ʿArab*, from the original Persian word meaning "he who finds gold."
49. Bolens, *La cuisine andalouse*, pp. 28–31.
50. Ishāq ibn Sulaymān al-Isrāʾīlī, *Kitāb al-aghdhiya* (*Book on Dietetics*), ed. Fuat Sezgin, Johan Series C (Frankfurt: Institut für Geschichte der

Arabisch-Islamischen Wissenschaften, 1986), vols. 30, nos. 1, 2, and 3: facsimile edition of manuscripts 3605, 3606, and 3607 in the Fath Collection, Süleymaniye Library, Istanbul.

51. The characteristic ingredient in all the stews called "sour dishes" (*hawāmid*) was not always vinegar. Often it was yogurt, sumac, or a sour fruit juice such as pomegranate, lemon, sour orange, or sour grape. There were also "plain" (*sawādhij*) dishes that did not have a sour flavoring.—*Trans.*

52. Giovanni Rebora, *La cucina medievale italiana tra Oriente e Occidente* (Genoa: Department of Modern and Contemporary History, University of Genoa, 1996), 58. [See also Anna Martellotti, *Il Liber de ferculis di Giambonino da Cremona: La gastronomia araba in Occidente nella trattatistica dietetica* (Fasano [Brindisi]: Schena, 2001), which argues that the influence of *sikbāj* on European cuisine extends beyond escabèche to include aspics as well. Charles Perry's culinary experiments have led him to conclude that if no escabèches today are served hot, this is because *sikbāj* was usually served as a cold gelatin.—*Trans.*]

53. This is a four-day festival that takes place every year.

54. Modern attempts to make *murrī* suggest that it tasted like soy sauce. The term *kāmakh* referred to a group of condiments for bread, almost all of them (with the exception of certain recipes in the tenth-century *Kitāb al-tabīkh*) based on milk. *Kāmakh ahmar* was salted milk flavored by the addition of moldy bread—a semiliquid blue cheese, in effect. In *kāmakh rījāl*, the salted milk was aged until bacterial action produced the characteristic flavor of cheese, with the salt preventing spoilage in the interval; the result must have been a sort of semiliquid Boursin.—*Trans.*

55. Jacques Véhel, *La véritable cuisine tunisienne*, ed. Yassine Essid (Tunis: Médiacom, 2003 [orig. 1922]).

MATERIALS, TECHNIQUES, AND TERMINOLOGY

1. Ibn Sayyār al-Warrāq, *Kitāb al-tabīkh*, p. 8.

2. Abū Marwān ʿAbd al-Mālik ibn Zuhr, *Kitāb al-aghdhiya (Tratados de los alimentos)*, ed. and trans. García Sánchez (Madrid: Consejo Superior de Investigaciones Científicas, 1992), p. 136.

3. Ibn Zuhr advises that "the best cookware, if it were lawful, would be made of gold, and after that of silver. But as the use of these [materials] is considered to be illicit, one must therefore make use of ceramic utensils and the like"; see ibid.

4. Ibn Sayyār al-Warrāq, *Kitāb al-tabīkh*, pp. 11–12.

5. Michel de Montaigne, *The Complete Essays of Montaigne*, trans. Donald M. Frame (Stanford, Calif.: Stanford University Press, 1957), 1.55, p. 229; original text quoted by Ernest-Gustave Gobert, "Usages et rites alimentaires des Tunisiens," *Revue de l'Institut des Belles Lettres Arabes* 1 (1942): 52ff.

6. Ibn Khalsūn, *Kitāb al-aghdhiya*, ed. Suzanne Gigandet (Damascus: Institut Français de Damas, 1996). [*Al murrī al-naqī'* was the characteristic soy sauce of North Africa; cookbooks from Syria and Iraq also give recipes for it. It differed from Iraqi-style soy sauce in that larger numbers of aromatic ingredients (coriander seeds, caraway, nigella, fenugreek, anise, fennel seeds, carob, fennel leaves, citron leaves, and pith of orange branches) were infused in the liquid while it aged. Iraqi cooks were content to infuse their soy sauce with fennel and nigella alone, and then add a few more spices at the end.—*Trans.*]

7. Ibn Razīn al-Tujībī, *Fadālat al-khiwān*, p. 175.

8. Al-Jāhiz uses the Arabic word *bāridjīn*, which some scholars take to be derived from the Persian *bartchidan*, meaning "to pick up." However this may be, the purported identification with a Western-style fork evidently cannot be sustained.

BREAD AND BROTH

1. *Tharīd* was not always bread and meat piled in a pyramid; sometimes it took the form of a stew mixed with bread crumbs, sometimes of bread in broth. In some dialects *tharīda* was taken to be *thuraīda*, the diminutive of a word such as *thurda*, which subsequently became the name of the dish. From this word, *al-thurda*, came the Portuguese word for soup, *açorda*—evidence that, in medieval Iberia, *tharīd* was similar to European soups, which originally consisted of broth with a piece of bread (a "sop") in it.—*Trans.*

2. Today the word *shāshiyya* refers to the green fez with a white tassel that is characteristic of southern Morocco. Why this cap should have come to be associated with Ibn al-Wadī' is inevitably a matter of speculation, since we do not know who this man was, or indeed whether he and Ibn al-Raf ī' were the same person.—*Trans.*

3. In other collections, as is often the case with medieval recipes, the pieces of bread—referred to as "the *tharīd*"—are mentioned only at the end of the recipe, with the instruction that the contents of the *mithrad* be strewn over them. Thus in the *Manuscrito anónimo*, for example, when the stew is done the cook is told to "moisten the *tharīd* with it."—*Trans.*

4. Ibn Abī Dinār, *al-Mu'nis fī akhbār ifrīqiyya wa tūnis*, ed. Muhammad Sham-

mām (Tunis: al-Maktaba al-Atīqah, 1967), 306. *Kunāfa* was an ultra-thin crepe cooked on a griddle, which was often waxed rather than oiled. In the medieval period the crepe was sometimes cut into small pieces; today the batter is drizzled onto the griddle to make a vermicelli-like ingredient that is used in pastries similar to baklava, known in the eastern Arab countries as *kunāfa* and in Greece and Turkey as *katayif.* The fact that *dawīda* is a diminutive of *dūd* ("worms") suggests a resemblance to modern *kunāfa,* except that it does not seem to have been sweetened; apparently it was a sort of crispy vermicelli served as a side dish. If so, as Charles Perry points out, *al-faṭīr wa-mā yaṭīr* (literally "unleavened bread and that which flies") may not have involved moistening the *faṭīr,* in which case its similarity to *tharīd* is doubtful.—*Trans.*

5.   Ibn Abī Dinār, *al-Muʾnis,* pp. 310–313.

SWEET-AND-SOUR DISHES

1.   The spelling of the name of this dish in *Kanz,* with a long second syllable in the final word, is quite unusual; in both *Wusla* and *Kitāb Wasf* this syllable is unmarked. The presence of the macron here (*shanāʿ*) signifies a rare verbal noun, from the verb meaning "to be ugly, loathsome."—*Trans.*

2.   A recipe named *sitt al-nūba* is found in *Kitāb Wasf al-Aṭʿima al-Muʿtada.* It calls for serving chickens boiled in water that have been flavored with soy sauce and lemon juice with a preparation of purslane milk, honey or syrup, pistachios, rose water, and musk.—*Trans.*

ROASTS, MEATBALLS, AND SAUSAGES

1.   What makes the dish Frankish is that it is cooked over an open charcoal fire, as in a European baronial hall, rather than in an oven.—*Trans.*

MEAT, POULTRY, AND VEGETABLE STEWS

1.   This distaste was probably due to ignorance of the proper way to cook eggplant in order to eliminate its bitter flavor (according to an anecdote reported in *Muhadarat al-Udaba,* by Abu al-Qasim Husain ibn Muhammad al-Raghib al-Isfahani, "its color is like the scorpion's belly, and its taste is like the scorpion's sting"). Additionally, it was believed by medieval Arab physicians to cause cancer and madness, a reputation that eventually made its way to Europe. Only a handful of recipes in Ibn Sayyār's book call for eggplant, but by the thirteenth century the proportion had risen considerably,

with many recipes endorsing the seasonal substitution of eggplant for carrots.—*Trans.*

2. Ibn al-ʿAwwām, *Le livre de l'agriculture,* trans. J. J. Clément-Mullet (Arles:
    Actes Sud; Paris: Sindbad, 2000), 693.

3. Thus the text—but it seems likelier that "for the twenty pieces of eggplant"
    is meant.—*Trans.*

FISH

1. It was nonetheless far more honored in Spain and North Africa, with their
    fertile fishing grounds, than in Baghdad, which had only a few species of
    freshwater fish, and particularly in Syria, where stocks in the Mediter-
    ranean are poor. Only four species of fish are mentioned in the eastern Arab
    cookbooks, and of these only one is specified for a dish; the books from
    Moorish Spain name seventeen varieties. Forty-eight fish recipes in all are
    found in the five medieval cookbooks from the eastern Arab world, as
    against fifty-six recipes in the two Spanish books. Fish mostly appears in
    dried form in the east, whereas there are only two such recipes from An-
    dalusia.—*Trans.*

2. It is not clear that *sīr* always referred to salted fish. On the one hand, the
    name has been plausibly connected with the Hebrew word for brine, *tzūr,*
    which would have become *sīr* in Coptic. On the other hand, some recipes
    call for salt to be added to *sīr* in such substantial quantities that the term
    could not have been used in every context to mean fish that had already been
    salted. Moreover, the fact that *sīr* is often called for in ground form (*mathūn*)
    suggests an unsalted product, for fish cured without salt must be as hard as
    rock in order to prevent spoilage and then pounded to a meal, fine or
    coarse, for use in cooking.—*Trans.*

3. The title of this recipe is disputed. Instead of *murūj* (which means "mead-
    ows" in Arabic), Ambrosio Huici Miranda reads *murawwaj* ("put out for sale
    in the market"), suggesting a dish that could be bought in the souks. There
    is also a dish by this name, though of different recipe, in the eastern book
    Kitāb Wasf al-Aṭ°ima al-Muʿtāda.—*Trans.*

CHEESE AND OTHER DAIRY DISHES

1. How the eastern term *brīk* (from the Turkish *börek*) came to be applied to
    such dishes in North Africa is unclear. The sheets of pastry used to make
    briks in Tunisia are made out of semolina and known as *warka malsuka,*

whereas the stuffed and deep-fried pastry known today as *brīk dannūni* consists of thin leaves made from flour paste, different from *warka malsuka*, and is called simply *warka*. Nor is there anything Turkish about the pie known as *briket el-hamm*, made with twenty *warka* arranged in two layers and stuffed with meat and brains.

2. In its simplest version, *sikanjubīn safarjalī* is made with "the juice of Isfahan quince and white purified sugar, with or without vinegar—all of it cooked"; see Manuela Marín and David Waines, eds., *Kanz al-Fawāʾid fī tanwīʿ al-mawāʾid* (Berlin and Stuttgart: Franz Steiner Verlag, 1993), 131.

SOUPS

1. Ernest-Gustave Gobert, "Usages et rites alimentaires des Tunisiens," *Revue de l'Institut des Belles Lettres Arabes* 1 (1942): 52ff.

PASTA

1. Note, too, that topping grain with meat was (and remains still today) the classic presentation of couscous. This recipe appears in the section on couscous in *Wusla;* in fact, it comes before the recipe for "couscous of the North Africans."—*Trans.*

2. In many places *muhammas* refers to a large-grained couscous, but the term is still used for a kind of pasta in parts of Algeria (Kabylia and the Mzab Oasis) and among the Tuaregs (who pronounce it "tikhemzin"). "Bullets" is, of course, a European epithet.—*Trans.*

COUSCOUS

1. See Bernard Rosenberger, "Consommer les céréales," in *Société, pouvoir et alimentation: Nourriture et précarité au Maroc précolonial* (Rabat: Alizès, 2001), 173. [One notices a certain vacillation in the manuscript tradition between couscous proper (made by sprinkling flour with water and stirring it, then steaming the grains) and something called couscous that is actually a kind of pasta (made from kneaded wheat dough, as in the case of *muhammas*, for example). In *Kitāb al-Wusla* a distinction is made between *kuskusū* (a small pasta) and *kuskusū al-maghāriba* ("couscous of the North Africans," which is to say the stirred and steamed kind). The speed of the latter method, mentioned approvingly in one recipe, has led Charles Perry to suggest that the North African version arose as a quick way of making the pasta sort of couscous, and reached Syria and Iraq only later.—*Trans.*]

2. The real reason for this name is that in the eastern Arab world the word *kuskus* has a vulgar meaning.—*Trans.*

RICE AND OMELETS

1. *Wusla* says of a recipe it calls Indian rice (*arruz hindī*) that the rice comes out *mufalfal*, which recalls the Arabic name for pilaf, *arruz mufalfal* ("rice [grains as separate as] peppercorns"). But this by itself is not enough to show that the pilaf technique came from India, where pilaf (*pulao*, the Middle Persian word still used in India) is considered a Muslim dish and most pilaf dishes have Persian names.—*Trans.*

SAUCES

1. Other authorities indicate that *sahnā* was not a sauce, but a fish-based condiment or seasoning. The fourteenth-century dictionary *Lisān al-ʿArab* defines it as salted fish, which is the older meaning of the word; Ibn Sayyār gives instructions for drying fish into *sahnā*. On the other hand, the fifteenth-century dictionary *Al-Qāmūs* defines it as "an appetizing condiment of fish," which agrees with the preparations found in all the cookbooks of the thirteenth and fourteenth centuries, where *sahnā* always involves adding flavorings to dried fish. The recipes in *Kitāb Zahr al-Hadiqa* (which calls for sumac rather than sumac flour) and *Kitāb al-Wusla ilā l-habib* (which calls for sumac flowers) both list more extensive combinations of herbs, spices, and aromatics than *Kanz al-Fawāʾid.*—*Trans.*

PASTRIES AND JAMS

1. Ibn Sayyār al-Warrāq, *Kitāb al-tabīkh*, 270.
2. This lattice effect is what is meant by the description of these fritters as "intertwined" in the poem quoted by Ibn Sayyār.—*Trans.*

PART THREE. CONTEMPORARY NORTH AFRICAN CUISINE

Charles Perry contributed details on spices to the opening text of this section.

GLOSSARY

Arabic terms are given throughout in the singular to facilitate reading.

aruzziyya: a dish of rice cooked in broth with seasoned meatballs.

atrāf ṭīb: a condiment composed of a mixture of various spices, mentioned in *Kanz* and *Wusla.* The latter source lists a dozen ingredients, among them spikenard, betel, bay leaf, nutmeg, mace, cloves, rosebuds, pepper, ginger, and cardamom.

banādiq: a contemporary meatball dish popular in Tunisia.

bārida: a general name for cold appetizers, the style of which varied by region throughout the Islamic world.

basbāsiyya: oven-baked fish with fennel.

bestilla (b'steeya): Moroccan pigeon pie.

birāf: a custard made by repeatedly skimming the surface of curdled milk, served with honey or powdered sugar.

brīk: a sort of turnover made with tissue-thin layers of dough, filled with seasoned meat or fish and deep-fried; of Turkish origin, it quickly spread to the Muslim West.

dak (or *dag*): a cooking utensil (the name comes from the Middle Persian word *dēg,* for pot), found still today in Iraq, equipped with a grill made from carved willow stalks on which meat is placed. The meat is steamed, and its fat and juices drip into a broth or into rice that is cooked at the bottom of the pot.

dakbaryān: the name of the dish (literally, "pot-cooked") that was prepared in a *dak,* typically steamed meat and rice in meat broth.

dāniq: a unit of measure for both volume and weight, specifically the weight of a single grain of barley, about 0.5 gram.

dast: a tinned copper tray with high sides used for cooking over a fire or in an oven in the Middle East.

dīnār: the weight of the gold coin bearing this name (from the Latin *denarius*), about 4.5 grams.

dirham: unit of measure equal to six *dāniq;* also the name of a silver coin (from the Greek *drachma*), weighing about 3 grams.

duwīda: a contemporary dish of angel-hair pasta served with lamb and saffron.

fatīr: thin flat breads of unleavened dough, similar to matzo.

fidāwish: a term used in the Muslim West to designate a kind of short pasta, similar to present-day Tunisian *halālim* or Italian *trofie* (served with pesto in Liguria); in a recipe from Ibn Razīn, they have the shape of a grain of barley with very tapered ends. In the Muslim East, pasta similar to *fidāwish* are called *shaʿīriyya* (from *shaʿīr,* meaning "barley").

furn: an oven made from brick and used for baking bread (placed on the floor of the oven). Compare *tannūr.*

futāt: the pieces of bread used to make *tharīd.* The ancient Arab recipe calls for crumbled *fatīr* (see part two). Later recipes use other types of bread, described in the chapter devoted to *tharīd.*

ghannāy: a pottery dish used to cook thin flat bread in the Maghreb.

hasu: of Berber origin, a large-grained couscous (known in North Africa also as *barkūkish*).

isfunj: sponge cake.

iskirfāj: a cheese grater.

itriya (or *itriyya*): a term used across the Muslim world in the Middle Ages to designate a kind of hard-grain pasta (from the Greek *itrion,* which originally referred to a Greek flat bread made with sesame, but by the third century it was being boiled; Ibn Razīn's cookbook is the only one that gives instructions on how to make it—and then only "if it is not available," suggesting that it was mostly sold in shops). According to Andalusian accounts, *itriya* had a shape similar to that of spaghetti ("it is rolled out with both hands as thinly as possible and then dried in the sun"). In the medieval period this pasta was sold in local markets and exported abroad. A document from the fourteenth century refers to a cargo of pasta in a ship sailing under the flag of Granada from Hunayn (in what is now Algeria) to Almería, for example. In southern Italy today, the term *tria* designates a kind of artisanal pasta.

jām: a bowl or jar used as a serving dish in Iraq. In Safavid examples from the fifteenth century, it assumes the form of a rounded metal tray with chiseled designs.

jashīsh: a coarsely milled semolina often made by grinding barley and used in winter soups.

jūdhāba: a term of Persian origin, said by Lane's *Arabic-English Lexicon* (1865) to refer to "a pudding of bread [*khubza*] put into the oven [*tannūr*], and having suspended over it a bird or some flesh-meat, the gravy of which flows upon it as long as it is cooking." Often, though not always, the pudding was arranged between layers of thin flat bread. See also recipe 22.

kāmakh: a dairy-based condiment or spread served with bread.

khabīs: a kind of pudding, normally thickened with flour, but sometimes with cornstarch.

khātūnī: a dish of rice with pistachios.

kibrītiyya: a dish of meatballs and eggplant.

kofta: a popular contemporary dish in Egypt and North Africa consisting of disks of seasoned ground meat (or sometimes fish) dredged in flour and fried in oil, often served with a sauce.

kunāfa: a kind of pancake, piled high on a plate and moistened with honey or butter and sprinkled with cinnamon.

labaniyya rūmiyya: a Greek (or Byzantine) yogurt stew prepared with meat, chard, garlic, and rice.

līmūniyya: fish cooked in lemon juice, crushed safflower, and seasonings.

maqrūd: a semolina cake, filled with date paste and either fried or baked.

maʾqūda bir-ringa: a kind of herring and potato pie popular in North Africa today.

marwaziyya: a dish, made with or without meat, that assigned a prominent place to prunes in its classical presentation, but alternatively to cherries or raisins; a modern Tunisian and Moroccan version (*murūziyya*) uses dried chestnuts and almonds instead of fruit.

mdarbil: a contemporary dish of stewed veal and eggplant flavored with vinegar and seasonings.

minqāsh: a wooden stamp used to decorate cakes.

mithqāl: a less common name for *dīnār.*

mithrad: a basin used for crumbling bread for *tharīd* (and apparently also for kneading) in Andalusia, made of glazed porcelain, flared and resting on an annular base. The cover has a similarly bulging shape, reminiscent of the conical *tājin* used in Morocco to cook the stews of the same name (tagines).

mufalfal: literally, "peppercorns," signifying grains of rice that do not stick to one another after cooking; the basis of a technique better known in the West as pilaf.

muhammas: in parts of North Africa, a kind of dry pasta shaped like peppercorns and served with beef, mutton, or chicken; in other parts of this region the term refers to a large-grained couscous.

mujabbana: typically Andalusian, the name of this dish comes from the incorporation of cheese (*jubn*) into a stuffing. Ibn Razīn gives several recipes, some of which are cooked in the oven (like quiches and pies today), others being fried like beignets.

mulūkhiyya: a dish of seasoned meatballs (made from beef, lamb, or fowl) with chopped jute leaves.

murrī: another long-keeping condiment (see recipes 137 and 138).

murūj: a dish of fish (or sometimes sardines or eels) cooked in an aromatic broth.

nabatiyya: a soup of chicken broth and *itriya,* the earliest one known to incorporate cooked pasta.

nabīdh: "near wine" made from dates or grapes that, because it was fermented only overnight, could be considered nonintoxicating under Islamic law.

nisha: a starch made by kneading a stiff dough and then kneading it again under a stream of water, so that the starch dissolves. In this liquid form it is called *malban;* dried, *nisha.* Because there is some gluten in it, it is not pure starch.

nuwāsir: a contemporary dish in which thin square pieces of pasta are steamed, moistened with chicken broth, and garnished with chickpeas and chicken.

qālib maqrūd: a wooden stamp, slightly more than two feet long, about two inches wide, and an inch and a half in thickness, and incised with geometric patterns. It was used to imprint semolina dough that had been stuffed with date paste.

qamhiyya: a puree of whole wheat that has been cooked in milk after being rinsed in rose water.

qatāʾif: in its modern North African form, a sweet and savory pastry made with tissue-thin layers of dough and sprinkled with nuts and sugar syrup; originally an ultra-thin crepe, also known by the Coptic word *kunāfa,* which in the eastern Arab world evolved into the modern dish of this name (see above). In Turkey today it is called *kadayif,* and in Greece *kataifi.* In medieval Spain and North Africa the crepe was sometimes clipped with scissors into flower-petal shapes.

ratl: a rather variable unit of measure, in Baghdad very close to one pound avoirdupois (about 450 grams) and elsewhere equal to as much as 2.25 kilograms.

rhagīf: the sort of ordinary flat bread that was eaten every day, often a round and rather thick loaf (like *jardaq*) cooked in the oven.

rishtā: a term of Persian origin referring to pasta cut into strips, like Italian fettuccine or linguine. In contemporary Muslim cooking it refers to homemade noodles of this sort.

rukhāmiyya: rice cooked with meat and broth, milk, sheep tail fat, and white sugar.

rummāniyya: literally, "a dish with pomegranate"; in medieval recipe collections, typically described as meatballs in pomegranate juice.

ruqāq: a term derived from *raqīq* ("thin"), referring to a very thin bread similar to one still made today in the Middle East (also called *marqūq*) that is cooked on a *sāj,* a convex griddle of Turkish origin.

rutābiyya: a dish of meat and dates.

sahnā: according to some authorities, a sauce (as in its Egyptian version); according to others, a fish-based condiment or seasoning.

samn: clarified butter, often salted.

shaʿīriyya (or *shaʿriyya*): pasta that may have had the shape of a grain of barley in medieval times. Today it refers to vermicelli.

sharmūla: a fish sauce of raisins and various seasonings associated particularly with contemporary Tunisian cuisine.

shaubak (or *shawbak*): a rolling pin.

shibtiyya: a modern dish of fried cakes made with ground sardine fillets or other fish, served with a savory (often tomato-based) sauce.

sibāgh: the general Arabic term for sauces.

sikanjubīn: a syrupy drink thought to have medicinal properties.

sikbāj: a Persian word denoting a dish made with vinegar whose popularity reached its height in Baghdad under the ʿAbbasids.

sīr: according to some manuscripts, a salted fish that formed the basis for a condiment; other authorities suggest the term referred to fish cured without salt and pounded to a meal before cooking.

sitt al-shanāʾ: a dish of fried meat and taro mixed with *tahīna* and toasted hazelnuts.

tabāhaja: a beef dish meant to honor guests by its use of pistachios.

tahīna: sesame paste.

tājin: a type of pot or casserole; also the name of the stew cooked in it. Both are known today in English by the term *tajine* (or *tagine,* the French spelling of contemporary pronunciation).

tājīn: a cooking pot with straight sides.

tannūr: a bell-shaped oven, essentially a large clay pot in which a fire was built, for baking flat breads (against the inner wall) or roasting meats (on skewers, in the manner of the Indian tandoor today). It could be freestanding or set into the floor or wall.

tayfūra: a large serving dish used in Iraq.

tharīd: a classic Arab dish of the medieval period, favored by the prophet Muhammad and the object of a great many recipes that have in common only the soaking of crumbled bread in meat broth.

tiltīn (or *taltīn*): leavened dough that was kneaded, cut into squares two fingerwidths on a side, and then dried in the sun.

ʿujja: the generic name for omelet, of which a large number of types are recorded.

ūqiya: a unit of measure equal to ten *dirham.*

uskurruja: a cup used as a measure (an *uskurruja* of honey or vinegar, for example), but sometimes for the purpose of serving condiments. It must have been a very small sort of bowl, like the ones used in the Far East to bring sauces to the table.

zabībiyya: a fish dish served with a spicy sauce of vinegar and raisins.

zīrbāj: a sweet-and-sour dish of meat or poultry prepared with fruit or nuts.

zrīr: a honey-based dessert enriched with butter and flavored with nuts and seeds that have been toasted and crushed.

zubdiyya: a serving dish used in Egypt and the Middle East.

zulābiyya mushabbaka: a kind of fritter made by dripping batter into hot oil to form intricate latticed designs, then dipping the pastry in flavored honey and coloring it with turmeric and other spices; known in Syria today simply as *mushabbak,* and in Tunisia as *zlābiya.* In Indian restaurants it is familiar as *jelebi.*

INDEX OF RECIPES

GENERAL INDEX

ʿAbbasids: Baghdad caliphate of, xii, 4–5, 13; culinary interests of, 10, 22, 41, 43–44; golden age of, 13; pastries of, 131; recipe books of, xxiii; revolts against, 38; sauces of, 129; sequence of courses, 56; sweet-and-sour dishes of, 77; table etiquette of, 57

Abu al-Alaʿ al-Maʾarri, 30–31

Abū Harb, 38

Abū al-Hindī, 20, 28–29

Abū Ishāq. See Ibn al-Mahdī, Abū Ishāq Ibrāhīm

Abū Yaʿqūb al-Dhaqnān, 20–21

Afghanistan: cookware of, 125; Islam in, 5; sugar production in, 131

Africa Nova, 25. See also North Africa

agriculture: of Asir, 26; treatises on, 42

ʿAʾisha (wife of Muhammad), 68

Akhbār as-Sīn wa-l-Hind (manuscript), 17

alcohol, taboos concerning, in Islam, 31–34. See also wine

Aleppo: recipe books of, 6; rise of influence, x

Alexandria, sauces of, 129, 130

Algeria: Berbers of, 7; cuisine of, 47, 77,

82, 192n2; festivals of, 73; meat dishes of, 69; Romans in, 25

alica (soup), 114

Almohad dynasty, 7; conquests of, 32

almonds: fish with, 102; in sweet-and-sour dishes, 80, 84–85

Almoravids, 15

America, vegetables of, 46, 59

al-Amīn, Caliph, 39, 40

ʿAmr bin ʿAbd Manaf, 68

Andalusia: Almohad conquest of, 32; Asian influence in, 7; Berber influence in, 13, 15; feast days of, 73; Umayyad control of, 13. See also cuisine, Andalusian

André, Jacques, 186n25

Apicius, Marcus Gavius, 22, 23, 63; sauces of, 41, 54; use of spices, 24

appetizers: bārida, 63, 64–65; carrots in, 66–67; cold, 12, 63–67; eggplant in, 63, 66; fava beans in, 66; hazelnuts in, 66; leeks in, 66–67; tahīna in, 66; yogurt in, 66

apricots: lamb stew with, 151; in sweet-and-sour dishes, 81–83, 85

Arabian peninsula, freedom from foreign domination, 25

Arab language: food in, 20; poetry, 26; scientific treatises in, 5

Arabs: cultural influences of, 26; dietary obsessions of, 20–25; eastern vs. western, xii; nomadic culture of, 26; Shuʿūbiyya movement opposing, 19–20; trade routes of, 16–18, 26, 27; trade with China, 16–18; tribes of, 25

Arberry, A. J., 11

aromatic substances: ancient, 22; Andalusian, 43; herbs, 54; in medieval Islamic cuisine, 52–53, 189n6; pepper, 144

aruzziyya (rice), 40–41, 127–28

ʿĀshūrāʾ, festival of, 71, 72

Asir, agriculture of, 26

aspic, 188n52; origins of, xiv. See also *sikbāj*

Asyut, recipes of, 14

Atlas Mountains (Morocco), 8

atrāf ṭīb (condiment), 54, 58; with eggplant, 95; in sweet-and-sour dishes, 78, 79–80

Avicenna. See Ibn Sina

Ayyubids, end of reign, 14

baba ghannouj, 66

Babylon, cuisine of, 23–24

bādhinjān (eggplant), 92; *būrān*, xvii–xviii

Baghdad: ʿAbbasid caliphate of, xii, 4–5, 13; *bārida* of, 63; cuisine of, ix–x, 6–7, 13, 14, 40–41; culinary literature of, 9, 14; cultural diversity of, 4; decline of, x, 4; elite of, 40; freshwater fish of, 191n1; gastron-

omy of, 41; House of Wisdom, 5, 185n3; professional chefs of, x; urban culture of, 5–6

al-Baghdādī, Muhammad ibn al-Karīm al-Kātib, 55. See also *Kitāb al-ṭabīkh*

bahārāt (spice mixture), 145

Bahdal, Maysūn bint, 18–19

banādiq (meatballs), 153

bananas: cakes, 43; fried, 83–84, 133; in sweet-and-sour dishes, 82, 83–84

Banū Ghassān. *See* Ghassanids

Banū Hilāl tribe, 13

bārida (appetizers), 63, 64–65; chicken, 64; fish, 64–65

barkūkish (couscous), 119

al-Barmakī, Ahmad: *Kitāb al-ṭabīkh al-laṭīf*, 10; *Kitāb faḍāʾil al-sikbāj*, 10

basbāsiyya (fish dish), 102–3

Bashshār ibn Burd, 19

Basra: Buyid emirs of, 5; recipes of, 15

bawārid (appetizers), 12

bazergān couscous, 175

Bedouins: diet of, 19; eloquence of, 18; lamb dishes of, 89; way of life, 26

beef: with pistachios, 79–80; with rosebuds, 93

Benchecroun, Mohamed, 104

Berbers: influence in Andalusia, 13, 15; influence of, xii, 7; language of, 25; tribes of, 44. *See also* cuisine, Berber

bestilla (pigeon pie), 158

bharat (spice mixture), 145

Bidʿa (chef), 12, 38–40; recipes of, 40, 41

birāf (dairy dish), 110
bizār (spice), 145
Bizerte, fish dishes of, 64, 165
Bolens, Lucie, 41
bread: and broth, 68–75; condiments
    for, 188n54; *fatīr*, 72–73, 74, 75,
    190n4; in sequence of courses,
    56–57
bread crumbs, in soups, 111–12
bream, with grape juice, 64–65, 99
Brethren of Purity, 5
brīk, 108, 191n1; in contemporary
    North African cuisine, 146, 156,
    158, 163, 182; *dannūni*, 107, 156,
    192n1; tuna and, 163
broth: bread and, 68–75; chicken,
    119–20; couscous in, 123; *itriya*,
    119–20; rice and, 125–26
al-Bukhārī, 28
bunn (condiment), xi, 55
Būrān, Lady, xvii, xviii
burghul (soup), 114
butter, salted, 24. See also *samn*
Buyid emirs, 4, 186n12; wine con-
    sumption under, 33
Byzantium, culinary traditions of, 37

Cairo: al-Azhar mosque, 5; recipe
    books of, 6
cakes: cheese and egg, 109; *falūdhaj*,
    27; fish, 103; layered, 108; *mersu*, 23;
    salty-sweet, 48; sponge, 136
calendar, lunar, 34–35
calzones, stuffed with fish, 104
candies, in Arab cuisine, xvi. *See also*
    desserts
Canton, Iraqi merchants at, 17

cardamom, eastern use of, 53
carrots: in appetizers, 66–67; in jams,
    134–35
Carthage, Romans in, 25
cereal preserves, 44
cheese, 106–9; dry, 109, 138–39;
    dumplings, 44, 106; and egg cake,
    109; in fish balls, 100; *masliyya*, 28;
    shirāz, 58, 138; on skewers, 109; in
    Tunisian cuisine, 107
chefs, professional: of Baghdad, x
Chelebi, Daud, 10
cherries, *marwaziyya* with, 79
chicken: in *bārida*, 64; broth with
    bread crumbs, 111–12; broth with
    itriya, 119–20; in contemporary
    North African cuisine, 148; with
    Seville oranges, 93–94; in sweet-
    and-sour dishes, 80, 81–83,
    84–85, 190n2; in *tharīd*, 70, 72–73,
    74–75
chickpeas: puree of, 65; with rice, 126
China: Arab trade with, 16–18; cui-
    sine of, 16–17; tableware of, 18
Christianity, dietary rules of, 29, 30
Christians: Armenian, 92; taxation
    of, 38; wine production by, 32
Christians, Ethiopian: ban on pork,
    187n35
cinnamon: fish with, 100; in rice
    dishes, 125
citron peels, candied, 134
coconut, in pastries, 132
condiments: in Andalusian cuisine,
    54; *atrāf tīb*, 54, 58, 78, 79–80, 95;
    for bread, 188n54; *bunn*, xi, 55;
    cheese, 109; disappearance of, 46;

condiments (*continued*)
fermented, 53, 54–56, 60, 139–40; *kāmakh*, 46, 47, 54, 140, 188n54; *khall al-mazza*, 145; Mediterranean Muslim, 43; *murrī*, xi, xii, 46, 47, 54–55; recreation of, 54–56; *sahnā*, 105; *shiqqu*, 23–24; in sweet-and-sour dishes, 77; in *Wusla*, 54
confectioners, Middle Eastern, xvi
Constantine the African, 43
cookbooks: European, 45; medieval Arabic, ix–x. *See also* recipes
cooking: duration of, 58; simplicity in, 7
cookware, 4, 11, 49–52; cleaning of, 3; iron, 50; materials for, 188n3; types of, 50–51; utensils, 51–52
Córdoba (Spain): cuisine of, 42; Islamic culture of, 5
coriander, 24
couscous, 121–24, 192nn1–2; *barkūkish*, 119; *bazergān*, 175; in Berber cuisine, 121; in broth, 123; in contemporary North African cuisine, 173–75; European recipes for, 45–46; lamb, 173–75; with meat, 121–22; Moroccan, 124; with mutton, 123–24; North African, xiii, 121; origins of, 121; pot for, 122; *samn* in, 122, 124; semolina in, 121; with walnuts, 123; and yogurt, 124
Crusades: prohibition of wine following, 32; recipes from, 14
cuisine: Algerian, 47, 77, 82, 192n2; Asian nomadic, 7; Babylonian, 23–24; Byzantine, 37; Chinese, 16–17; of Fertile Crescent, 65;

Mamluk, 43; Mesopotamian, 23–24; of Muslim West, 44; Nabataean, x, xi; Ottoman, xviii, 13; of Sfax, 113, 114; of Sicily, 45; Uzbek, 125
cuisine, Andalusian, 6, 41–42, 43; Berber influence on, 15; condiments in, 54; dumplings in, 106; eggplant in, 92; fish in, 96; of Murcia, 6, 15–16; pasta in, 111, 118–19; soups in, 112, 113; spices in, 42; sweet-and-sour dishes in, 82–83; *tharīd* in, 44, 72
cuisine, Berber, 44; couscous in, 121; dumplings in, 106; influence on Arabs, xii; vinegar in, 23
cuisine, Christian, 187n35; during Lent, xxiii; *tharīd* in, 69, 75
cuisine, Egyptian, 44; condiments in, 54; eggplant in, 92; jute plant in, 93; meat in, 88–89; pasta in, 116; spices in, 145; taro in, 84; vinegar use in, 23
cuisine, European: Arab influence on, xiii–xv; couscous in, 45–46; fish sauce in, xiv; French, 144; influence of *sikbāj* on, 188n52; influence on Arabs, xiii–xiv; *tharīd* and, 189n8. *See also* cuisine, Italian
cuisine, Greco-Roman: influence on medieval Islamic cuisine, 22–25; spices in, 63. *See also* Apicius, Marcus Gavius; cuisine, Roman
cuisine, Greek: influence on Arabic cuisine, xi; Ottoman influence on, xviii; yogurt stew in, 90–91
cuisine, Indian, 44, 95, 125, 126; pilaf in, 193n1

cuisine, Italian, 45–46, 116; crayfish in, 104; eggplant in, 92; Mahgrebi influence on, 24; pomegranates in, 78; regional, 24; *salmoriglio* in, 129

cuisine, Jewish: in medieval Arabic texts, xxiii; *tharīd* in, 75

cuisine, medieval Arab: of Baghdad, ix–x, 6–7, 13, 14, 40–41; Berber influence on, xii; candies in, xvi; Chinese influence on, 16–17; criticism of, 18–20; cultural borrowings in, 7; eggplant in, xvii–xviii; European influence on, xiii–xiv; evolution of, xvii–xviii; grains in, xiii; influence in Europe, xiii–xv, 44–46; Mediterranean, 43; molds in, xi–xii; and Persian cuisine, 40; pork in, xxiii; presentation of dishes in, 53; sequence of courses in, 56–57; spices in, xvi, 46, 47; staple crops of, xv; sweeteners in, xvi; terminology of, 57–58; in tradition of the Prophet, 25–29; weights in, 58

cuisine, medieval Islamic: aromatic substances in, 52–53; diversity in, 8; early, 25–29; eastern vs. western, 15; exoticism in, 16–18; fish in, 96; Greco-Roman influence on, 22–25; manuscript sources of, 8–16; Qur'anic proscriptions concerning, 29–36; regional differences in, 13–14; sauces in, 129

cuisine, modern Arab: medieval heritage of, xv, 59; national, 47; spice mixtures of, 145. *See also* cuisine, North African contemporary

cuisine, Moroccan: couscous in, 124; fish in, 101; mutton in, 47; pies in, 48, 158; stews in, 150

cuisine, North African, xii, 13; couscous in, xiii, 121; fish in, 191n1; grains in, xiii; influence on Italian cuisine, 24; *murrī* in, xii; pasta in, 117; salt in, 144; soups in, 111, 113; soy sauce in, 189n6; spices in, 24; sweet-and-sour dishes in, 76; *tharīd* in, 44; vinegar in, 47; in *Wusla*, 14; *zulābiyya* in, 132

cuisine, North African contemporary, 144–84; *brīk* in, 146, 156, 158, 163, 182; chicken in, 148; dates in, 178–79; desserts in, 177–84; eggplant in, 149, 164; fish in, 161–66; jute leaves in, 146; lamb in, 151–52, 173–75; meatballs in, 153; *mulūkhiyya* in, 146, 157; pasta in, 117, 169–72; *qatā'if*, 182; quince in, 184; salt in, 144; semolina in, 178–79; spices in, 144–46; squab in, 159; stews in, 149–51, 155; tahini in, 146; veal in, 149; vegetarian dishes in, 167; *zulābiyya* in, 181

cuisine, Persian: and Arab cuisine, 40; of Baghdad, 6–7; influence of, 24; stews in, x

cuisine, Roman, 22; honey in, 24; vinegar in, 24. *See also* Apicius, Marcus Gavius; cuisine, Greco-Roman

cuisine, Syrian: fish in, 191n1; *tharīd* in, 70

cuisine, Tunisian, xix, 52; *bārida* in, 64; bird stew in, 42; cheese in, 107;

cuisine, Tunisian (*continued*)
fish in, 97, 166; meatballs in, 153;
Montaigne on, 52; *mulūkhiyya* in,
157; national, 47; salt in, 144;
sausages in, 88; semolina in,
191n1; soups in, 112; stews in, 150;
tableware in, 51; *tharīd* in, 69, 71–
73
cuisine, Turkish, 5; *boranis* in, xviii
culinary history, sources of, 8–16
culture, Arab: food in, 20–22
cumin, fish with, 102

dairy dishes, 106–10
dakbaryān (steamed meat and rice),
125–26
Damascus: economy of, 37; gastronomy of, 18, 36–38; Umayyads of,
36–37
dashīsh, 113
dates: and milk, 28; paste, 178–79; in
porridge, x; squab with, 159;
stuffed, 180; in sweet-and-sour
dishes, 84
al-Daula, Saif, x
dawīda, 72
deg (steamer), 125
desserts, in contemporary North
African cuisine, 177–84. *See also*
specific desserts
dhimmī (infidels), 37–38
diet: Arab, 20–25; asceticism in, 21; in
hadith, 28; treatises on, xxiii–xxiv,
13
Dioscorides, 43
Dīwān, 186n19

drunkenness. *See* intoxication
dumplings: cheese, 44, 106; fried,
106; semolina in, 106–7
duwīda (pasta), 170

East, Muslim: cuisine of, 44
eggplant, 41; in Andalusian cuisine,
92; in appetizers, 63, 66; *atrāf tīb*
with, 95; in contemporary North
African cuisine, 149, 164; in Italian
cuisine, 92; meatballs with, 93; in
medieval Arab cuisine, xvii–xviii;
prejudice against, 92, 190n1; *sikbāj*
with, 77–78; stuffed, 94; in sweet-
and-sour sauces, 94–95; tuna and,
164; veal and, 47, 149
eggs: and cheese, 109; *mujabbana*
with, 108–9; toppings, xix
Egypt: peasant revolts in, 38; Roman
domination of, 25; sugar cultivation in, 131; Turkish influence on,
13. *See also* cuisine, Egyptian
epicureanism, 21–22. *See also* gastronomy
escabèche (cold dish), xiv, 44; variants
and related dialect names, xiv–xv,
45
etiquette: table, 57, 69, 189n8; of
wine, 33, 34
exoticism, search for, 17

fākhitiyya (stew), xvi–xvii
fālūdhaj (cake), 27
farina, cream of, 112
fasting, 30; during Ramadan, 29
Fatimids, 5, 7, 42; serving dishes of, 51

fatīr (flat bread), 72–73, 74, 75, 190n4

al-fatīr wa mā yatīr (pasta and chicken), 71

fava beans, in appetizers, 66

fennel, fish with, 102–3

fenugreek, in soup, 113

Fertile Crescent: cuisine of, 65; nomadic influence in, 7

Fez, Islamic culture of, 5

fidāwish (pasta), 116–17

fish, 96–114; balls, 100, 102, 103, 104–5; *bārida*, 64–65; bream, 99; cakes, 103; in calzones, 104; with cinnamon, 100; in contemporary North African cuisine, 161–66; with cumin and saffron, 102; with fennel, 102–3; with fruits, 46; with ginger and cheese, 100; in grape juice, 64–65, 99; herring, 161; in Islamic cuisine, 96; with lemon, 97; marinated, 46; in Moroccan cuisine, 101; mullet, 103–4; with *murrī*, 98, 99, 100, 139; with nuts, 46; and pickled vegetables, 47; and potato pie, 161; with raisins, 96; in raisin sauce, 43, 165–66; roasted, 98, 100; salted, 47, 166; salted and seasoned, 97; sardines, 100–1, 102, 103, 162; shad, 101; *sikbāj*, 98; *sīr*, 97, 139; as starters, 63; in Syrian cuisine, 191n1; in Tunisian cuisine, 97, 166; *zirbāj*, 97

fish sauce, 65, 130; European, xiv; Roman, 22, 54

fonio (millet), 121

food: in Arab culture, 20–22; coloring of, 53; as divine reward, 31; imported, 16, 18; public distribution of, 37

food culture: Arabic, 20–22; of Nabataea, x, xi; Persian, ix–x; Turkish, xiii, 5

food terminology: ʿAbbasid, 43–44; Aramaic, x

forks, Western-style, 189n8

France, Arab cuisine in, 144

Franks, cuisine of, 14, 89–90, 190n1

freeloaders (*mutataffil*), 21

Fridays, meatless, 30

fritters, 193n2; honey, 36

fruits: apricots, 81–83, 85, 151; bananas, 43, 82, 83–84, 133; cherries, 79; dates, x, 28, 84, 159, 178–79, 180; grapes, 23, 45; lemons, 97, 148; with meat, 46; oranges, 93–94; in paradise, 31; pears, 177; prunes, 79; in stews, xix; in sweet-and-sour dishes, 76, 79, 80, 81–82, 83–85. *See also* quince

ftāyr (cream puff), 132

fulyātil (pastry), xii

Galen of Pergamum: *On the Properties of Foods*, 9

garlic, in soup, 112

garum (fish sauce), 22, 54

gastronomy, 16–18; in Arab literature, 8, 9; of Baghdad, 41; of Damascus, 18, 36–38

Gelder, Geert Jan van, 185n5, 186n19

ghannāy (pan), 72

Ghassanids, 7, 26

mad al-Muzaffar: aristocratic background of, 186n10; profession of, 11. See also *Kitāb al-tabīkh*

Ibn Shahma al-ʿAnbarī, Thawb, 21–22

Ibn Sinā, 5; *Canon of Medicine*, 115

Ibn Sīrīn, 20

Ibn Sulaymān al-Isrāʾīlī, Abū Yaʿqūb Ishāq, 42–43; *Book on Dietetics* ("The Book of Foods and Cures"), xxii–xxiv, 9, 43; on pasta, 115

Ibn al-Wadīʿ: and Ibn al-Rafīʿ, 189n2; *shāshiyya* of, 70, 189n2

Ibn Zarqūn: *Burning of the Embers for Prohibiting Wine*, 32

Ibn Zuhr Abū Marwān ʿAbd al-Mālik: on cookware, 188n3; on hygiene, 50

ibrāhīmiyya (recipe), 12

ʿid al-fitr (festival), 36, 47, 166

identity conflicts, culinary traditions and, 18–20

incense, trade in, 27

India: in Arab manuscripts, 17; cuisine of, 44, 95, 125, 126, 193; spices of, 16, 24, 41, 144; trade with, 18

Indian Ocean, ports of, 18

intoxication: public displays of, 32; Qurʾanic proscriptions concerning, 31–34

invalids, vegetarian dishes for, x–xi

Iran: Persian conquest of, ix; pilaf of, xiii

Iraq: crops of, 38; intellectual preeminence of, 5; nomadic Asian influences in, 7; trade with China, 17

Isfahan, *sibāgh* from, 130

isfunj al-qulla (sponge cake), 136

iskirfāj (grater), 75

Islam: culinary history of, 8–16; cultural centers of, 4–5; East-West divide in, 15; food literature of, ix; Jewish scholars of, 42; tradition in, 27. See also cuisine, medieval Islamic

Islam, Sunni: Hanafi rite of, 31

Italy, Arab cuisine in, 45–46, 116. See also cuisine, Italian

itriya (noodles), 115–16; with chicken broth, 119–20

Izz al-Dīn al-Wāsitī, 95

jāhiliyya (age of ignorance), 27

al-Jāhiz: *Kitāb al-Bukhalāʾ*, 20–21, 40; table etiquette in, 189n8; *tharīd* in, 68

jams, 133–36; carrot, 134–35; squash, 135

jashīsh (semolina), 113–14

jelly, quince, 184

Jews: dietary rules of, 29, 30; expulsion from Granada, 73; festivals of, 35; and Islamic scholars, 42; taxation of, 38; wine production of, 32

jizya (tax), 38

jūdhāba (pudding), 125–26

Jurjan (Persia), 14

jute leaves, 44, 48, 146; in Egyptian cuisine, 93; meatballs with, 95

kabkābu (fish dish), 47

Kabylia, 192n2; Berbers of, 7

kahla (mullet), 103–4

Kalah, Arab trade at, 18

Kalb tribe, 18

kāmakh, 54, 140, 188n54; disappearance of, 46, 47; sequence in serving, 56; in *tharīd,* 70

kāmak rījāl (condiment), xi–xii

Kanz al-Fawāʾid fi tanwīʿ al-mawāʿid, 10; regional diversity in, 13–14; sweet-and-sour dishes in, 77

khabīs (pancake), 136

khall al-mazza (condiment), 145

kharāj (tithe), 37

al-Khatib, Durriyya, 186n14

khātūnī (rice dish), 127

Khosrau I (king of Persia), xiii, 39

Khosrau II (king of Persia), 27

Khusrau i Kavātān u Rētak Ē, ix

Kippur, Hebrew festival of, 35

kishk (cereal preserves), 44

Kitāb al-aghdhiya wa-l-adwiya, 45

Kitāb Fadālat al-khiwān fi tayyibāt al-taʿām wa-l-alwān (Ibn Razīn al-Tujībī), 10; cookware in, 51; couscous in, 10, 121; eggplant in, 94; fish in, 63; *murrī* in, 55; purpose of, 11; sequence of courses in, 57; *shāshiyya* in, 70; shrimp in, 96, 104

Kitāb al-tabīkh (al-Baghdādī): Iranian influence in, 10–11; *murrī* of, 55; *sikbāj* in, 14

Kitāb al-tabīkh (Ibn Sayyār al-Warrāq), 10; composition of, 185n7; cooking equipment in, 4, 11, 52; eggplant in, 190n1; "false" dishes in, xxiii; fish in, 63; hygiene in, 11, 49; omelets in, 128; pasta in, xiii; recipe details in, 12; roasts in, 86; *sahnā* in, 193n1; steaming in,

125; *tharīd* in, 69; on utensils, 52; wine in, 32–33; *zulābiyya* in, 131

Kitāb al-Wusla ilā habīb fi wasf al-tayyibāt wa-l-tīb. See *Wusla*

kofta, 87, 154

Kulam Mali (India), 17

Kulthum, Umm, 36

kunāfa (pancakes), 136–37, 190n4

Kurdistan, 23

Kushājim (poet), x, xvii

kushkāt (soup), 111

Kutāma tribe, 44

Lakhmids, 26

lākhshā (pasta), xiii

lamb: in contemporary North African cuisine, 151–52; couscous, 173–75; and pasta, 169, 170; roast, 89–90; soup, 169; stew, 151. See also mutton

Lebanon, 48

leeks, in appetizers, 66–67

lemon: in chicken stew, 148; fish with, 97

Lent, Christian cookery during, xxiii

Lévy, Jacques-Victor: *La véritable cuisine tunisienne,* 47

Liber de coquinaria, 78

Libya, 97

līmūniyya (fish dish), 97

liquamen (sauce), 54

literature, Arab: gastronomy in, 8, 9; poetry, 26

locusts (*ghathīma*), x, 140

maʿāsim el-bey ("king's wrists"), 152

madqūqa (pounded meat), 86–87

Maghreb: Almohad conquest of, 32;

feast days of, 73. *See also* cuisine, North African; North Africa

Mago of Carthage, 114

Mahjūb, Sulaymā, 186n14

malsuka (pastry), 152

Mamluks: beginning of reign, 14; cuisine of, 43

al-Ma'mūn, Caliph, xvii, 185n3; recipes of, 64

Manuscrito anónimo (thirteenth century), 11, 16; *tharīd* in, 189n3; Ziryāb in, 42

maqrūd, 132, 178–79

ma'qūda (fish dish), 103; *bir-ringa*, 161

Marín, Manuela, 186n13

marqa hluwwa (sweet stew), 69

marqit 'asāfīr (bird stew), 42

marrow, artificial, 90

Martellotti, Anna, xiv, 188n52

marwaziyya, with cherries, 79

Mashriq, extent of, 15

Masinissa, King, 25

Maslama, Abū: *Garden of Joys in the Description of the Reality of Wine*, 32

masliyya, 6–7, 28

al-Mas'ūdī: *Meadows of Gold*, 5

Mauritania: Berbers of, 121; mutton in, 123

mdarbil (veal and eggplant), 47, 77, 149

meat: beef, 79–80, 93; couscous with, 121–22; in Egyptian cuisine, 88–89; hygiene surrounding, 49; *kofta*, 154; lamb, 89–90, 151–52, 169, 170, 173–75; minced, 48; with nuts, 46; pork, xxiii, 29, 187n35; pounded, 86–87; roasted, 86–87;

sauces for, 43; sugared, 69; veal, 47, 149

meatballs, 48; with eggplant, 93; fried, 87; with jute leaves, 95; in pomegranate juice, 78–79; Tunisian, 153; with vinegar, 87–88

Mecca, caravan trade of, 27

medical texts, Arabic, xiv

Medina, Muslim community of, 28

merguez, 155

mersu (cake), 23

Mesopotamia: Asian influence in, 7; cuisine of, 23–24; cultural diversity in, 7

Middle East: anti-alcohol attitudes in, 32; contemporary cuisine of, 6; couscous in, 121; influence in Sicily, 45; *samn* in, 24; spices of, 53; tableware of, 51; *zulābiyya* in, 132

milk: curdled, 110; and dates, 28. *See also* dairy dishes

mint, in sweet-and-sour dishes, 78, 79

mithrad (vessel), 51; in couscous preparation, 122; for dumplings, 107; in soup preparation, 112; for *tharīd*, 71, 72, 74

moghrabiyyeh (pilaf), xiii

molds, in medieval Arabic cuisine, xi–xii

Montaigne, Michel de, 52

Morocco: Atlas Mountains of, 8; Berbers of, 7; spices of, 24, 46; tableware of, 18. *See also* cuisine, Moroccan

Mosul, cuisine of, 14

Mroueh, Sahban, 185n2

pasta, 115–20; in Andalusian cuisine, 111, 118–19; angel-hair, 170; and chicken, 71; in contemporary North African cuisine, 117, 169–72; Greek origins of, xiii; *hasu*, 111, 118–19; *itriya*, 115–16; lamb and, 169, 170; *muhammas*, 118, 119; of Muslim West, 44; *nuwāsir*, 171–72; *rishtā*, 115; semolina in, 119; *sha'iriyya*, 117–18; sparrows' tongues, 169; *tiltīn*, 118; *treyya*, 116

pastries, 131–33; coconut in, 132; honey in, 132–33, 135; *malsuka*, 152; quince in, 133–34; Sasanid, 27; semolina in, 132, 136

pears, candied, 177

peasant revolts, 38

pepper: Aleppo, 144; in modern cuisine, 53, 144

Perry, Charles, 11, 55, 185n8, 188n52; on *fatīr*, 190n4

Persia: food culture of, ix–x; language of, 5

Persian Gulf, ports of, 18

petonciano (eggplant), 92

Phoenicians, spread of culinary traditions, 23

physicians: Christian, x; culinary interests of, 8–9

pies: Andalusian, 82–83; fish and potato, 161; pigeon, 158; salty-sweet, 48

pilaf, 193n1; Iranian invention of, xiii

pine nuts: fish with, 102; pancakes with, 108

Pisa, Almohad relations with, 16

pistachios: beef with, 79–80; pancakes with, 108; rice with, 127

Pliny the Elder, 114

poets, Arab, 26

pomegranate juice: meatballs in, 78–79; in sauces, 129–30

pork: Ethiopian Christians on, 187n35; in medieval Arab cuisine, xxiii; prohibition of, 29, 187n35

porridge, dates in, x

prunes, in sweet-and-sour dishes, 79

puddings, 81; *fālūdhaj*, 37; *jūdhāba*, 125–26; *muhallabiyya*, xvi

puff paste, in *tharīd*, 71

qamhiyya (puree of wheat), 113–14

Qarqannah Islands, cuisine of, 113, 166

qatā'if (dessert), 182

qawalib (incised stamp), 178

Qayrawan, Islamic culture of, 5

qidr (tableware), 51

quarry, Qur'anic proscriptions concerning, 30

quince: in contemporary North African cuisine, 184; jelly, 184; in meat stew, 150; in pastries, 133–34; in sweet-and-sour dishes, 80; syrup, 134; tagine, 150

Quraysh tribe, 27, 37

raisins: fish with, 96; honey wine with, 140–41; sauces, 43, 165–66

Ramadan, 34–36; culinary tradition of, 36; evening meal during, 35–36; fasting during, 29; recipes for, 113, 166; rhythm of, 35; *sahūr* during, 35; *zulābiyya* during, 132

ras el-hanut (spice mixture), 146

al-Rāzī, Abū Bakr: *Manāfiʿ al-aghdhiya wa madārrihā*, 9; on wine, 33

recipes, medieval Arabic: anonymous texts, 16; of caliph al-Maʾmūn; of caliph al-Wāthiq, 64, 81; circulation of, 42; disappearance of, 46, 47; Greek influence on, xi; male authors of, 16; medicinal, xiv, 13; names of, xvi; for Ramadan, 113; recreation of, 54–56, 58–60; for special occasions, xv–xvi; survival of, xvii; transmission of, ix, 46–48; utensils in, 51–52. *See also* cookbooks

Red Sea: Arabs of, 25; ports of, 18, 26

rice, 125–28; *aruzziyya*, 40–41, 127–28; chickpeas with, 126; cinnamon in, 125; Indian, 126, 193n1; *khātūnī*, 127; marbled, 126–27; in meat broth, 125–26; *mufalfal*, 126, 127; with pistachios, 127; rose water in, 125; *samn* in, 126; in soup, 114; with spinach, 128; yellow and white, 127; with yogurt, 127

rishtā (pasta), xiii, 115

roasts: fish, 98, 100; lamb, 89–90; meat, 86–87; mutton, 86; scented stuffing for, 90

Roman Empire, influence in Arabia of, 25. *See also* cuisine, Roman

rosebuds, beef with, 93

rose water: in rice, 125; syrup, 78

Rufus of Ephesus, 9

Sabbath, *tharīd* of, 75

al-Safasī, Ahmad, 110

saffron, 24; fish with, 102; in me-

dieval Arabic cuisine, 53; in sweet-and-sour dishes, 83

sahnā (condiment), 105, 140, 193n1; from Baghdad, 130

salads, 92

salmoriglio (sauce), 129

salt: in contemporary North African cuisine, 144; shad in, 101

Samanids, Islamic culture of, 5

Samarkand, 14

samn (butter), 24, 58; in couscous, 122, 124; in griddle cakes, 137; in rice, 126; in *tharīd*, 73

Sanhāja tribe, 44

San Vito (Italy), Cuscus Fest, 45

sardines: in contemporary North African cuisine, 162; fried, 102, 103; grilled, 100–1; with nuts, 102; *shibtiyya*, 162; timbale, 101

Sasanians/Sasanids: culinary traditions of, 37; cultural influence of, 7; food culture of, ix; pastries of, 27

sauces: ʿAbbasid, 129; Alexandrian, 129, 130; of Apicius, 41, 54; chicken fat, 129–30; fish, xiv, 22; meat, 43; pomegranate juice in, 129–30; raisin, 43, 165–66; soy, 189n6; sweet-and-sour, 47, 94–95. *See also sibāgh*

sausages, 52; liver, 88; mutton, 44; in *tharīd*, 69; in Tunisian cuisine, 88

Sauvaget, Jean, 186n17

scallops, smoked, 88–89

seasonings, compound, 53–54

Seljuks, consumption of wine, 33–34

semolina: caramelized, 135–36; in contemporary North African cuisine, 178–79; in couscous, 121; in dumplings, 106–7; in pasta, 119; in pastries, 132, 136; in soup, 113–14; in Tunisian cuisine, 191n1

serving dishes, 50, 51

sesame: paste, 44; in *zrīr*, 183

Seville (Spain): Almohads of, 7; cuisine of, 13, 92

Sfax, cuisine of, 113, 114

shad, in salt, 101

shaʿīriyya (pasta), 117–18

sharmūla, 47, 166

shāshiyya, 189n8; of Ibn al-Wadīʿ, 70, 189n2

shibtiyya (sardines), 162

shiqqu (condiment), 23–24

shirāz (cheese), 58, 138

shiwā ifranjī (Frankish dish), 14, 89–90, 190n1

shorbā (soup), xvi

shrimp, 96, 104

Shūʿūbiyya movement, 19–20

sibāgh (sauces), 129; for fish, 65, 130; from Isfahan, 130; for long-distance travel, 129, 130. *See also* sauces

Sicily, cuisine of, 45

sikanjubīn, 110, 184; quince, 133; *safarjalī*, 192n2

sikbāj, xiv; of Baghdad, 6, 7; al-Baghdādī on, 14; with eggplant, 77–78; etymology of, 185n1; fish, 98; influence on European cuisine, 188n52; olfactory elements of, 39; original forms of, 77; popularity of, 8, 39, 44; preparation of, 3; in Spanish cuisine, 44; *tharīd* in, 40; vinegar in, 22

sīr (fish), 97, 139, 191n2

sitt al-nawba (sweet-and-sour dish), 84–85

sitt al-nūba (sweet-and-sour dish), 190n2

sitt al-shanāʿ, 83–84

slaughter, ritual, 29

slaves: exploitation of, 37; Zanj, 38

sman (butter), xii. *See also samn*

soups, 111–14; in Andalusian cuisine, 112, 113; *burghul*, 114; fenugreek in, 113; garlic in, 112; lamb, 169; in Maghrebi cuisine, 111; rice in, 114; semolina in, 113–14; sourdough, 112–13; with sparrows' tongues and lamb, 169; wheat with meat, 111

sour dishes, 43, 188n51. *See also* sweet-and-sour dishes

soy sauce: Chinese, 54; infused, xii; Iraqi-style, 189n6. *See also nuoc mam*

Spain: Almohad dynasty in, 7; Arabic cuisine of, xii. *See also* Andalusia

sparrows' tongues (pasta), 169

spice mixtures: *bharat*, 145; *offah*, 145; *ras el-hanut*, 146

spices: in Andalusian cuisine, 42; in antiquity, 24; in Arab cuisine, xvi, 46, 47, 145; availability of, 144; *bizār*, 145; in contemporary North African cuisine, 144–46; coriander, 24; in Egyptian cuisine, 145; Indian, 16, 24, 41, 144; Maghrebi, 24; mixtures, 53–54, 145–46; in modern cuisine, 53; Roman, 63; saffron, 24; trade in, 27; turmeric, 24; in Yemeni cuisine, 145 spinach, rice with, 128

squab, with dates, 159

squash: in jams, 135; in *murūziyya*, 167

starch, in griddle cakes, 137

stews, 92–95; bird, 42; in contemporary North African cuisine, 149–51, 155; fruit juice in, xix; lamb, 151; lemon chicken, 148; meat with quince, 150; in Moroccan cuisine, 150; in Persian cuisine, x; pickled vegetable, 155; sour flavorings of, 188n51; sweet, 69; sweet-and-sour, 81; taro in, 92; in Tunisian cuisine, 150; yogurt, 90–91

stoves, medieval Arabic, 52

Strait of Gibraltar, 7

sturgeon, proscription of, 30

sugarcane, cultivation of, 38, 131

sumac, eastern use of, 53

sunna (tradition of Muhammad), 27; *tharīd* in, 68

sweet-and-sour dishes, 76–85; acidity of, 76; almonds in, 80, 84–85; in Andalusian cuisine, 82–83; apricots in, 81–83, 85; *atrāf tīb* in, 78, 79–80; bananas in, 82, 83–84; chicken in, 80, 81–83, 84–85, 190n2; condiments in, 77; dates in, 84; fruits in, 76, 79, 80, 81–82, 83–85; mint in, 78, 79; in North African cuisine, 76; onions in, 81; prunes in, 79; quince in, 80; saffron in, 83; stews, 81; *zirbāj* in, 80–81

sweet-and-sour sauces, 47; eggplant in, 94–95; thickening of, 76

sweeteners, in medieval Arab cuisine, xvi

syrups: Mediterranean Muslim, 43; quince, 134; rose water, 778; vinegars in, 76

tableware: Tunisian, 51; types of, 50–51; *zubdiyyas*, 90, 91

Tacuinum sanitatis, 45

tagines (stews), xix

tahīna (sesame paste), 44, 58, 95; in appetizers, 66

tahini, in contemporary North African cuisine, 146

tahīniyya, 66

tājīn (tableware), 51

tājin malsuqa, 82

takhmīr (egg topping), xix

Tamerlane, 4

Taqwīm al-sihha, 45

Tāriq ibn Ziyād, 7

taro, 83; in Egyptian cuisine, 84; in stews, 92

tayfūra (vessel), 107

al-Thaʿālibi, 20

tharīd, 6–7, 68–75; in Andalusian cuisine, 44, 72; chicken in, 70, 72–73, 74–75; in Christian cuisine, 75; consistency of, 69; etymology of, 189n1; and European soup, 189n8; *kāmakh* in, 70; in Maghrebi cuisine, 44; in *Manuscrito anónimo*, 189n3; Muhammad's fondness for, 8, 28, 68; *murrī* and, 75; as national dish, 68, 75; of Nawrūz, 73–75; puff paste in, 71; Sabbath, 75; *samn* in,

73; sausages in, 69; in *sikbāj*, 40; in
sunna, 68; Syrian, 70; with truffles,
70–71; in Tunisian cuisine, 69,
71–73
The Thousand and One Nights, 9
tiltīn (pasta), 118
Toledo, culinary traditions of, 44, 107
tomato juice, in Arab stews, xix
trade: caravan, 27; and spread of culinary traditions, 23
trade routes, Arab, 16–18, 26, 27
transhumance, 29
treyya (pasta), 116
truffles, *tharīd* with, 70–71
Tuaregs, *muhammas* of, 192n2
tubers, in meat dishes, 92
tuna: and *brīk*, 163; and eggplant, 164
Tunis, feast days of, 73. *See also*
cuisine, Tunisian
Turks: food culture of, xiii, 5; influence in Egypt, 13
turmeric, 24
tzūr (brine), 191n2

ʿūd (galangal), 78
ʿujja (omelets), 128
Umayyads, 13; of Damascus, 36–37;
food distribution by, 37; gastronomy of, 36–37; overthrow of, xii
Umm al-Fadl, 41
United Arab Emirates, 46
ʿusbān (sausage dish), 88
Uzbeks, cuisine of, 125

Vacca, Virginia, 187n30
Vallaro, Michele, 187n30

veal: in contemporary North African
cuisine, 149; with eggplant, 47, 149
vegetables, 66–67; American, 46, 59;
eggplant, xvii–xviii, 41, 63, 77–78,
92, 93, 94–95, 149, 164, 190n1; in
meat dishes, 92; pickled, 47, 155;
spinach, 128; squash, 135, 167;
stuffed, 48
vegetarian dishes, 43; for invalids,
x–xi; *murūziyya*, 167
vegetarianism, 21; in Qurʾanic tradition, 30–31
Venezuela, pasta consumption in, 115
Venice, cuisine of, 24, 82
vinegars: in Berber cuisine, 23; in
Maghrebi cuisine, 47; meatballs
with, 87–88; Mediterranean Muslim, 43; in Roman cuisine, 24; in *sikbāj*, 22; in syrups, 76; in *zirbāj*, 22

Waines, David, 186n13
walnuts: couscous with, 123; in *tharīd*,
74
warka malsuka (pastry), 191n1
al-Wāthiq, Caliph: recipes of, 64, 81;
zulābiyya of, 131
weights, in medieval Arab cuisine, 58
West, Muslim: cuisine of, 44; culinary
literature of, 42
wheat: cultivation of, 26; puree of,
113–14. *See also* semolina
wine: in cooking, 187n40; Egyptian,
23; etiquette of, 33, 34; grape, 140;
honey without raisins, 141; honey
with raisins, 140–41; Ibn Sayyār
on, 32–33; medicinal use of, 33;

DESIGNER
J. G. BRAUN
TEXT
11.5/13.5 VENDETTA MEDIUM
DISPLAY
INTERSTATE, VENDETTA
COMPOSITOR
BINGHAMTON VALLEY COMPOSITION, LLC
PRINTER AND BINDER
MAPLE-VAIL MANUFACTURING GROUP